LITERACY IN THE DISCIPLINES

Also from the Authors

Effective Instruction for English Language Learners:
Supporting Text-Based Comprehension and Communication Skills
Julie Jacobson, Kelly Johnson, and Diane Lapp

Exemplary Instruction in the Middle Grades:
Teaching That Supports Engagement and Rigorous Learning
Edited by Diane Lapp and Barbara Moss

Teaching New Literacies in Grades 4–6:
Resources for 21st-Century Classrooms
Edited by Barbara Moss and Diane Lapp

Transforming Writing Instruction in the Digital Age:
Techniques for Grades 5–12
Thomas DeVere Wolsey and Danà L. Grisham

LITERACY IN THE DISCIPLINES

A Teacher's Guide
for Grades 5–12

Thomas DeVere Wolsey
Diane Lapp

THE GUILFORD PRESS
New York   London

Copyright © 2017 The Guilford Press
A Division of Guilford Publications, Inc.
370 Seventh Avenue, Suite 1200, New York, NY 10001
www.guilford.com

Printed in the United States of America

This book is printed on acid-free paper.

Last digit is print number: 9   8   7   6   5   4   3   2   1

Library of Congress Cataloging-in-Publication Data

Names: Wolsey, Thomas DeVere, author. | Lapp, Diane, author.
Title: Literacy in the disciplines : a teacher's guide for grades 5–12 /
    Thomas DeVere Wolsey, Diane Lapp.
Description: New York, NY : Guilford Press, a Division of Guilford
    Publications, Inc., [2017] | Includes bibliographical references and index.
Identifiers: LCCN 2016013132| ISBN 9781462527922 (pbk. : acid-free paper) |
    ISBN 9781462527939 (hardcover : acid-free paper)
Subjects: LCSH: Content area reading. | Language arts (Secondary)
Classification: LCC LB1050.455 .W65 2016 | DDC 372.47/6—dc23
LC record available at *https://lccn.loc.gov/2016013132*

With special thanks to Michelle McLeod and the Annenberg Foundation for sharing
their Disciplinary Literacy videos, which offer concrete examples of the purposeful instruction
presented in this book.

To the disciplinary and literacy professionals
who have helped to shape this book,
and to the teachers who, as experts, do the work of ensuring
the learning of every student, every day

About the Authors

Thomas DeVere Wolsey, EdD, teaches online courses at Portland State University and elsewhere and is the founder of a consulting firm, the Institute to Advance International Education. Previously he worked in public schools for 20 years, teaching English and social studies. Dr. Wolsey's research explores how language informs thinking about content and how the interactions of students in digital and face-to-face environments change their learning. He is also interested in the intersections of traditional literacies with digital literacies, focusing specifically on how those literacies affect teacher preparation and professional development.

Diane Lapp, EdD, is Distinguished Professor of Education in the Department of Teacher Education at San Diego State University. She has taught elementary and middle school and currently works as an instructional coach at Health Sciences High and Middle College. Dr. Lapp's research and instruction focus on issues related to struggling readers and writers who live in economically deprived urban settings, and their families and teachers. Widely published, she has received the Outstanding Teacher Educator of the Year Award from the International Literacy Association, among other honors, and is a member of the International Reading Hall of Fame and the California Reading Hall of Fame.

Contents

PART III. ROUTINES THAT SUPPORT LEARNING IN THE DISCIPLINES

Purchasers of this book can download and print enlarged copies
of select practical tools at *www.guilford.com/wolsey2-forms*
for personal use or use with individual students.

PART I

THE LITERACY
OF THE DISCIPLINES

Chapter 1

What Is Disciplinary Literacy?

What's the difference between content-area literacy and disciplinary literacy? The concepts seem to be synonymous, don't they? For more than three decades, teachers of content have been told that they are all teachers of reading, and while students do read, write, and communicate in every discipline, the focus of content teachers is on instructing within their discipline. However, teachers of the content who are the experts in these fields are the ones who should be supporting literacy learning within these disciplines because they know exactly the type of literacy processes that are needed to succeed within their discipline. So to answer the initial question, the difference between content-area reading and discipline literacy is that

> disciplinary literacy is more aimed at what we teach (which would include how to read and use information like a scientist), than how we teach (such as how can students read the history book well enough to pass the test). The idea of disciplinary literacy is that students not only have to learn the essential content of a field, but how reading and writing are used in that field. On the other hand, content-area reading focuses on imparting reading and study skills that may help students to better understand and remember whatever they read. (T. Shanahan, 2012)

In this text, we posit the idea that science teachers are the best teachers of the literacies needed to understand science. We go after the notion that social studies teachers are best suited to help students understand how professional historians make sense of the historical record and mathematics teachers should support their students' close analysis of math problems. Even though physical education should be about physical activity during the school day, we argue that there is a literacy of health- and sports-related professions that might really hook some students in grades 5–12 to think critically and deeply about what it means to be healthy and fit. Insights about the arts should be shared by teachers in those disciplines as they expose students to the literacy practices most common among artists and musicians. The idea that teachers of specific content may connect and engage students with the nature of the discipline and how novices, amateurs, informed citizens, and professionals in each discipline make sense of the world through that disciplinary lens is at the heart of this book.

Here it is, in short: Experts and professionals think in specific ways about their fields. As professionals, they understand information within their disciplines; they often expand it through the books and articles they write, the scores they compose, the inventions they create, and the problems they solve. To create, they first must understand the knowledge of a discipline. Words help us understand the discipline, and the discipline informs how we understand the world. The essence of our message is that neither we nor our students can be an expert in every discipline, but every student can better comprehend the fascinating world we inhabit by looking at it from the perspectives of experts who know their parts of the world well.

Read more complex texts, and read more often within all disciplines is the call (National Governors Association Center for Best Practices & Council of Chief State School Officers [NGA & CCSSO], 2010), perhaps even the mandate, teachers hear. For teachers who primarily teach within the disciplines associated with content areas (e.g., science, mathematics, physical education), the increase in reading goes beyond the traditional reading associated with English literature coursework. However, more teachers are finding that when they help readers to make sense of disciplinary texts, their students make leaps toward learning the content. Simply put, students who understand how historians engage in thinking through reading, writing, and discussion tend to understand history better. The same is true for science, math, the arts, and even physical education. This book addresses disciplinary literacy and academic language needs for students and their teachers in grades 5–12.

 To support your understanding of disciplinary literacy beyond the information included in this text, we invite you to explore an Annenberg Learner video series titled *Reading and Writing in the Disciplines* that can be found at *http://www.learner.org* (left). Diane Lapp was one of the consultants to their program, so throughout this text we also refer you to several of the videos in the series because we believe they illuminate many of the ideas we're sharing. To get started understanding discipline literacy, begin with the Overview video at *https://www.learner.org/courses/ readwrite/video-detail/overview.html* (right).

The challenge for content-area teachers is to put literacy in service of learning information by thinking (i.e., reading, composing, viewing, listening) through a disciplinary lens. In turn, students' literacy improves. At the same time, students are not usually experts in each of the fields that schooling requires of them (Heller, 2010). Rather, they are aspiring novices or sometimes amateurs seeking to make sense of what their mathematics, art, and social studies teachers ask of them. Teachers must leverage students' reading skills to help them make sense of often complex content knowledge. Fortunately, many familiar instructional routines (sometimes called "strategies") are easily adaptable by teachers who want to clear the haze from the discipline-specific lens of learning and literacy in the content areas.

Researchers (see Moje, 2007; Shanahan & Shanahan, 2008) have identified the need for increased attention to the means by which teachers can build literacy capacity in their students and, at the same time, more effectively teach the content and the thinking patterns of the discipline. However, much of the current literature describes the nature of disciplinary learning or how the areas of content learning overlap (e.g., Wolsey, 2010) rather than how to develop literacy abilities and content knowledge. In fact, we have been unable to identify texts of the kind advocated by researchers, namely those for the teacher-practitioner, that comprehensively demonstrate how to teach students to use their disciplinary habits of thinking to improve what they learn about content. Moreover, teachers need resources that address literacy through a comprehensive and disciplinary approach to learning, receptive and expressive practices through a comprehensive literacy (e.g., Brozo, Moorman, Meyer, & Stewart, 2013), and a disciplinary approach to learning (rather than separating reading from writing as if there were no relationship between the two and how content is learned [e.g., Shanahan, 2006]). This book proposes to fill the gaps.

We wondered whether we really have to choose between content literacy and disciplinary literacy. Do we have to abandon the tools and routines we know in order to get on the disciplinary literacy bandwagon? We don't think so. Those familiar routines can often be the bridge our students need from understanding and creating texts in general ways to a more diverse way of looking at the world through the lens of each discipline as we come to understand the literacy practices used by experts in each discipline.

DISCIPLINARY LITERACY AND CONTENT-AREA LITERACY

Like most of you, we have found that effective teachers typically integrate and learn from each new iteration of the ideas they encounter. They use their training, experience, and wisdom along with genuine caring and knowledge of the students in their classrooms to teach about an ever-changing world. With a focus on disciplinary literacy, this text delves into what it means to be an effective communicator and producer of information in several of the disciplines—mathematics, history/social studies, science, English, the arts, physical education, and technical subjects—and looks at strategies that support building students' communication/literacy skills within each. Although each discipline has its own particular literacy demands, understanding the differences and commonalities can help teachers build upon the relevant skills and strategies that students bring with them to class.

Throughout this book, we have avoided what we call the "versus" syndrome. Choosing between content literacy and disciplinary literacy seems counterproductive. Binary constructions that force us to choose between two seemingly opposite choices rarely produce understanding, we think (Hayakawa & Hayakawa, 1990). Both have a place and a purpose for some students at some times during their educational journeys. But what do we mean by content literacy or disciplinary literacy? The terms are not interchangeable, and one does not mean the other has no place. We teach general learning strategies when that is appropriate, and we look more specifically at the disciplinary or content approaches when that is more likely to engage students and improve learning. Like most things in life, words are often quite complex. The same word can be used in different ways depending on who speaks or writes the word and what the context is for its use. Let's take a quick tour of the terms *content, content areas,* and *disciplinary literacy.*

A Brief Tour of the Terms

Content

What the words are all about, really. Every text is about something. Stephen Hawking wrote about the universe and how it came to be (1996). That's content. Ernest Hemingway (1952) wrote about life through the allegory of a fisherman confronting challenges at sea. That is also content. John Wesley Powell (1895) wrote about his expedition down the Colorado River and what is now known as the Grand Canyon. Yes, what we learn about that voyage and the geology and people of the region is also content. Put perhaps a bit too simply, content is the *what.* Of course, we agree with Rosenblatt (1995) that how we respond to the words and how our own experiences inform our reading are vitally important to how we make sense of content. Content is what the author, using words and other modalities (such as images or sounds), tries to convey to the reader while the reader brings experiences of her or his own to that content. This interaction of reader and text is more important than we might think, and we will return to this idea in Chapter 2.

Content Areas

Now here is a tough one, because the term includes the word *content* but it is more than, and less than, the word *content* all by itself. *Content area* is really a school term that one encounters only in teachers' lounges and colleges of education. Sometimes the term *subject area* is used interchangeably with *content area.* Most students we know have not heard the term and wouldn't understand it. That is okay because the words and syntax teachers use is necessarily important to the students who benefit from the ideas embedded in those words. When our doctors talk among themselves, they sometimes use words that we would not understand because we are not trained or experienced in the field of medicine. When they speak with us, they use different terms or they explain the terms they use. Teachers are really not any different. Content area refers to school subjects—mathematics, science, history, literature, arts, and so on. These subjects are often put into containers or silos by grade level and by course numbers. Organizing content into these "areas" is a way of keeping the entire enterprise of schooling moving forward. We may argue about the way the content is organized or how students move through the system, but content area is just a means of thinking about the way content (what we learn) is organized during the school day or year. It is the *how* of content as it appears in school.

Disciplinary Literacy

Shanahan and Shanahan (2008) suggested a pyramid model for the increasing specialization of literacy development that shows the relationship between basic literacy skills, intermediate or generic literacy skills, and disciplinary literacy skills. They write that disciplinary literacy skills are those that are "specialized to history, science, mathematics, literature, or other subject matter" (p. 44). This definition captures the essence of disciplinary literacy to us. Moje (2013), in a webinar on the TextProject site, equated *subject area* with the term *discipline*. Her insight here is that subject areas are how the disciplines are experienced in schools. Wow, that is an insight! It would not be useful to expect students in 10th grade to be conversant with every conceivable discipline that exists or might exist in the world. Those subject areas provide a scaffold for students as they enter and explore the disciplines as they encounter them in school, and as they find them in the world of work and as informed citizens later in life. One other notion Moje explains is worth our attention, too. She tells us, "Subject matter learning is not merely about learning the *stuff* [emphasis added] of the disciplines; it is also about the processes and practices by which that stuff is produced. . . . Some of the power of knowledge comes from being an active part of its production, rather than from merely possessing it" (Moje, 2013, time index 10:48).

We are going to come back to this later because the idea that students can produce knowledge is particularly worthwhile when we talk about disciplinary literacy. Producing knowledge means that learners have some command of the concepts and they can add their voices to the discussions that are appropriate for their own disciplinary thinking.

While we agree with Brozo and colleagues (2013) that generic literacy skills that work across content areas are worthwhile for students, too, teaching students to understand how experts in the disciplines think, approach texts in their fields, and organize their parts of the world have an important place in the curriculum.

Put simply, we need not choose between broadly applicable content literacy approaches and those specific to any given discipline.

One question teachers at any level face is just what does disciplinary learning look like for students of different age levels and in different grades? And what a good question it is. We teachers often tell students that they should think like a scientist, a historian, a mathematician, or an author of fiction. But what do we mean by that? It seems quite improbable that most students would actually be experts in all those fields, doesn't it? It also seems unlikely that students in high school, for example, could usually emulate the thinking habits of someone with multiple university degrees and years of experience in specialized fields. What does a teacher in any subject area do? Let's explore that in the next section.

One of our favorite websites is TextProject, where teachers may find a wealth of information and resources about many aspects of literacy instruction and standards alignment. We recommend checking it out at *http://textproject.org*. As mentioned earlier, throughout this book, we also include links to video resources from Learner.org and our own Disciplinary Literacy channel on YouTube, which can be found at *https://literacybeat.com/literacy-in-the-disciplines*.

Disciplinary Literacy across Grade Levels

Imagine a young child who can explain the scientific concept known as Bernoulli's principle she had learned through investigation in preschool. Moje (2013) describes just such an event as her preschool daughter questioned a phenomenon and attempted to explain it as she sat in the bathtub with a squeeze bottle. You can hear Moje describe it at *https://youtu.be/8fMncjLc1iQ?t=12m46s*. Even at a very young age, children are interested in the world and question why and how things work.

Diagrams often help us conceptualize our ideas, so we created one in Figure 1.1 that we think may help us consider literacy growth as a function of increasing specialization in school settings. We agree with Shanahan and Shanahan (2008) that literacy learning is increasingly specialized and occurs in different ways depending on where learners are in their own growth. At the same time, we wanted to represent the idea that disciplinary learning occurs pretty much throughout children's lives. We tipped their literacy pyramid on its side, then split it apart to show a continuum. It is, of course, a rough model, but perhaps it can help us think through just where and when disciplinary learning can and should occur.

Because we think of the literacy skills as interlocked and overlapping, we reconceptualized the pyramid in this way. Disciplinary thinking and the associated literacies may start and be fostered quite early in a child's life. At the same time, the basic literacy skills (alphabetic principle, letter–sound correspondences, sight words, and so on) are of particular importance early in life. As intermediate and general proficiencies in comprehension, fluency, and other thinking strategies improve, so do disciplinary literacies. Over time, and depending on the demands of

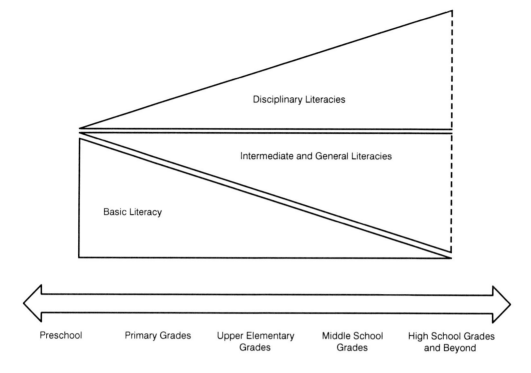

FIGURE 1.1. Continuum of literacy specialization.

curriculum, the workplace, and the needs of individual students, disciplinary literacies might be a greater focus for students.

A Question of Questions

A couple of paragraphs ago, we recounted Moje's story of her preschool daughter who questioned a phenomenon she encountered in the bathtub. We are reminded that schools often turn the idea of questions upside down. The teacher becomes the one with the question and the students must produce a suitable answer. Holt (1982) poignantly explained how children often become fearful of not knowing the answer expected and their natural instincts to explore and question the world blunted as a result. Mehan (1979) identified the input–response–evaluate format identified as characteristic of oral classroom discussion, where the teacher asks a question to which the teacher already has an answer in mind. The student responds and the teacher then evaluates the degree of correctness. Under such circumstances, how would a student ever develop the habit of mind of asking questions to which the answer might require investigation? We argue that the disciplines demand that students be the ones with the questions, that they be taught to navigate (Moje, 2013) the complex worlds of the disciplines, and to take the risks that all experts in any field take when confronted with challenging problems.

In addition to being able to ask and frame questions or identify worthwhile problems, all the disciplines typically represented in school (as subjects or content areas) tend to use data to inform decisions. They present and evaluate arguments, but the manner of making or evaluating the argument may be different for mathematicians than it is for authors of fiction, for example. Experts and students working in the disciplines often use language and other symbol systems in ways that are unique to that discipline. They work with multiple texts that often provide differing points of view, and they are able to summarize them in ways that are familiar to those who think about and communicate in that discipline. Finally, and most important, experts and students know how to produce knowledge and communicate that knowledge in ways that are distinctive to that discipline.

So let's see where we are in our thinking about disciplinary literacy. We proposed the ideas that:

1. Thinking skills expressed through language are useful in ways specific to the school-oriented disciplines.
2. Students benefit from learning through disciplinary lenses, but they are not experts in most cases.
3. There are some common attributes to the disciplines that cross all of them, but the way professionals and experts approach those attributes varies from one discipline to another. For example, historians tend to approach the use of data in ways that are very different from the methods scientists use.

As a result, the way literacy informs and is informed by the disciplines has unique qualities to a mathematician, a social scientist, an author of fiction, an artist, or an athlete. We're about to go on a journey to discover some of the many ways that scientists read a report or a historian evaluates a source of information. Throughout our journey, we hope you will recognize familiar instructional routines and adapt them to help your students more thoroughly understand the nature of the disciplines and produce knowledge in the best traditions of those disciplines. We also hope that you find a unique place for your voice as an advocate for your discipline and the literacy practices that inform it as we go along.

Just How Many Literacies Are There?

In this book, we focus on the literacies of disciplines commonly found in schools. These include the disciplines of mathematics, history and the social sciences, the arts, literature, and the sciences. The disciplines specific to physical education and athletics and music have found their way into our exploration, as well. Of course, we subscribe to the notion of "new literacies" that generally refer to the means by which digital technologies are infused into our ways of knowing and understanding the world (e.g., Lankshear & Knobel, 2006). You will find the idea of new literacies

---

Many Literacies

- Financial literacy:
  www.usmint.gov/kids/teachers/financialLiteracy

- Cultural literacy, often associated with the works of E. D. Hirsch, takes on a global context in this article from the *Houston Chronicle*:
  http://smallbusiness.chron.com/important-gain-cultural-literacy-international-business-69605.html

- Visual literacy, a topic about which Diane and DeVere have written often:
  www.humanities.umd.edu/vislit
  http://ivla.org/new/what-is-visual-literacy-2

- Environmental literacy:
  http://enviroliteracy.org

FIGURE 1.2. Many literacies, with example websites. Of course, there are many more.

throughout this book infused into the disciplines. However, there are other literacies as well. It is beyond the scope of this book to explore the possibilities of just how many literacies there are and what disciplines are represented therein. We point out a few to highlight the idea that the language and symbols used in a variety of fields, professions, and businesses are worthwhile even when they are typically not traditional subjects taught in schools on a sustained basis. Some examples are shown in Figure 1.2.

How Does Disciplinary Literacy Help Teachers Teach Content More Effectively?

Earlier in this chapter, we suggested that there is the "stuff," or content, to be learned. There are also ways of knowing, learning, and communicating that are frequently specific to the disciplines as they are taught in schools. Disciplinary literacy helps us get to the very soul of what we learn, why we learn it, and how that learning informs our ability to navigate the world and, most important, navigate the world of ideas and people who produce those ideas. Disciplinary literacy gives students a voice, sometimes as informed novices and sometimes as aspiring experts, to understand ideas from many perspectives and as knowledgeable participants in the public sphere (see Habermas, 1991).

Standards and curricula increasingly demand that students learn the ways of knowing and communicating that are specific to the disciplines they encounter in schools. What's more, students are asked to look at the world through multiple lenses as they integrate what they know from their studies in one discipline with those of other disciplines to solve the complex problems that society faces. To accommodate their developing understandings, we have considered the roles literacy plays in the lives of those working within each discipline. Then we have addressed this understanding through the information and examples shared in this text. We hope this approach will support you, the teachers of all disciplines, in expanding your students' literacy skills within the context of your discipline. We believe the results will be well-prepared and well-informed students who have the literacy prowess needed to succeed in any career they choose.

HOW TO READ THIS BOOK

Although the nuances of each discipline are unique, some aspects of literacy provide a lens through which we might examine the uniqueness of each. In the chapters that follow, we look at those aspects.

This chapter has provided an overview of disciplinary literacy and of essential concepts related to proficient reading, writing, and communication that support literacy development. Next, in Chapter 2, several experts focus on the literacy demands of each discipline. Teachers respond to each of the experts and suggest ideas based on their readings from this chapter. Let's start our journey.

CHAPTER 1 ACTIVITY:
A Graphic Organizer to Guide You through Your Reading

A common approach for decades, known as content-area literacy, benefited many students as they learned to navigate texts in science, mathematics, and other disciplines. The approach relied on general strategies to help students work with texts they encountered in their classwork.

Getting the content right is our goal, and using language specific to the discipline is one way to accomplish that. Literacy in the disciplines (or disciplinary literacy) goes a step beyond general approaches that may be used across disciplines. Whereas content-area reading (or content-area literacy) focused on strategies that build students' skills with any text, disciplinary literacy homes in on what makes each discipline unique in the ways experts and professionals approach the field. It is important that students—novices in fields such as history, art, or mathematics—learn to work with texts that will lead them to better understand the content.

Figure 1.3 can help you isolate the unique features of language as they are used in your discipline or content area. Here is how you can use the chart:

1. Choose a literacy-related task that is specific to your discipline or content area.

2. In column A, indicate the most common practices relative to the four areas: Vocabulary, Reading and Writing, Using Visual Information, and Using Sources. A few blank rows are also included so you can study other aspects of

What Literacy Looks Like in My Discipline

My discipline or content area:	A My discipline usually:	B An example literacy task in my content area or discipline	C Differences between usual and specific task (columns A and B)	D Contrasting example from another discipline
Approach to Vocabulary → Word origins → **Discipline-specific vocab** → **Academic vocab across disciplines**				
Approach to → **Reading** → **Writing**				

(continued)

FIGURE 1.3. Disciplinary comparison chart.

	A	B	C	D
My discipline or content area:	My discipline usually:	An example literacy task in my content area or discipline	Differences between usual and specific task (columns A and B)	Contrasting example from another discipline
Approach to Visual Information → Charts → Graphs → Images				
Approach to Sources → Relative importance → How attributed → Perspective				

(continued)

FIGURE 1.3. *(continued)*

A	B	C	D
My discipline usually:	An example literacy task in my content area or discipline	Differences between usual and specific task (columns A and B)	Contrasting example from another discipline
My discipline or content area:			

FIGURE 1.3. (*continued*)

language in your discipline, such as presentations, interdisciplinary connections, and so on.

3. In column B, note the literacy aspects of the specific task you chose to study.

4. In column C, compare the common practices in your discipline with those in this specific task.

5. In column D, contrast information in the first three columns from an example task in another discipline. You may want to work with a colleague who works in another content area or discipline to collaborate with you. The filled-in example for vocabulary in Figure 1.4, using an article about plankton study from *Science* magazine, may guide you.

 To support you in identifying the features of your discipline, refer to *www.learner.org/courses/readwrite/media-index.html*. Once there, view the video related to our discipline. You'll be able to choose from many videos, including:

- Reading and Writing in Science
- Reading and Writing in English
- Reading and Writing in History
- Mathematics in the Real World: An Epidemiologist
- Science in the Real World: A Biotech Startup
- English in the Real World: A Sports Journalist
- History in the Real World: A Documentary Filmmaker

What Literacy Looks Like in My Discipline

	A	B	C	D
My discipline or content area:	**My discipline usually:**	**An example literacy task in my content area or discipline**	**Differences between usual and specific task (columns A and B)**	**Contrasting example from another discipline**
Approach to Vocabulary → **Word origins** → **Discipline-specific vocab** → **Academic vocab across disciplines**	*Relies on Greek and Latin roots.* *Uses very specific vocabulary that other disciplines don't use, but uses Tier Two words (see Chapter 4) to make connections, etc.*	*Read Tara Oceans article.* *Uses discipline-specific words with Greek and Latin origins such as heterotrophic, microscopy, eukaryotes.* *Also uses Tier Two words such as lineage and in situ.*	*This article is challenging to read but I can use my knowledge of words from Greek and Latin roots as well as my knowledge of words I have encountered in other disciplines to make sense of the vocabulary.*	*In The Old Man and the Sea, Hemingway's language choices are not very difficult or specific literature, but the words he chooses convey emotions such as hope and desperation. The words are not specific to any one discipline.*

FIGURE 1.4. Example of a disciplinary comparison chart. The source for column B is an article on plankton from *Science* magazine (Bork et al., 2015).

17

Chapter 2

What Are the Literacy Demands of Experts in the Disciplines?

Talking with Scientists, Historians, Mathematicians, Authors of Fiction, Musicians, Artists, Athletes, and Technical Experts

What exactly are the literacy demands of scientists, sociologists, chefs, and every other person who heads out for the workplace each morning? The answer to this question is one that educators must consider when planning instruction for their students. Are we preparing students to have the literacy skills they will need to function in the workplace? We have had many opportunities to collaborate with others throughout our careers, but one of the most intriguing collaborations occurred recently as we've listened to how literacy professionals, professors, practitioners, and teachers come together to inform each other and us about the role language plays in their discipline and subsequently in the future careers of their students. Their conversations highlighted how those who work in each of the disciplines use language, how teachers in content areas and in literacy education might collaborate to design instruction to ensure that their students are prepared for the workplace, and what that means for students (Draper, Broomhead, Jensen, & Siebert, 2010).

These collaborations were compiled as narratives or transcripts of each conversation between a practicing expert or professional in the discipline and a professor of literacy. Teachers then responded to the conversation describing how they prepared students in each discipline to use language in the ways described by the practicing experts.

You may be tempted to turn to the section of this chapter that addresses just your discipline, and we hope you do, at first. However, there is much to be learned by comparison with the other disciplines. Read them all to get a firm grasp on just where your discipline is among the others. Of course, this is only a representative sample because there are many disciplines and specialties within disciplines that we might address. This is a good place to get started. Have fun!

MATHEMATICS

Dana L. Grisham Interviews W. David Scales[1]

W. David Scales is a colleague and fellow researcher in the Teacher Education Research Study Group, or TERSG, a special-interest group of the Literacy Research Association. David's expertise has been invaluable to our group as we conducted longitudinal mixed-methods research. Although I am a Californian and David is located on the East Coast, he generously made time to talk to me via Skype with video enabled. We talked for the best part of an hour as I interviewed him and I learned a great deal about how he views literacy, mathematics, and psychology.

David doesn't regard himself as a mathematician, although mathematics is a large component of what he does, or as he termed it, "a means to an end" or a very necessary and "cool" tool. Instead, a psychometrician is a measurement "expert." David regards his job as matching or adapting research questions to the best research methodology and design to gain the maximum knowledge from the collection and analysis of mostly quantitative data. He works to understand "constructs" and then to measure them effectively, always asking himself these questions: How do I do it? What are the mechanics?

When asked about how he reads various texts, David talked about reading an article from a scholarly journal in his field, stating that there were at least two types of articles (practical and theoretical) and that he read them differently. He laughed as he noted that there might be more formulae than words in some of the texts, but for both, he skims the abstract to find out where the article is heading because that makes even the "heavily technical" parts more understandable. Unless the theoretical topic is truly essential for him to know, he prefers to read articles for a "practicing psychometrician." He lives in both worlds, of course, but he talked about the courses he teaches and that the articles he prefers to read are practical, much like the way he teaches his courses—to practitioners, not to "hardcore math stat geeks." As a teacher, David states, "I'm trying to explain to students that it's actually a language that is to be read and they don't see it." And so when he reads these articles, he skims through the abstract first to ask himself basic questions: "Do I already have a good working knowledge of where I'm going? Do I understand all the moving pieces before I get into it, or do I need to go hit that great big collection

[1]**Dr. Dana L. Grisham** is a retired Professor in the Department of Teacher Education at California State University, East Bay (Hayward). **Dr. W. David Scales** is Assistant Professor of Psychology at Western Carolina University in Cullowhee, North Carolina.

$$\sqrt{\dfrac{\sum(X-\bar{X})^2}{N-1}}$$

FIGURE 2.1. Example of mathematics as a collection of symbols.

of references that I have sitting right there, up and down, and go look stuff up? Because if I see something that is mind-bogglingly complex, I'm going to have to go dig in my books and find out what it is."

For David, learning in psychology is almost purely Skinnerian behaviorism. He tells me he is not a behaviorist of any kind but feels that Skinner was "dead on with shaping." Mathematics and statistics, in particular, are a collection of symbols, and the student must learn what each piece does and how they may be combined (put together or chunked) to see how the whole thing works. He provided the example in Figure 2.1, which shows the formula for the standard deviation.

David stated he sees this formula as a single communication, but that the uninitiated will instead observe that X has eight moving parts. The formula makes use of PEMDAS, the order of operations. PEMDAS is parentheses, exponents, multiplication, division, addition, and subtraction. And so we can read this, which is a score, minus the mean to get the difference. So literacy is indeed involved in math. Students may disagree at first, but my insistence is that it absolutely is—because it's shorthand, the same now as "LOL" or "LMAO" when texting: "It's a way of getting from point A to point B without having to write out the entire thing."

As far as learning to communicate mathematically, David argues that one must first acquire it using "short-term memory," in that a formula is like a telephone number that must be memorized and eventually becomes automatic. He stated, "And so it comes from having to work on these rooting pieces to begin with to understanding that single thing. This is now not a collection of moving pieces, it's a 'known' phenomenon that makes sense because, in my experience, having looked at this formula 28 billion times in my life, I know how it works. I see the bigger picture."

When talking about writing, he notes that the *Publication Manual of the American Psychological Association* (APA, 2009) is a "formula" for how to write, although you must consider the audience and the message as well—the purpose is communication, or, as David notes, "Absolutely, because what we do is no secret. People think that much of what I do involves witchcraft. But the magic, such as it is, occurs in being able to explain to somebody what I do because if you understand this after you and I have talked, I have done my job correctly. If you don't, I have not." In fact, he keeps the equivalent of a psychometrician's "bible" on his desk, *The Visual Display of Quantitative Information*, by Tufte. From the APA "formula" to the formula for standard deviation (above), is a stretch, but the comparison is strangely apt when the sole purpose is communication between individuals and groups. David switches from Skinner to Vygotsky—using it as a verb, noting, "Let's Vygotsky this bad boy out!" In other words, step back, think again, and try again to communicate.

When asked specifically what teachers need to know to communicate the language demands of a psychometrician's work, he stated that flexibility is the key in communications. Flexibility is necessary for anyone who wants to communicate his or her expertise to another because individuals come with strengths and needs, as well as (in mathematics, surely) fear of failure. This heterogeneity means that some learners will have "aced" calculus, while others "freak out" when they must add a string of numbers together: "Flexibility is absolutely mandatory, and people can often be afraid of the subject matter or the tools that in my trade are necessary to convey that information and these tools because . . . we're not just talking about oral communication and written communication, we're talking about manipulation of software as a form of communication."

In running a statistical program such as SPSS, the results are provided in tables and graphs, which are another means of communication. The psychometrician must find multiple ways to convey meaning to his or her audience. Developing the expertise to communicate a message (information) accessibly to a variety of learners must be developed over time and becomes part of a professional expertise, which the psychometrician may call upon. A qualification essential to David is open mindedness: "There is more than one way to get to an answer. Rigidity is a fear of mine in thinking." Another element that is important in communication is that there are no absolutes in research. He talks about the fact that there is only one rule: "You're gonna die." That's why researchers and psychometricians don't talk about rules and laws. They talk about probabilities, likelihoods, and tendencies. They characterize using the terms *most, some,* and *few.* But they never talk about *all* or *none.*

The learner in working with mathematics, statistics, and computer programs must first put the pieces together in a hierarchical manner. David talks about putting the smaller pieces together and that there must be patience in the explanations because you have to break things down. Losing one's place along the way can be dangerous because it is difficult to learn the new without the necessary background knowledge. Thus David provides a routine for the learner: "A structure. We talk about it. I show you how to do it by hand. I show you how to do it in Excel. I show you how to do it in SPSS [a statistical analysis program]. I do Excel and SPSS because I need [students] to understand how to do it in more than one program or format. Excel is universal, SPSS costs."

David is funny and thoughtful as he describes what a psychometrician does and how a person who uses mathematics as a tool (or language) for communication accomplishes it. As I look back over the interview, it seems to me that mathematics is a semiotic system of communication, akin and related to what human beings do: use language to express and exchange ideas. The idea of social semiotics seems very important here—each of us belongs to groups that have specialized language for communicating the knowledge base of our specialty . . . and mathematics is one more "system" for communicating knowledge.

A Teacher Reflects: Faith Bass-Sargent, Middle School Mathematics Teacher[2]

The changes in the new California Common Core Standards (CCSS) and other standards have sparked a conversation in the math community regarding the role of language in the development of conceptual understanding in math. In addition to concepts to be taught by grade level, the CCSS articulates a set of Standards for Mathematical Practice (NGA & CCSSO, 2010), the first of which is a student's ability to "make sense of problems and persevere in solving them." The sense-making portion of the Standards is what drives the conversation about language and how math teachers can use it as a feasible tool to create honest understanding of the math they are practicing. In the traditional view of math education, there was emphasis on "answer getting." For example, all that is asked of the student is to show the proper steps while solving a problem.

However, with the Standards, the mood in math has shifted to understanding and critical evaluation of the work product. For example, a teacher may ask students how they know their answer is correct and whether they can predict a rule that would work in similar situations. As educators have moved away from traditional numerical answer getting, students are struggling with how to articulate themselves inside the classroom. Under the Standards, teachers impress upon students the need to use precise vocabulary to describe and defend their work. This question arises: When do teachers begin implementing necessary vocabulary, start treating the numerical values as a bridge to a greater discussion on what principles are at work, and what conjectures can you make? As middle school teachers, we have found that strong, consistent vocabulary development and a focus on common language throughout sixth, seventh, and eighth grades has vastly improved student learning. In addition, as we work closely as a team, we prepare lessons that specifically refer back to concepts taught in earlier grades that have different applications.

For example, prime factorization is taught in sixth grade. When a teacher asks a student to factor, the student may take the number and create a factor tree that breaks it down to the number's prime factorization. In one case, the teacher may assign additional practice in "prime factorization." Prime factorization lays the groundwork for the Algebra 1 concept of polynomial factorization. In order to have an effective and descriptive conversation about the new concept of polynomial factorization, we have carefully scaffolded our lessons specifically to refer to the earlier lessons on prime factorization. For students to make sense of the problem, they

---

[2]**Faith Bass-Sargent** teaches mathematics at Elsinore Middle School in Lake Elsinore, California.

need to be engaged in the full story of what is happening in the math. Much like a story or movie, the pieces of math interconnect at multiple grade levels in a variety of ways. The student should be able to get a sense of the "big picture" and be able to carefully articulate its story from the beginning. The consequence of students focusing on communication and dialogue versus answer getting has led to the realization that students who traditionally have been successful in concept development are making greater strides in their classes.

We have seen the benefit of focusing on creating a clear vertical articulation of language. As such, part of the vertical articulation process is to collectively start creating meaning regarding what a vocabulary word represents. As educators, we discuss the progression of a specific concept and how it represents itself at each grade level. We diligently discuss what the word means and collectively commit to encouraging the students to use that word with precision. When we find a student using a word incorrectly, we should use it as an opportunity to fill out the meaning of the word completely. For example, when a student says he or she is going to factor, the teacher should ask clarifying questions, such as, "Are you factoring to find prime numbers, or are you factoring to find the binomials?"

In addition, when a student encounters a cognate (in this context, a polysemous term that is used in different ways depending on the disciplinary context) that has a different meaning in another field of study, it is important to address its similarities and draw connections. For example, the words *difference* and *share* have multiple meanings. Asking a student what the difference between two numbers is can be a daunting task if you do not establish clear parameters to the question. It seems simple—if you are looking through the lens of a math teacher, then the teacher assumes the student knows he or she is being asked to subtract. However, if the student has just come from language arts class and been asked to discuss the difference between the roles of adults and children in the novel *The Giver,* he or she has now been asked to use the same word in two very different applications. The teacher can use these situations to carefully articulate that, in math, an entire concept can be attached to a single word. Without knowing the students' experience with the vocabulary, a single word could be misleading or confusing. These misunderstandings can be the difference between having only procedural understanding of the steps versus making sense of the concept.

With the CCSS, math teachers have had to thoughtfully reevaluate their role in language development. For a student to receive full and well-defined mathematics stories, the conversations held in classrooms throughout a student's career must be clearly connected. This connection can be achieved, in part, through the vertical articulation process that starts in kindergarten and ends with calculus. If they can craft a way to establish what each concept looks like in fruition, and create a common language, the students will be able to cross the crevasse from procedural understanding to being able to talk about math in a way that communicates deeper thinking and understanding.

ATHLETES AND OUTDOOR EDUCATION

Steve Mogge Writes about Adventure Sports, Outdoor Physical Education, and Literacy[3]

Research has examined the literacy practices of professionals and academics in order to understand successful participation in different disciplines (Moje, 2008; Shanahan & Shanahan, 2008; Shanahan, Shanahan, & Misischia, 2011). T. Shanahan (2012) explains that experts' use of literacies in unique ways stems from appreciation of different research traditions and ways of knowing, an effort to ensure expert participation, and as a means to protect power and authority in the discipline. The CCSS being implemented across the United States identify literacy practices in social studies/history and science and technical content areas (NGA & CCSSO, 2010) that are informed by disciplinary research. Teachers in these content areas are called on to build bridges between students' out-of-school discourses, general academic discourses, and the disciplinary discourses.

Of course, there are other disciplines and subject areas to consider. Adventure sports are part of the outdoor recreation industry, which has enjoyed increasing popularity in recent years. The "No Child Left Inside" (Louv, 2008; Orion, 2013) and environmental advocacy movements have led many states and schools to expand outdoor experiences through outdoor and physical education. Some states have adopted standards that include exposure to outdoor natural environments (Lieberman, 2013). School leaders and teachers may look to outdoor education and physical education as subject areas worth comprehensive, integrated curricular attention. This chapter focuses on one sector of the outdoor industry—whitewater adventure sports—in an effort to learn about the unique literacy practices so that these can be considered for K–12 education.

Research Methods and Interview Participants

The research that informs this chapter involved participant observation in a community college whitewater adventure program as well as interviews with six leading professionals in the whitewater adventure sports industry. As Table 2.1 illustrates, the six interview participants are highly accomplished, representing world-class competitors, international explorers, and industry-leading businesspeople. Their experiences and insights can be taken seriously by anyone aspiring to succeed in those fields and by K–12 educators who want to expose youth to outdoor experiences.

---

[3]**Dr. Stephen Mogge** is Associate Professor in the Graduate Reading Education Program at Towson University, in Towson, Maryland.

TABLE 2.1. Careers, Backgrounds, and Accomplishments of Whitewater Industry Interviewees

Current whitewater profession	Professional background and accomplishments
Executive director, whitewater park	• U.S. national kayaking team • Four-time national C2 champion • Two-time Olympic competitor
Co-owner, high-end whitewater garment manufacturer	• Kayaking instructor • U.S. national kayaking team • Three-time national K-1 champion
Co-owner, high-end whitewater garment manufacturer	• Kayaking instructor • International "alpine kayaking" explorer • First whitewater/river explorations of Baffin Island and Borneo
Owner, whitewater rafting and adventure company	• First and largest whitewater adventure outfitter in the northeastern United States • Interpretive history scholar and leader • Industry leader and education advocate
River safety expert, author, and river products representative	• Early Appalachian river explorer • River safety teacher and author • Guidebook author • Member of the Whitewater Hall of Fame
Rodeo competitor and multisport expeditionary summit-to-sea adventurer	• Professional rodeo kayaker • Teacher at a world-class kayak academy • Adventure sports marketing manager • Summit-to-sea adventures: Mt. Denali to the ocean

Findings and Implications for K–12 Schooling

Below are key findings from interviews with the adventure sports professionals along with suggestions for K–12 curricula. While "physical literacy" (Whitehead, 2001)—learning to read natural or man-made environments and move with purpose, efficiency, and success to meet the challenges encountered in the environment—may be a valuable construct for adventure sports and outdoor education (and will be pursued in other writing), the focus here is on the role of more traditional (print and digital information) literacies. As will be shown, traditional reading and writing can complement an outdoor and physical education curriculum, although it certainly should not replace time and experience in the outdoors and in physical education activities. In schools where these are valued, cross-curricular collaborations with language arts, social studies, and science teachers will likely be more successful.

Formative Experiences in the Outdoors: Outdoor Awareness, Confidence, and Competence

In childhood, three of the interviewees attended after-school and summer camps where exploration, adventure, and outdoor play were important additions to their September–June school-focused lives. They lived in urban or suburban settings, but each summer left their families for weeks-long immersion in wilderness camps where whitewater river paddling captured their attention. The other three participants grew up in the whitewater country of north central Appalachia, where this research study is focused. They came of age in an environment where whitewater play was regular part of after-school and weekend life as well as summer adventures. Immersion and interaction in wilderness environments were a foundation for their future adventures and professional pursuits.

SUGGESTIONS FOR K–12 SCHOOLING

As Louv (2008) and others point out, a fully formed, healthy childhood requires not only that children be active in physical education courses but that they also have the opportunity to explore wilderness, become comfortable in natural environments, and engage the outdoors in physically and emotionally challenging ways. The excitement and interest launched through outdoor experiences can be foundational to many social, cultural, historical, geologic, geographic, ecological, and biological inquiries conducted in classrooms, libraries, and online. Collaborating with school colleagues, outdoor and physical education teachers can provide the field experiences that catalyze further disciplinary inquiry in social studies, science, and literacy classrooms.

Formative Experiences and Adventure Literature

Five of the six interviewees claimed to be avid readers throughout childhood. Two genres that captured the participants' attention were adventure literature and world history and cultures. Stories of Ernest Shackleton's expedition to Antarctica and Joe Kane's book *Running the Amazon* were frequently mentioned, as were *National Geographic* magazine and, more generally, fiction reading. Through escapist literature they were able to transport themselves to distant lands for exploration and excitement. These types of reading experiences aligned with their outdoor adventure interests and helped them to establish their identities and ambitions for the future. The Executive Director of the Whitewater Park explained: "You can't expect everybody to go on these amazing adventures, so both literature and art are kind of our bridge to real-life experiences." The alpine expeditionary explorer added, "The idea of using kayaking as a tool for exploration, that's what I love doing. And that whole self-image was completely formed by these explorers [I was reading about]. . . . I have this culture in my mind of what exploration means, and I want to be part of that."

SUGGESTIONS FOR K–12 SCHOOLING

Again, it is not suggested here that schools replace guided outdoor experiential or physical education time with reading literature. Rather, adventure literature can complement outdoor experiences and expand on the excitement derived from time in the outdoors through stories of those who push adventure boundaries. Schools that adopt outdoor and physical education as a priority should integrate adventure literature in the language arts curriculum, thereby promoting students' interest and engagement with literature, reading achievement, and physical development.

Adventure Guides, Exploration, and Trip Reports

The interview participants confirm that guidebook and, more recently, Web-based information from sources such as American Whitewater (see *www.americanwhitewater. org*) is essential to outdoor adventure planning. Before contemporary paddlers put out on a whitewater river, they consult these guides to learn about transportation shuttle requirements and access, river levels, topographic gradients, the difficulty of rapids (based on an international rating scale), significant hazards, and navigation time. The international expeditionary explorers claim to having spent months and even years studying the history, culture, politics, geography, geology, and watershed environments of the regions they explore. They take copious notes and make detailed written plans—most of which are left behind once the formal adventure is underway. These professional explorers often document their adventures in magazine articles and videography. Even recreational paddlers frequently write up "trip reports" to share with fellow paddlers in club newsletters and online forums.

SUGGESTIONS FOR K–12 SCHOOLING

While direct experience and activity are the foundations upon which many outdoor experiential and physical education curricula are built, information is still critical to successful and safe outdoor experiences. Students should be exposed to information sources and read about the outdoor environments they visit. Small groups can take part in drafting trip plans, anticipating the physical environment, flora and fauna, and important safety precautions. Reflective journaling has long been recognized as an important learning tool for helping outdoor learners contemplate the physical, emotional, and psychological challenges they experience (Bennion & Olsen, 2002; Rapparlie, 2011). More conventional narratives of personal adventure can support sustained interest and fascination with outdoor experiences and encourage creative storytelling among some reluctant writers. K–12 language arts curricula can expand on students' initial excitement with outdoor activities through nonfiction and fiction accounts. Combining student trip reporting and adventure literature with outdoor experiences can foster successful collaborative themed units and guided creative outdoor explorations.

Writing

When asked specifically about the role of literacy in K–12 schooling, the interviewees were unanimous in declaring that success in the profession requires good writing abilities. The market for guidebooks and adventure stories in a relatively small niche arena is highly competitive. High-quality adventure writing, most of them claimed, is rare but essential in the field. On the business—retail garment, equipment, and outfitter—side, marketing is everything. One of the garment manufacturers asserted that millions of dollars in business transactions depend on successful communication with suppliers and customers, most of it via email. "Strunk & White, Strunk & White," he repeated over and over. The outfitter explained that his river guides need to be able to write up trip reports and accident reports that can withstand critique in the event of a lawsuit. The Summit to Sea adventurer explained that in the competitive sponsorship world, the adventurer who has a strong social media presence and can capture the experience through engaging adventure stories wins the grants.

SUGGESTIONS FOR K–12 SCHOOLING

As discussed earlier, outdoor and physical education teachers can incorporate reflective and adventure writing on their own but also collaborate with language arts colleagues to help students move from direct field experiences to reflection and writing. Outdoor experiences can spawn creative writing and, as shown above, involve business and technical writing. Students should be informed that, "even in the world of adventure sports," observation, creativity, and concision in writing are highly valued.

Experiential-Literacy-Learning Guides/Guidance

Because adventure sports and outdoor experience programs privilege direct field experiences as the foundation upon which other learning occurs, various texts (simulation, drama, audiovisual media, pictures and audio, traditional print) play a supplemental but essential role in curriculum design. The community college adventure sports program, in which participant observation was carried out for this research, sequences the curriculum first to prioritize immersion in outdoor field experiences; then promote reflection through discussion, simulation, and video; and finally, introduce text for more formal learning of concepts and professional preparation.

Rous (2000) offers examples of literature and writing integration with environmental and adventure activities. These can be presented through traditional before, during, and after strategic frameworks that prioritize students' outdoor engagement throughout the learning experience and then incorporate reading and writing. Teachers can construct learning guides that sequence outdoor experiential observations; data collection; audiovisual documentation; reflective, analytical, and exploratory writing; as well as adventure, science and social studies readings to expand on field observations and incorporate advanced disciplinary understanding across curriculum areas.

Conclusion

The CCSS (NGA & CCSSO, 2010) initiatives may well guide youth toward college and career readiness, but they still focus only on traditional school disciplines and content areas. This limited emphasis leaves many stones unturned, many forests, mountains, and rivers unexplored and underappreciated, and many children staring out of classroom windows longing to be in the outdoors as explorers and adventurers. Collaborations across the school curriculum that link literacy with outdoor and physical education may lead these students to embrace academic achievement as a means for participation in the great outdoors.

A Teacher Reflects: Kathy Blakemore, Physical and Outdoor Education Teacher[4]

My most gratifying teaching experiences have come not from covering the standards in my classroom or in the gym, but from getting my students outside the classroom to directly interact with nature. It's always surprising to me that so many of my students have never ventured beyond our little town, have never seen the ocean, or hiked in the local mountains. While it can be a frustrating and time-consuming task making these excursions happen for our students, the seemingly insurmountable challenges surrounding the planning and approval process melt away once we see our students' smiling faces as they experience nature and return to our classrooms with a wealth of new experiences to draw from.

As a life science and physical education teacher, I have had the pleasure of taking my students to the Catalina Island Marine Institute (CIMI) for more than a quarter century. My students have the opportunity to experience firsthand what we have been learning about in our seventh-grade classroom. Imagine my joy as I'm mobbed by my students excitingly telling me about the bioluminescence they

---

[4] **Kathy Blakemore** is an outdoor education enthusiast who also teaches science and physical education at Elsinore Middle School in Lake Elsinore, California.

observed on their nighttime snorkel adventure. Their use of the academic language of science and outdoor education was proof of their enthusiasm: "We waved our hands around and kicked our fins and the plankton lit up beautiful blue! Seeing bioluminescence was one of my bucket list experiences, Mrs. B."

My students also noticed distinct differences between the aquatic environments of Long Beach Harbor and the coves at CIMI and were able to describe their observations. "If everyone could see how beautiful and clear the water was at Catalina, they would take better care of the ocean," Marlee said.

My favorite camp experiences with students include our full-day kayaking adventure and our snorkeling trips. Sahar shared that not only had she never kayaked before, but also she had never swum in the ocean before: "Now I want to go ziplining and skydiving! It's fun to be active."

Even my wheelchair-bound students were able to experience camp this past year. Working with our chaperones and aides to get these kids suited up in wetsuits and out in the ocean to snorkel was a worthwhile endeavor. Janelle smiled as she proudly announced that she "got to snorkel for the first time, something I never dreamed I would be able to do." As I stood on the pier at camp overlooking Janelle and Gabby snorkeling with their classmates, tears came to my eyes, and I still get misty thinking about making this experience happen for them.

Even students who did not have the opportunity to attend camp were able to learn about the experience through the eyes of their classmates. My language arts colleague has the CIMI students write about a day at camp from the perspective of a moray eel. As the students share their stories in class, the kids who did not have the opportunity to attend camp get to live vicariously through their peers' written observations.

As teachers, we have a tremendous responsibility, as we power our students' connection to the world. Although my students remember, first and foremost, how much fun their visit to the Catalina Island Marine Institute was, I know how these firsthand experiences act as a bridge to scientific literacy. I truly believe that sharing our love for the great outdoors might be the most important lesson of all.

HISTORY AND THE SOCIAL SCIENCES

Donna Ogle Interviews Susan J. Pearson[5]

I met Susan on a blustery November afternoon as she dismounted from her bike, took off her helmet, and locked it to her front wheel. She was just finishing a day working at the university and had made time to talk with me. As we settled into a

---

[5] **Dr. Donna Ogle** is Professor Emeritus of Literacy Education at National Louis University in Chicago, Illinois.
Dr. Susan J. Pearson is Associate Professor of History at Northwestern University in Evanston, Ilinois.

cozy corner restaurant table I turned on my tape recorder and asked her to describe her work as an academic historian. Susan explained that she combines her own research and writing with her responsibilities developing and teaching courses in American history.

Her training is as a United States cultural historian with a focus on the 18th to 19th centuries. In graduate school she researched issues of animal protection from 1865 to 1920, and through her research identified a connection between the development of societies designed to protect animals and those advocating for children's rights. She pursued this connection in her doctoral dissertation research and was the first scholar to establish the relationships between the animal and child rights movements. This research is also the topic of her recently published and award-winning book, *The Rights of the Defenseless: Protecting Animals and Children in Gilded Age America* (Pearson, 2011).

Currently, Susan is researching the history of mandatory birth record-keeping in the United States, a practice that didn't begin until the beginning of the 20th century. Her research involves identifying and searching government archives, periodicals and contemporary press, and personal papers. Many of the resources she needs are in the National Archives in Washington, DC, and the Library of Congress. She also uses other libraries and searches for notes from historical writings that provide leads for additional sources. In addition, she sometimes uses the Central Archival Catalog, which is now available online.

Susan explained that her approach as a researcher involves finding and reading sources pertinent to the problem she is investigating and always asking two questions: What point of view is represented in the text, and what is its context? After identifying the perspective of a text she checks to see whether the view is reliable and can help her more deeply understand the problem she wants to study. She explained that all source texts do reflect the author's perspectives, and we need to understand them to make credible interpretations.

It is also important to Susan to contextualize each source; she asks herself what the source is and how it fits within its own time, who the intended audience was, and what the text can or cannot reveal. It isn't enough to read a text from a 21st-century point of view because that can really distort an author's point. Historians need to have a clear understanding of the issues and contexts within which the texts they use were written. Only then can they begin to make reasoned interpretations and build strong arguments.

In order to contextualize sources, Susan explained that is it important to know the basic debates in the field at any particular time—what questions were being grappled with during the time a text was written, and how the sources she studies reflect these debates. "In fact," according to Susan, "75% of graduate school is learning the debates in the field." For her, "the fun part is that people disagree, and I like to find the different perspectives." By understanding the factors that influenced the debates and putting the different source documents in context, "you find the con-tribution you can make" by more deeply understanding and interpreting the issues.

When asked about her own reading, Susan responded that she reads in vari-ous ways. In looking for details while researching a topic, she may use the index first and then locate specific information. At other times, she reads with the intent of both identifying and understanding the argument and content of the piece and then contextualizes it: "Interpretation—that's what we do."

Susan explained that, for historians, a key to historical reading is understand-ing arguments; in fact, that is a focus of her work with graduate students. She explained that, generally, undergraduates come in with little experience or under-standing of how to identify arguments and evidence provided by authors. She wants them to become familiar with both primary and secondary sources and use both types of texts because her goals for their reading include both developing a deeper understanding of the content and the details surrounding an issue and also looking for arguments. She thinks it is important that undergraduate students read to build a good foundation in knowing the content and contexts in which historical issues can be addressed.

Susan shared how she helps build this orientation with freshmen and sopho-mores who are in her course "United States Women's History to 1865." Each week, she addresses a particular topic and has assigned readings that include both primary and secondary sources. The secondary source generally provides a historical context for the topic, and the primary sources bring in voices with particular points of view. For example, the week that the class explores "Women's Work and Industrializa-tion," the readings include a chapter from the book *The Bonds of Womenhood* (Cott, 1997) and two primary-source documents: *Rules of the Mill, Lowell and Lancaster, 1820–1840* (Woloch, 2014) and Harriet Farley's "A Letter from Lowell" (1844).

When she assigns primary and secondary sources, Susan expects students to know that each text has an argument or point that is supported with information. She also expects them to find the relationships between the primary and second-ary sources; sometimes these are complementary and at other times different. She explained, "That's what historians do; we compare our evidence with other people's findings." A tension for undergraduates is that they are often overwhelmed with the amount of information presented; however, by junior or senior year they are better able to look for arguments in the texts they read.

Developing her students' writing skills is very important, so each week Susan has them write an argumentative essay based on the readings. She poses a ques-tion and they draw on the sources they have read to construct their arguments. For example, when reading four chapters from *The Bonds of Womanhood* students were asked to respond:

"The author argues that domesticity is both a constraint and empowers women. How is it so? Explain in 500 words or less."

In writing these essays students must focus on both the relevant content (identifying issues and details from the text) and do the thinking to formulate their own argument and use relevant evidence in response to the author's statement.

Susan explained that she actually thinks more actively about students' writing than their reading. Her course syllabus also reflects her expectation that students write each week and also compose a final memoir paper. Her directions read:

"For this paper, you will read the memoir of an American woman and make an argument about how she exemplifies, defies, or otherwise relates to the historical context in which she lives. You will choose your memoir during the first week of class. For each memoir, I will hold a writing workshop during a regularly scheduled class meeting. Memoir papers are due on the last day of class. Choose one of the following selections: Mary Jemison, Abigail Bailey, or Elizabeth Keckley."

Conclusion

Susan Pearson is a historian active in her own scholarship as well as fully involved with teaching history to university students. During the interview she explained in some depth the types of reading and writing she expects of herself and her students. For those teachers who read this from the frame of the CCSS there are clearly some important issues to consider:

1. A historian doesn't read a text without first determining the authorship, context, and the larger setting from which it emerged. The terms—author's perspective or point of view and contextualizing a text—are central to her ways of thinking about texts she reads.
2. Interpretation means understanding the perspective of the author in relation to how it fits with its own times.
3. Developing enough knowledge of the context from which sources emerge is important in understanding them.
4. Identifying and evaluating the evidence provided by authors is central to historical thinking.
5. Writing argumentative texts using accurate historical data is at the heart of historical work.

A Teacher Reflects: Javier Vaca, 11th-Grade Social Studies Teacher[6]

In her interview, Susan J. Pearson talks about the importance of contextualization when studying any issue or document. The idea of identifying the context is one that I emphasize in my 11th-grade United States history class.

I teach my students that when preparing to read historical documents, it is important to familiarize oneself with the societal, political, and financial issues of the time. With these contextual parameters they are better able to evaluate the document. As we study a topic I often model through thinking aloud how I contextualize or consider what was happening in America when a document we are studying was created, and how that context affects my interpretation of the document.

For example, when we study early American history, my students read about and discuss the effects of the Great Awakening, a sweeping religious movement. My purpose is for them to understand how this movement spread and influenced society during the 18th century. We often view photos of this period. While doing so I might think aloud and wonder about all of the folks gathered around George Whitefield as he preached. I might share that I had read that he had such a power of persuasion that even Benjamin Franklin, who is often described as a scientific skeptic, emptied his change purse into the collection basket after hearing the preaching of Whitefield, a British minister who toured the colonies to enlighten folks about religion.

Once students understand the importance of contextualizing all types of documents, they are better able to consider the possibility of persuasion as a factor that could fuel a 21st-century religious movement. They understand the Enlightenment period in the timeline of American history and contrast it with current religious persecution and newly developing ministries. My students recognize there was no social media in the 18th century and the spread of information and ideas today is completely different because one can daily hear a contrastive perspective. Understanding contextualization allows my students to more effectively evaluate the information.

The other portion of Dr. Pearson's interview that relates to my teaching and my students is the idea of prompting students to write as historians. It is important for my students to synthesize their ideas and thoughts through writing. After studying a particular time period through reading primary sources, my students need to show their understanding and learn from their writing. They are able to make better connections to the historical time periods we are studying when they are prompted to look for evidence from primary and secondary sources to support their claims in writing. Like Dr. Pearson's students, my 11th graders are taught how to identify as well as write convincing arguments.

---

[6]**Javier Vaca** is a teacher of social studies at Health Sciences High and Middle College in San Diego, California.

After reading this interview I realized the power a teacher has to prepare students for real-life participation and the positions they must take in society. By teaching students in high school these principles, they might be better prepared to learn in university settings that demand even more from them. They are on their way knowing how to contextually study an issue from many perspectives, share a well-documented interpretation, and identify new areas for investigation. I hope I am preparing my students so they will want to continue deepening their historical thinking under the guidance of university professors like Dr. Pearson.

LITERATURE AND THE ENGLISH LANGUAGE ARTS

Denise Johnson Interviews Steve Sheinkin[7]

Steve, what is involved in your daily work? In what way do words matter in your job?

The funny thing about doing this work, even though it's called being a writer, is that most days aren't writing days. Most days are research or organizing and outlining days. I find that's what takes the most time and actually that's probably what I enjoy the most. The actual writing process is hard. I find it hard to get started. It's easier to do the research and then say, maybe I'll just do one more outline or maybe I'll just read one more book. I really have to force myself to sit down and write. That first draft is by far the hardest part, and that is about words. I already know at that point exactly what the story should be, but now I have to translate it from my head to this two-dimensional piece of paper and somehow keep it as exciting as I think it should be. That's by far the hardest part. But in terms of words, it's just a matter of seeing it and then writing it and describing it as simply and as clearly as I can.

How do you read texts in your discipline? What processes do you use?

A big part of my job is reading and taking notes. So when I'm reading, I'm always writing at the same time. I'll read with my notebook or usually a computer open and have the book open and take notes because I know that is all the raw material that I might use. I will take hundreds of notes and most of it or some of it won't make it in, but I feel like I need to have a record of where I got everything. That file gets very big and unwieldy by the end of the project. I think of it as a series of steps in solving

---

[7]**Dr. Denise Johnson** is Professor and Director of the Literacy Leadership Program and Department Chair of Curriculum and Instruction at the College of William & Mary in Williamsburg, Virginia. **Steve Sheinkin** is the author of several award-winning nonfiction books for young adults: *The Notorious Benedict Arnold: A True Story of Adventure, Heroism & Treachery*; *Bomb: The Race to Build—and Steal—the World's Most Dangerous Weapon*; and *The Port Chicago 50: Disaster, Mutiny, and the Fight for Civil Rights.*

a mystery. Each book is almost like a witness to me—they present ideas almost like an interview—through the quotes within the book or source notes at the back. That's a big part of the reading for me—letting one source lead to the next, and to the next, and to the next, and sometimes to surprising sources.

If you were to interview a candidate for a job, what demands for reading and writing (and perhaps discussion or speaking/listening) would you expect people to know that are specific to your type of work?

To me, the ability to write clearly and concisely, that's where I don't regret my whole textbook life. [Steve wrote material for history textbooks before becoming a full-time author.] You know that piece of wisdom that says you need to work at something for 10,000 hours to get good at it? That was my 10,000 hours. I want somebody who has put in a lot of time. People do ask me how they can become a writer, and really, the only thing you can do is just put in that time. Nobody can really help you that much until you've really put in that time, which some people don't want to hear. Writing doesn't come easily for most people, at least not to me.

What cognitive tasks are involved, such as synthesis? What are the demands of reading and writing for you in your job?

The thing I love doing most of all is taking massive amounts of information and then thinking of it as a puzzle or parts of a movie and trying to figure out how to fit it together. That's where index cards come in, because I think that really helps—to have something in your hands to move around just like the pieces of a puzzle. There's a scene or a piece of information I have—maybe 50 things—and just moving them around where they go because I think the biggest challenge with writing nonfiction for this age is that you can't assume they already know about anything. So the *Port Chicago* book starts at Pearl Harbor, and if I say that to an older person, they have a million associations, but a kid—you never know—maybe they do and maybe they don't. So how do you work in the basics of what was going on in December 1941 and what the Japanese were doing and what we were doing? I have to include enough background information so that it makes sense in context while still keeping the story. That, to me, is the biggest challenge—figuring out how to synthesize the stuff you need to know and the stuff that's going to make it fun to know.

What would you say to teachers about the language demands (reading, writing, discussion, etc.) of your particular discipline or job?

The number one thing teachers ask me to talk about is the editing process and the fact that just because you hand a paper in doesn't mean you're done. That's true of the best writing you can think of, just like it's true for your seventh-grade paper. When I hand something in, I get it back full of comments. One of them is: This isn't working. That's a big, big part of the process. You must be open to revision. By all means, get it down. That's the hardest part. But once you do that, show it to people and don't get defensive if they point out things that don't work or aren't clear. I'm just so glad nobody ever sees first drafts that I write except my editors. Published work is so good because so much revision has been done. It's that back-and-forth with my editor where she'll say, "If you really feel strongly about this piece, tell me what you think," and we'll go back and forth. It's important to be able to express what the book is really about, and if that's what it's really about, how does this part fit into the core story and how does it advance that story? That's what good editors will do—they say that's a great scene but it doesn't advance the story.

A Teacher Reflects: Stacy Miller, High School Teacher[8]

I love that Steve Sheinkin refers to the 10,000 hours to be successful. I first read about this theory in Malcolm Gladwell's *Outliers: Stories of Success* (2008). I like to read about people applying it to their own lives, to include reading and writing. Often we see the successful result of something—even an essay or an op-ed piece—without seeing the 10,000 hours behind it. It's like that cliché movie storytelling technique where shortly before we see a character achieving success we see a montage of "this is the character working hard" scenes that comprise, maybe, 30 seconds of screen time. Of course, the soundtrack swell helps as well. I have to remind students that 30 seconds of screen time is not the same as 10,000 hours or practice and real work.

The index card thing. I get that. As a tactile, visual learner who likes to see things, to manipulate them, index cards are a great tool. It is literally hands-on. It's important not to overlook the myriad ways to learn something or process information, and I like that Steve Sheinkin mentions the cards and puzzle pieces.

Steve Sheinkin makes some great statements about the editing process. I agree that we need to teach students more about that and to appreciate good editing—and editors—for what they do. It's the difference between writing something to turn in for credit and writing something to really express yourself. As a full-time educator, I wish I had more time for the revision process with my students. I wish we had more time for drafts and revisions. The funny thing about teaching honors and advanced courses is that you are preparing students to write an exam answer (I'm referring to the College Board and the AP Exams) that cannot be edited or revised. Students get one shot to express their thoughts intelligently and cogently. There are no drafts.

---

[8]**Stacey Miller** teaches at Stuttgart High School (U.S. Department of Defense Education Activity [DoDEA]) in Germany.

SCIENCES

Maria Grant Interviews Devin Burr[9]

I interviewed Devin Burr, a medical student, on a gray May day from my home in San Diego. Devin and I talked by phone. He was residing in Oregon at the time of our conversation, poised to graduate from Western University of Health Sciences in June, and ready to move to Jefferson City, Missouri, where he would begin an intern year followed by either a dermatology or emergency medicine residency. Grateful that a busy medical student would make time for a lengthy conversation about "literacy in his life," I proceeded to barrage him with the queries on my mind. His responses were not only insightful, but they were also thought provoking, so much so that I was compelled to make significant connections to my own area of passion—instructional practices in the discipline of science teaching.

A Day in the Life of a Physician

Devin began by clarifying his educational background to date. As mentioned, he's a medical student, currently focused on disease processes and how the human body reacts. The first 2 years of his course of study were spent in the class—brick-and-mortar studies to build background knowledge and expertise. The next 2 years were spent in the field, engaged in "rotations" as a way to encounter all areas of medicine. Through this experience, Devin was able to visit with patients under the guidance of physicians, report findings back to physicians, and practice making diagnoses under the guidance of mentors. As a future intern, he will be tasked with more responsibilities that might include ordering labs and giving medications. He'll be on duty for longer periods of time and will stay with a particular rotation for at least a month. As he continues to progress, he'll conduct exams and will recommend treatments.

 In my own attempt to better understand the role reading, writing, and academic language might play in the life of a medical student, I questioned Devin about his daily routine. He let me know that the morning hours spent in the hospital consisted of visits to patients, consultations with night nurses, and writing notes that would later be presented to a resident or attending physician. By afternoon he might be working in the emergency room to help with examinations. His time in the hospital was variable—sometimes he'd be at the clinic from 8:00 A.M. until 5:00 P.M., other times he'd be at the hospital until 10:00 P.M. After each rotation, Devin was required to complete an assessment (a test) with content based on his experience. The test was designed to assess his acquired skills proficiency and

---

[9] **Dr. Maria Grant** is Professor of Education at California State University, Fullerton, and a physics teacher at Health Science High and Middle College in San Diego, California. **Dr. Devin Burr** is a resident physician at Aspen Dermatology in Spanish Fork, Utah.

content knowledge. An exam might cover the treatment of appendicitis or surgery for a gall bladder issue. Devin would read up on the area of focus to become expert in whatever discrete area of study he was tackling for the rotation.

Literacy Practices in a Doctor's Day

As soon as Devin mentioned books and reading, I knew it was my cue to delve deeper with my interrogation: "How do you read texts in your discipline? What processes do you use?" In response, Devin clarified that when he reads a text he often follows his self-developed protocol. He provided me with an example, stating, "I might have to read a book with pages and pages about a topic or a disease—heart attacks, for instance." Devin clearly outlined his protocol for me, adding that it's really effective for him. Here's how it works:

1. The first read is a general read. Devin reads the text like a storybook. There's no highlighting, and it's done only one time during the first day of study.
2. The next day, he rereads, this time looking for findings, labs for a disease, medications, and so on. He highlights these for future reference.
3. Devin says he begins to focus his reading, from big ideas to smaller details. He calls this "reading like a funnel." He was definitely engaged in close reading.
4. Next, he studies the highlights for the exam.
5. For any subsequent readings, Devin clarifies that he often will take notes. He adds that the note-taking helps him to focus and then he has the notes for future study, as a tool. That reminded me of the need for K–12 classroom science teachers to think of note-taking as both beneficial in terms of the process and the product. Students learn when they take the notes and they have a product—the notes—that they can use to study for a test, write a paper, or develop a podcast or poster.

Noticing that Devin emphasized how essential it was for him to do a general read followed by a series of detailed, focused readings, I felt compelled to ask him about the complexities of the texts he studies: "Do you encounter diagrams or charts? How do you deal with these and with other difficult areas of text?" Once again, Devin's response offered insights into this issue of science literacy.

Devin often comes upon tough areas in his readings—technical terminology, academic styles of writing, and content that requires strategies in order to negotiate meaning. To wade through this high water of struggle, Devin often turns to podcasts about particular medical topics. In this way, he augments his reading with audio content that is clarified by an expert in the field. Devin enthusiastically tells me that he "likes diagrams," adding that they break up the text and provide alternative ways to understand the content. In other words, diagrams help Devin to augment his learning. He even admitted that sometimes he uses them to bypass the complex, tedious text that accompanies a diagram. He has copious amounts of reading, and a diagram can provide a shortcut to understanding—one that Devin enjoys taking if it leads to learning in a more abbreviated manner. Since Devin does place such importance on his reading of diagrams and since they are numerous in medical books, he added that he finds meaning in the details: the captions, the labels, the arrows, and so on. He truly *reads* a diagram just like he might a paragraph or a page, first paying attention to the generalities, then homing in on details. He added that his math background is helpful when reviewing graphs and charts.

Impressed with Devin's ability to articulate his reading strategies in such a metacognitive manner, I asked him to share his thoughts on the literacy expectations in his field of study: "What demands for reading, writing, and speaking-listening are there in the medical profession and within the studies that lead up to a career in this field?" Devin had clear thoughts on this topic of discussion, replying, "For medical school and to be an intern you need to know how to read technical texts." He added, "When it comes to writing, there is much more involved than I ever thought." Dwelling a bit on the topic of writing, Devin reflected, "What a medical professional writes on a patient's chart is the path that will be followed for treatment. It needs to be clear and coherent. Medications need to be clearly described and this all needs to be interpretable." Devin closed his thought, noting with a serious tone, "You're dealing with people's lives." It became clear to me that the topic of *writing in the medical* profession was one that Devin had given considerable thought to, realizing that the degree of clarity and precision could mean life or death for some patients. In a cursory manner, I had always thought of medical writing in terms of my own personal experiences as a patient—scribbled code on a slip of paper called a prescription.

Devin made clear that complex descriptions that paint a picture of a patient's history and current status need to be composed with detail in a coherent, understandable way. As Devin underscored, many people, including doctors, nurses, pharmacists, surgeons, and others, might need to review a patient's profile. Unclear writing puts a patient at risk. Devin added that sometimes bullet point notes are acceptable, especially when it comes to listing treatments. In addition, it is essential that a doctor justify requests in his/her writing. If a doctor wants to order an expensive test or treatment, the request should be made using detailed, precise language. For instance, a request that states "Patient has a dark mole, with an irregular border that has increased in size. It requires an incision," is more compelling and clearer than a request that notes "Patient has a brown mole, needs incision." Writing for the profession is often an expectation and/or interest of medical students and doctors. Devin has publications in professional journals, in print and in the works, one article on the topic of treatments for feet of diabetics and another on the topic of minimal-incision extraction for large lipomas.

As our conversation proceeded, Devin made sure I also knew that strong oral communication skills—listening and speaking—are critical to the medical profession. He clarified this by describing the importance of probing questions, especially when it comes to a patient's illness and treatment: "As medical students and interns, we must listen carefully to get a picture of the patient. Then we must be able to verbally convey the information to doctors." He also commented that sometimes patients don't reveal enough and doctors need to rethink their questions. Often they have to reframe the question in a way that delves deeper. Sometimes a doctor may even need to contact others who can contribute more to the understanding of a patient's condition and needs. This might include family members or even nursing facility personnel. Conversations with different people require different registers. For example, when discussing issues with other medical experts, a doctor can speak in more academic, topical terms; however, when speaking with family members, the dialogue may need to be tempered by compassion and understandable layperson's terms.

Medical students are constantly engaging in high-level cognitive tasks, including analysis, synthesis, and evaluation. Devin provided an example of this by describing how doctors conduct physical exams when they are trying to diagnose a person's condition. He explained that doctors often use data from a physical exam, along with labs, to determine a disease or patient issue. They analyze the data and evaluate the condition of the patient; then they can outline next steps for treatment. These thinking skills are intimately integrated with the literacy demands of the profession.

Devin provided me with valuable insights into the requirements for reading, writing, and oral communication. Consequently, I thought it greatly appropriate that I ask him to provide future medical students with advice, so I asked, "How could young people considering a career similar to yours best prepare for future study and career demands?" Without hesitation, Devin emphatically advised, "Develop a love of learning early on. Doctors who have had decades in the profession are still reading, still learning. There's always something new to learn." Devin didn't mince words with this advice. He emphasized that learning takes place in the class at the start and has to be a part of any doctor's personal goals throughout his or her career. Devin left me with a final thought, "Becoming a doctor requires more than just retaining information. You must apply your knowledge every day and your knowledge must continually grow."

Literacy to a Physician Is a Life-or-Death Matter

As I hung up the phone, reflecting on the conversation, I realized that expertise in all aspects of literacy is at the core of a doctor's daily life. It's the lifeblood of the profession. Being a highly literate expert in the medical field—one who reads, writes, and engages in professional, academic conversations—is the only way that a medical student and a doctor can flourish to offer patients high-quality medical care to treat illness and preserve health. I left more compelled than ever to promote the integration of discipline-specific literacy learning—*science literacy learning*—as means for our society's young people to become career and college ready for studies in science and related fields and to become informed global citizens who can have a voice in science issues that affect our planet. As Devin noted, the difference between life and death for patients rests on the literacy skills of their physicians.

A Teacher Reflects: Angela Hackman, High School Science Teacher[10]

As I read Devin's interview I was excited, as a science educator, to see how clearly he valued literacy in science as a medical student. I identified connections not only between the skills used by Devin and the activities in my classroom, but also with the need to continue sharing with my students the importance of literacy practices in the real world. My students gain so much by practicing literacy skills in class, but I believe they underestimate how valuable these skills will be to their future success.

In describing his reading of texts, Devin outlined a five-step procedure that allowed him to fully gain understanding for his daily activities and assessments. The steps he described are very similar to the process my students undergo when completing close reading in my classroom. The students begin by reading the text for general meaning and then begin to focus on details for a clearer understanding of the text. The students are also making notes, highlighting, and annotating the text while reading to ensure they know what to reference for future competencies in the class. Devin also mentioned how important diagrams can be to support the text. In class, we do close readings of diagrams, graphs, and tables. The students are able to process the text in a new way while learning the skills to analyze visuals so that in the future they can better understand information they read in college or their personal lives. We begin by generally looking over the visual, and then we begin to focus on details such as the title of the visual, the units on the axes, the labels, and any descriptions provided in the text. The students are able to recognize that a visual that initially seemed overwhelming can become understandable by breaking it down into smaller segments. The techniques my students learn, like Devin's practices, provide a foundation needed to process and use scientific information in their future workplaces, college, or when voting on a scientific ballot issue. I passionately believe in helping my students process scientific information with the intent of ensuring they will have the skills needed to become participating citizens involved in their community.

---

[10] **Angela Hackman** is a teacher at Health Sciences High and Middle College in San Diego, California.

In the interview, Devin also describes the importance of written and oral communication in addition to reading skills. The variety of literacy practices he uses is similar to the structure in my classroom. The students are required to read, write, and speak about science every day. To complete these practices, I must provide the structure to ensure they are using academic language as well as evidence to support their thinking. I expose my students to good and bad science so they can decipher what makes a good argument. My students are given sentence frames to help communicate their ideas. The vocabulary important for the topic is posted as a word wall in my classroom as a reminder of what scientific language should be used. I what them to see, learn, and use scientific language, so I must be sure they have a positive exposure to doing so.

Devin also stressed the need for clarity and detail in communication, which made me think of the students writing lab reports. When describing how to complete lab reports, I remind the students that detail is necessary because scientists must use their lab reports as evidence for studies in medicine and that the procedures must be replicable step by step. With patients' charts, Devin provides another example of the real-world necessity for explicit explanations that the students could relate to when completing in-class writing. In explanations, evidence and justification are necessary throughout the science world, which I stress in my classroom through using the Next Generation Science Standards (NGSS) and Engineering Practices. The students are required to use texts or labs as evidence when explaining their thoughts both in written and oral forms. For example, the students wrote argumentative letters to President Obama regarding solutions to global climate change. They described the problem by citing evidence from a speech by President Obama, an article from *Scientific American,* and labs completed in class about ocean acidification. The students continued the letter by providing a solution to carbon pollution using texts and online sources. They were able to see that, in order to make a valid claim, they needed to use detail and evidence just as Devin must use to ensure the patient gets the best care.

Ultimately the demands on a person to use science requires the ability to understand and express scientific thoughts through reading, writing, and verbal communication. Devin stressed a variety of ways science literacy affects his education and his future career. My students are practicing science literacy in the classroom. I believe my role as a teacher is to push my students to understand science through different types of communication while helping them see that by being able to truly understand and communicate science they can achieve more success in college classes and careers as well as better understand how the world around them works. My students are going to leave high school and become voters, leaders, and productive citizens, and I want them to be able to process difficult information to use as evidence to support their thoughts and actions.

MUSIC

Linda Lungren Interviews Tim Peterson[11]

Tim received his degree in visual arts (illustration, visual artist and storyboard artist) in 1998. He has worked on several projects and productions and television series and continues to do freelance arts projects in this area.

He has a passion for music and is part of a band formed in 2008 called Evertheory in Los Angeles, a semiprofessional band "hoping to make it big one day." His primary occupation is as a retailer at the Guitar Center, where he is surrounded by music and musicians.

As a retailer in the music store he uses language constantly. His knowledge of art and music is translated into sales on the floor. Words are absolutely important, as he has to be extremely clear and articulate with the customers. He feels 80% of his time with customers is spent listening, assimilating their thoughts, and interpreting their needs and directing them to find the best product for their needs.

His job in the Guitar Center involves a lot of reading. He has full certification in all areas of the store, which he achieved through demonstrating skills learned in required training modules, viewing training videos, listening to everything presented in the store, reading manuals and PDFs online, technical specifications of electronics, and so on.

As a member of a band, he is very involved with words and language. He must be an active listener of the world and translate that meaning into his lyrics and music.

Interviewing for members of a band is something that he does often, as members of the band come and go and must be replaced. He and his band partner have it down to a "science" with a list of questions distilled from things they have found to be important to the group. (e.g., expectations of rehearsal time; commitment to being available for rehearsals and performances; commitment to solo practicing outside of group rehearsal; willingness to collaborate). Reading music is a "plus," but not necessary in this type of band—much of today's rock band rehearsal is through listening, attaching chords, experiencing the music rather than note reading.

The actual work at the Guitar Center does not have to involve reading. However, to be skillful, an employee must be ready to meet, greet, listen, find the solution, and close the deal. To be knowledgeable, he must be able to read the specifications from manuals for the various instruments in the store (especially the electronic ones), finding the right equipment that works together through comparing specifications. These resources can also include websites, Google searches, and databases on the computer. Reading is one thing, but there is a need to interpret the words

---

[11]**Dr. Linda Lungren** is a music teacher for San Diego City Schools and a pianist, composer, and choral director. **Tim Peterson** is a bass guitar specialist in the Los Angeles area and a member of the popular band Evertheory.

for the customer. Experience is important, but being able to research the resources is also important. The customer is making an investment and wants to make the right choice based on information backed by literature, other people's experiences, and salesperson knowledge.

In the band, literacy is important in a variety of ways. Members must be able to read contracts and make sure the language is working to the band's advantage. They must be able to break down each part of the contract point by point so they can accept some and reject others.

In addition, social media plays a huge role in today's world. You must get your information "out there" and sound reasonably intelligent so you are giving your best impression and convincing people to listen to your quality of music. Social media is now "the press." In the past, publishers always had an editor to organize, check grammar, format, and conform to industry standards. There has been a deterioration of that model lately as the artist has become the social media creator, organizer, editor, formatter, and proofreader, so there is a far greater risk for error. It probably has to do with a change in the economy—doing away with jobs; doing more with less; using skeleton crews for jobs that are still big. Tim's graphic arts background has helped him in much of his social media design.

Writing has become interesting for the band artist. Sometimes you are asked to "post" something immediately on social media, and you have to make sure you are not misrepresenting something through hurried posts. You press "send" and it is gone. Tim's band has done several interviews where the interviewer typed out the questions to send to the band. The band typically divides it up and each member takes a few of the questions. They had an experience where the interviewer merely inserted his questions and their answers (typed as they had submitted) without really looking through and perhaps changing some of the grammar and spelling— not a good experience. A lot of interviewing is now done through written correspondence as opposed to face-to-face talking.

Tim is very involved in literacy and music and making commentary through his lyrics. He decides what kind of message he is trying to convey. It has to be concise, and he really has to condense and be frugal with his words like a poet. Songs are not like chapters or books—they need to be to the point. They have to distill their thoughts down to a song verse, simplify, find the exact words or phrases. Lyrics and songs are like sketches—the "underdrawing" of a sketch, expressing a lyrical idea, pulling out the purest form of language, refine, refine, refine, refine and layer, layer, layer, and revisit your original thoughts.

His band, Evertheory, is based on the Theory of Everything, and they love to investigate science within musical sounds, expressions, and words. They play with concepts and imagery of planets and the galaxy, the bell curve of knowledge, geometric shapes, and radiation belts. A listener must be willing to explore language with Evertheory's music, which can be quite complex and abstract; a superficial listener might just not "get it." The band has made a conscious effort to exclude swear words from their lyrics; even though swear words can be expressive, there often are other words that better express what they want to say.

A Teacher Reflects: Cameron Brown, Middle School Director of Instrumental Music[12]

Reading and interpreting music in the realm of instrumental music education comes about, in my opinion, similarly to the way the English language is taught to American schoolchildren. The first things that are mastered are the technical aspects of reading and writing, and how to do each of these correctly and effectively. Later, children are taught that reading and writing can also be artistic in the form of poems, lyrics, plays, and more. I would say that reading music and performing it on an instrument is taught in the same order, but the arrival at the performance of artistic elements, as well as evaluating of these elements, comes much sooner in music than it does for the English language.

Musical Language That Is Taught to Students

In the first year or two, music students are taught to read the two most basic aspects of music: pitch and rhythm. Pitch is the particular sound that is to be played on the instrument (A, B, C, D, E, F, or G, sometimes with a modifier such as flat, sharp, or natural). Rhythms are the symbols that tell the musician how long the note should be played in the number of beats it should receive. The basics are whole note (four beats), half note (two beats), and quarter note (one beat). It gets more complicated with both pitch and rhythm as students get older, continually progress, and advance their skill set to be able to encounter more difficult pitches and rhythmic patterns on their instruments.

In the first 2 years of music education, students also learn foundational artistic elements to performing as they continue to learn and grow with the basic pitches and rhythms on their instrument. The main artistic concepts taught in these early stages are the basics of dynamics (different levels of volume) and articulations (in band music) or stylistic bowings (in orchestral music), which are different ways to attack notes to achieve different effects.

As students progress into advanced middle school and high school music ensembles, and they learn many other stylistic markings that increase artistry and add emotional context. Examples of stylistic markings include the following: *appassionato* (impassioned), *cantabile* (play in a style as if the instrument were singing), *con fuoco* (with fire), *maestoso* (majestically), *marziale* (march-like), *scherzando* (playfully), and *tranquillo* (tranquil).

---

[12] **Cameron Brown** is Director of Instrumental Music at Thurgood Marshall Middle School in San Diego, California.

Language Used by Music Teachers and Conductors in Classrooms and Rehearsals

In addition to knowing the extensive lists of dynamics, articulations/bowings, tempo markings, and stylistic markings, teachers and conductors (who are the same person in a school music context) must convey artistic messages using spoken words to their students and/or ensembles (again, one in the same in a school setting). First, all of these artistic concepts must be taught effectively by the conductor/teacher. Once students master these concepts, teachers and conductors must utilize the terms in order for their students/musicians to perform these aspects of each piece of music accurately, as written by the composer and/or arranger, throughout the rehearsal process.

The descriptive, artistic language used by educators and/or conductors must effectively teach the concepts of the creative aspects of music. Once their students understand, educators/conductors must use the common language of the ensemble to convey their interpretation of the composer's and/or arranger's artistic vision for the music. I often find myself using metaphors and analogies to help communicate my interpretations of music to my students. In the past, I have said things like "This passage must be performed as if we're trying to put a baby to sleep," "We are sending soldiers off to war!", or "In this piece, we are attempting to recreate the beauty of a sunrise through sound." Other descriptive things I can recall saying to students would include "punchy" (to further emphasize some staccato markings), "lush" and "warm and cozy" (to describe a particular ballad), "soul lifting" (to describe an apex in an emotional), "vengeful" (to describe a particularly intense passage), and "snobbishly" (which is probably not a real word, but I used it to describe a march that was written for a royal family). Using these descriptors, and holding my students/musicians accountable for performing these artistic concepts as effectively as they can, is how I develop great musicianship in my students.

The Importance of Language in Music Education

The importance of both the common language spoken/written by students, as well as the multiple languages utilized in music (pitch, rhythm, and all artistic performance concepts), are imperative in both the learning, as well as performance, of music. There are so many dimensions in which language is used in music education that, without it, great music would be, in my opinion, impossible to make. Legendary conductor and composer Leonard Bernstein once said, "Music can name the unnameable and communicate the unknowable." Without the written and spoken language between musicians, I do not believe music of the caliber we know and enjoy in today's world could've been produced to such depths. I'm sure that, if language had never been developed, music would still happen in some way, shape, or form. I just cannot imagine it being performed to the levels that Mr. Bernstein described in his quote. Language and music are inseparable. Both allow humans to connect with one another. Without one or both of them, our lives would be empty and without much meaning.

LEARN MORE

 Go to *https://goo.gl/ttzQeg* on YouTube or *literacybeat.com/literacy-in-the-disciplines* to watch interview videos at our Disciplinary Literacy channel, including the following:

The Visual Arts

Interviewee: Liz Jardine, an artist in San Diego, California.
Interviewer: Dr. Barbara Moss, San Diego State University.
Teacher: Tim Benson, teacher and president of the San Diego Education Association.

Technology

Interviewee: Paul Hill, Film Editor.
Interviewer: Alex Gonzalez: Director of Technology, Health Sciences High and Middle
    College, San Diego, California.
Teacher: Annaleah Enriquez, Health Teacher, Health Sciences High and Middle
    College, San Diego, California.

Be sure to listen to the podcasts as well.

Literacy Meets Music

Teacher and musician Linda Lungren interviews
    musician Tim Peterson. Podcast.
A disciplinary approach to reading sheet music.
    Video resource from AdLit.

Evertheory

Engineering Education, Design, STEM, Mechanical Engineering, and Literacy

Cynthia Brock, Cal Anderson, and Joe Assof discuss intersections of engineering,
    mathematics, and literacy. Part I video.
Cynthia Brock, Cal Anderson, and Joe Assof discuss teaching implications from Part
    I regarding engineering, mathematics, and literacy. Part II video.
Ian O'Byrne and Kurt Becker discuss engineering education, design, STEM, and
    literacy. Video.
Classroom examples: Joe Assof uses close
    reading to understand word problems. Middle
    school example video. High school example
    video.

Joe Assof uses close reading in a
high school math class.

Students Use the Language of Science

High-school student-created video: Cyberbridge
Reading a graph like a scientist. Video contributed by Josh Lawrence at the University of California, Irvine and AdLit.

Be sure to listen to the podcasts as well.

CHAPTER 2 ACTIVITY

Read at least two of the interviews and teacher reflections in the chapter and create a graphic organizer that compares and contrasts the two disciplines. Use Figure 1.3 (pp. 13–15) for guidance about what to look for as you read. Possible columns include Discipline #1 Features, Discipline #2 Features, Similarities, and Differences. Focus especially on the unique features of each discipline that are not found in the comparison discipline.

Identify the literacy demands in your discipline and then write a concise paragraph that describes how you might apply the disciplinary features of learning content and language at your grade level and within your discipline. What would help you to demonstrate clearly for your students what makes your discipline unique?

PART II

LITERACY INSTRUCTION IN THE DISCIPLINES

Chapter 3

Saying It Well

Instruction That Supports Academic Language Development in the Disciplines

Students in Mr. Moore's eighth-grade United States history course are learning about legislative processes. Mr. Moore prefers the problem- or project-based learning (PBL) (see Hmelo-Silver & Barrows, 2006) approach to many learning outcomes because students learn to solve complex problems, use resources, and especially collaborate with each other both in and outside of the classroom. Groups of students are engaged in topical investigation. One group is at a computer station and all others are sharing tablets. The discussion is animated because they are exploring redistricting, the process of allocating seats to a legislative district based on census data and the many concerns of stakeholders within and outside the district.

As they work with an online simulation (*http://redistrictinggame.org*) they are engaging with the complex ideas involved in redistricting while considering the fields of politics, statistics, global information systems, the American legislative process, and geography. They use terms such as *GIS, census block, gerrymandering,* and *The Voting Rights Act.* To solve the problems the game presents to them, they must work together to make decisions. In other words, they are collaborating while learning. They are learning skills that will serve them well in careers, at home, as citizens, or in postsecondary school education.

Few job descriptions exist that do not call for the ability to work with others. Rigorous standards in many countries and states explicitly recognize the need for collaboration (e.g., NGA & CCSSO, 2010), involving communication in every discipline. In football, an elaborate language system is employed by coaches and quarterbacks and understood by the rest of the team to achieve a shared goal. Authors work as a team, as well. A popular notion is the image of the writer working alone at computer or typewriter, and it is true that some of the work is done in solitude. However, collaboration is at the heart of most writing events. To produce this book, we traded drafts of the chapters, worked with the contributors in Chapter 2 to provide specific examples for several disciplines, and coordinated with acquisition and production editors and the marketing department at The Guilford Press. Scientists work in teams, as do historians. We can imagine Indiana Jones in the field, on his own with only his wits to guide him, but archaeological work always involves collaboration and precise communication with a multidisciplinary team.

Many of the videos at *www.learner.org* illustrate the power of student collaboration.

 Be sure to view collaboration in math at *www.learner.org/courses/ readwrite/video-detail/collaborating-extend-mathematical-understanding. html*.

An example of collaboration in science is at *www.learner.org/courses/ readwrite/video-detail/creating-culture-collaboration.html*.

 To view a mathematics teacher engaging students in collaboration, visit *www.learner.org/courses/readwrite/video-detail/talking-mathematician. html*.

Look at the video and lesson at *www.learner.org/courses/readwrite/ video-detail/developing-questions-promote-discussion.html*.

LISTENING, SPEAKING, DISCUSSING: COLLABORATING

In schools, we frequently separate the receptive aspects and the expressive aspects of language into parts. Receptive literacy tasks include reading, listening, and viewing because they involve working with language generated by others and received by us. Expressive tasks are those where we produce language or some other expression that communicates, such as a work of art or a graphic. To be sure, there are skills specific to each aspect of language. However, in secondary schools, we tend to use multiple skills in a more integrated fashion. Discussion, engaging mentally through note-taking and self-questioning, and working in virtual environments are just some of the tasks that require students to collaborate while using their language skills.

Norms: That's How We Discuss Things around Here

Group norms, not rules, can promote effective interactions in collaborative group work (Cohen, 1994). Norms might include ensuring that each member of the group understands the task, assists other members of the group to stay on task, and helps each other to achieve the task. We developed a checklist we call Goal 18 to help students at any level evaluate how well the group is performing relative to these tasks. This form is shown as Figure 3.1. Students can work with their group to complete this tool. An alternative is to ask students to fill it out as a draft, then use their ranking to discuss further improvements to their group processes.

Accountable Talk

What students say in academic conversations is vital, but norms for the discussion are equally so. The Accountable Talk® approach (Michaels, O'Connor, & Hall, 2010) leads students to be accountable to the learning community for accuracy in their discussions, for rigorous thinking, and for attempting to make sense of what is said within the learning community. In the next sections, we explore some ways that can be done.

Goal 18 Discussion Evaluation				
The discussion Yes = 3; Almost = 2; No = 1			The group Yes = 3; Almost = 2; No = 1	
• Each person understood the concept.			• Everyone participated.	
• Wc used our time productively.			• We are pleased with the discussion outcome.	
• We built on each other's ideas.			• We are ready for the next discussion.	
Task total			Group total	
Job + Group =				

FIGURE 3.1. Group evaluation checklist. Adapted from Lapp, Fisher, and Wolsey (2009) with permission from the authors.

Groups and Discussions

Small groups for discussions throughout an instructional sequence promote topical and language learning and collaboration. Discussions are a bit messy. When the teacher does not have a purpose for the discussion, 35 or 40 peers engaged in a large-group conversation are likely to do several things.

- Compete for time to speak.
- Compete to gain the teacher's attention by stating what they believe the teacher wants to hear.
- Tune out.

 You might enjoy seeing small groups in action by viewing *www.learner. org/courses/readwrite/video-detail/blended-learning-using-technology-learn-math-concepts.html.*

Whole-class discussions are also problematic in other ways. Cazden (2001) and Mehan (1979) identified a discourse pattern called initiate (or input)–respond–evaluate, or IRE. It looks like a discussion, but it is not. In IRE, the teacher begins a verbal exchange by asking a question or making a statement that calls for a response from someone in the class (Cazden, 2001; Mehan, 1979). When a student responds, the teacher evaluates what the student said in terms of how close it comes to the predetermined response the teacher holds in mind. In short, the pattern is a kind of quiz to see how closely the student can come to what the teacher had in mind rather than to produce new understandings through a shared or co-constructed discussion. The pattern is so common that is called the recitation model because students are reciting what they have learned in response to the teacher's query, not what they have actually understood or learned. When the teacher already knows the answer that is expected, discussion takes a hike. Questions that elicit this type of response we think of as pseudoquestions because the reason for the discussion is to assess students, not to inspire inquiry and further learning. Authentic discussions tend to make use of the group dynamic to build new information collaboratively and initiate and engage students in conversation about the topic at hand.

An additional disadvantage of the whole-class discussion is that only one of 35 or 40 students can speak at a time. The mathematical odds in a 50-minute class period of having all students participate is reduced. If we begin to think of discussion as a collective endeavor to understand a concept or solve a problem, we can begin to understand why partner talk or collaborative conversations among groups of four or five students work so well. As students converse about a topic the teacher is able to circulate among them and listen to their discussions.

The Socratic Seminar

A useful whole-group discussion method is the Socratic seminar. In the seminar, students arrange themselves in a circle after they have read a text (or set of texts) to grapple with a problem posed in the form of a question. Socratic seminars work well when there are dilemmas or ethical questions involved. Adhering to the principle that we can adapt existing formats for specific disciplines, let's take a look at a scenario for science.

Scientists discuss the ethical problems posed by the knowledge they construct all the time. Consider the ethical problem that big data poses for society. Scientists and engineers make it possible to gather massive amounts of data about people, places, events, and so on, but sometimes what is done with that data is not what best serves the public interest. Suppose you were to gather a set of articles examining this issue and turn those over to students. After you give them time to read and question the articles, they gather in a circle in class and ask themselves, "How much data is too much?" You can likely imagine the spirited discussion that will take place. In the process of discussion, students will have to understand the scientific and engineering issues involved, the potentials for effective use and for misuse, and predict what the future might hold.

As important, the students will learn to:

- Consult sources to support their thinking.
- Change their minds as they listen to others.
- Listen respectfully even if their opinions have not changed.
- Identify the stratagems—the gambits that participants in a discussion use to further the conversation—they must employ, and name them, as they engage in the seminar.

We will return to the idea of discussion stratagems shortly, but we think it is important that students have a system for thinking about the moves they make in discussion and how those moves improve the experience and the learning for everyone involved. Doing so scaffolds the ideas for students rather than hoping that they pick these skills up just by participating. The teacher will also discover something quite useful as students become more proficient with the Socratic seminar approach; that is, she or he will need to guide the discussions less and less. Good teaching sometimes means knowing when to get out of the way.

> The University of Notre Dame maintains a list of ethical or controversial topics in science. Visit *http://reilly.nd.edu/outreach/emerging-ethical-dilemmas-and-policy-issues-in-science-and-technology.*

Throughout the remaining chapters, we invite you to view videos from Annenberg Learner (*https://www.learner.org*), that illustrate the principles we have written about. Navigate to *www.learner.org/courses/readwrite/*

video-detail/using-socratic-method-history.html to view a Socratic seminar in a high school classroom. See the "Learn More" section at the end of this chapter for other video links.

Large Classes

In large classes, it can be hard to involve all of the students in the class in a Socratic seminar. Sometimes, students also tend to be shy or to take over the discussion. The norms of participating by speaking and listening need a bit of reinforcement. Here are two techniques we use to guide students to better seminars.

CHIPS

Here's an idea for teaching students the routines of effective whole-class discussion and especially the Socratic seminar format. Give each student three chips, perhaps three small squares of paper on which they write their names. After each meaningful contribution (not just "I agree," but instead "I agree with _____ because . . ."), students place one of their chips in the center of the circle. When all students have only one or no chips left, the discussion can continue without the chips or they can retrieve their chips and start anew. In one useful demonstration DeVere observed, students simply tossed their chips onto the floor in the center of the circle. The students were responsible for cleanup, of course, but the slightly subversive act of throwing paper on the floor somehow made the chips gambit more fun even while meaningful discussion was encouraged.

Would a math teacher accept any answer a student proposed just because it counted as participation (Metzger, 1998)? When teachers or students respond, it may be in everyone's interest to probe for more information as to how the response was derived. Although it is popular to say, "There are no wrong answers," what we really mean is that there are multiple answers, but students should be prepared to defend those responses and consider new evidence. In some cases, an answer is actually wrong, so we ask our readers, "How do you handle incorrect or incomplete responses to encourage further inquiry?"

Eventually, students won't need the chips. Be sure to pull them back once students get the gist of the strategy, but also be sure to discuss with them why the chips are no longer needed.

INNER AND OUTER CIRCLE

If space allows, a useful technique is to put students in two circles for Socratic seminar (Metzger, 1998). We have also seen this process referred to as a fishbowl. The approach calls for the discussion group to be in the inner circle while students in the outer circle take notes, prepare questions, and share their feedback with the inner circle.

One innovative adaptation to the inner/outer circle approach is to pair students on the inner circle with those on the outer circle. At predetermined points called by the teacher or a student facilitator, students put the discussion on hold. The inner-circle peer turns to the outer-circle peer who shares ideas, arguments and counterarguments, and questions. In this way, every student can participate while student interaction is increased exponentially.

Watch this video from Learn English for an example of effective discussion practices with English language learners: *www.youtube.com/watch?v=YY2yjEEoB3U.*

Small Groups

Whole-class discussions that are intended to engage students and draw upon their knowledge even as they increase their mastery of that knowledge do have a place, as we just explored. Often small-group discussions offer an alternative that encourages most students to speak because the mathematical odds of doing so are improved. If there are 40 students in a class vying for the floor, in small groups the odds are vastly better to one in four or five. Of course, we hope to use techniques that are collaborative, and not a competition for attention.

In small groups, the teacher is no longer the center of attention, and the students in each small group are the locus of control. What students say in small groups matters when learning in the disciplines, and others can listen and participate. They can listen and contribute if appropriate norms are set up to encourage them to do so.

ROLES

Assigning students specific roles is a time-honored way of helping them understand the processes of discussion (e.g., Daniels, 2002; Wolsey, 2004). While care must be taken that roles do not become perfunctory or pro forma tasks that students just carry out because they were assigned, they can be useful ways to apprentice students into discussion processes. It makes sense to tell students that they will not always be relying on those roles.

How might teachers in the content areas move the idea of roles toward better understanding of the discipline? While a general study of a text might benefit from having a connector, a summarizer, or a vocabulary wizard for a while, these roles might be scaffolded. Like Candler (n.d.), we agree that roles have limited utility. But as a clear stepping stone, we think roles can be helpful. In Socratic seminars, for example, a few generic roles could help as they do in literature circles (Daniels, 2002), such as summarizer. Vocabulary wizards or masters might look at and highlight academic vocabulary that is used across disciplines or specific to a given discipline, perhaps considering the word origins or cognates as appropriate (see Chapter 4).

Beyond that, discipline-specific roles could be envisioned. If the discipline highlights statistical evidence, a role could be constructed to specifically question the statistics presented in a text. If artifacts from the past are valued, as in history, one student could ensure that the perspectives of the originator of that role be investigated and reported. Students must always understand that the role is temporary and the roles will be eventually adopted by everyone in the group in a more fluid manner.

 To help you understand the power of the Socratic method, please refer to the video at *www.learner.org/courses/readwrite/video-detail/using-socratic-method-history.html.*

Discussing Content in a Disciplinary Way

Discussion in class means that students must listen carefully to each other, and they must respond with useful contributions that the group may find useful. There is always an ebb and flow to discussion. We have developed some principles for discussion in academic contexts that we hope you find useful in the sections to follow. Some elements appear in online and face-to-face discussions, and some are more pronounced in one condition or another. Let's take a look.

Although the way disciplines use sources differs, the capacity to use many sources to inform discussion and other learning tasks is increasingly important in our schools. Watch this video from Learner.org to watch students use sources to support their claims during discussion: *www.learner.org/courses/readwrite/video-detail/building-knowledge-multiple-sources.html.*

In 2001, Anderson and his colleagues examined the discussion stratagems, or strategic moves, of more than 100 fourth graders. Anderson and team categorized the stratagems shared in Figure 3.2. It is important to note that students often made discourse moves through discussion that positioned their own experiences with those of classmates. As important, students also referred to the story they were discussing to support their arguments and make those arguments explicit. In this case, students were examining works of fiction, and it is in this context that Anderson and colleagues (2001) present their findings. However, we postulate that similar stratagems are used when the discourse takes other forms. Making students aware of these conversational moves can be very helpful in promoting classroom conversation. Turning these into sentence frames would be a first step toward offering this support.

Managing participation of classmates	• "What do you think, John?" • "Now let's hear what Samantha thinks."
Positioning in relation to a classmate's argument	• "I agree/disagree with Sabrina because. . . ." • "I've got something [an idea] for you, Tamika." • "Yes/no, but [counterargument]. . . ."
Acknowledging uncertainty	• "Probably/might/maybe [counterargument hedging the argument through conditional terms]. . . ." • "I am confused because. . . ."
Extending the story world	• "What if . . . [a scenario]?" • "Placing the self in the story: "I would still. . . ." • "Placing classmate in the story: "If you were. . . ."
Making arguments explicit	• "I think [proposition] because [reason given]." • Valid inference: "If [action], then [consequence], so [new action]."
Using story evidence	• "In the story, it said [cites evidence]."

FIGURE 3.2. Discussion stratagems.

Middle and high school students use many of these same moves in their discussions. As they develop the language of the discipline they need encouragement to share and to compare ideas with peers. Looking into Ms. Mitchell's ninth-grade classroom, we see the power of conversations that are grounded by other work products and sources. Students grow in their thinking when they are encouraged to move beyond personal experiences and support their hypothesizing with documentable evidence. As they do so, students incorporate sources from assigned readings and from their own investigations into their discussion responses and presentations.

We adapted the work of Alvermann, Dillon, O'Brien, and Smith (1985) into a checklist of behaviors you can use with your students to help them navigate the practice of discussion when working with sources. Figure 3.3 shows some of the strategies students might employ. Although Alvermann and colleagues were examining textbooks (texts specifically designed for use in a classroom, as compared to a "text"), these moves are useful in working with multiple sources.

Supporting discussion through connection to one's own experiences and to credible resources such as course texts is often encouraged in face-to-face classrooms. A student might say, "I read about this topic on page 27 of our textbook where the author suggested . . . " or an instructor might say, "I really like your idea. Did you find any support or counterarguments for it in what you read or in other discussions you've had with peers?"

To better understand how to teach students to utilize multiple sources, look at the lesson and video at *www.learner.org/courses/readwrite/video-detail/building-knowledge-multiple-sources.html*.

Verification	Check accuracy of a response ____
	Produce substantiating evidence in an argument ____
	Other (specify):
Indirect reference	Initiate a mind-set ____
	Trigger an image ____
	Other (specify):
Refocusing	End a straying discussion ____
	Signal a new topic of discussion ____
	Other (specify):
Paraphrasing	Emphasize text as the authority ____
	Synthesize text in one's own words ____
	Other (specify):
Closed book (when a text-book is used as a source)	Review for a test ____
	Use as comprehension check for did/did not read the assignment ____
	Other (specify):
Other	Specify:

FIGURE 3.3. Determining the role of the text in discussion. Based on Alvermann et al. (1985).

As students interact with their peers, with you, and with other sources, they will become increasingly proficient at thinking about the sources of information on which they rely, and that collaboration will encourage greater student participation.

We have suggested that teachers consider the following questions (Wolsey & Lapp, 2009, p. 373) as they plan for discussions in their classrooms:

1. What background knowledge do students have about the topic? How should the instruction be tiered to support these differences?
2. What knowledge might students need to be exposed to before they can engage in meaningful discussion about the topic?
3. What discussion skills might students need to develop in order to participate in an effective discussion?
4. Will discussion help promote learning and inquiry about this topic? Are multiple constructions of knowledge possible?

> A tactic for getting at important aspects of historical events is to consider the possibilities. For example, what might have happened if Colonel Joshua Chamberlain had retreated when his regiment ran low on ammunition at Little Round Top at the Battle of Gettysburg? Instead, his regiment mounted a charge with bayonets that is widely regarded as a turning point in the battle. By investigating multiple sources and discussing their fact-based thinking as they address this question and other related question such as "Does Chamberlain deserve the lion's share of credit for this victory? What role did Andrew Tozier play in this victory?" Students come to understand the power of communication, as well as issues of loyalty, leadership, and how the resolve of one can lead to the success of many.

THE POWER OF FRAMING IT: LANGUAGE FRAMES

Because students typically are novices in any given discipline, they need support. One useful way of providing support with the language of the discipline is through language frames, sometimes called sentence frames (Fisher, Frey, & Rothenberg, 2008; Graff & Birkenstein, 2007). Vocabulary (see Chapter 4) is vitally important as students become more and more proficient with language to understand and describe what they know of a discipline. But they must also know how to use those terms in meaningful ways in connected discourse—sentences, paragraphs, related critical thinking, and the like. Language frames provide students with a means of acquiring the language habits of the discipline. For example, any discipline that requires students to make sense of predictions may use frames like:

I can predict that. . . .

I believe that _____ will happen because. . . .

What might happen if . . . ?

They then fill in their own knowledge and contexts. Following the pattern of "They say . . . , I say . . . , " students can grasp the idea that what they learn from other sources can inform the assertions they make.

In geometry, a frame may help students think about proofs; for example:

A postulate is a _____ that is _____.

A postulate is _____ because it cannot be _____.

If a postulate is _____, the proof _____.

A historical explanation might make use of these frames paired with academic vocabulary, as shown in Figure 3.4.

For making inferences from literature, consider:

In the text it says [*text evidence*]. That makes me think that [*inference*].

When the author said [*text evidence*], it made me think [*inference*].

I think that [*character name*] is [*character trait*] because in the text it says [*text evidence*].

I can infer [*inference*] because in the text it says [*text evidence*].

I think that [*character name*] feels [*emotion*] because [*text evidence*].

In science:

As _____, then _____. *As more water flows over a surface, then more erosion and deposition occur.*

When I changed _____, then _____ happened. *When I changed the amount of water flowing down the stream table, then more erosion and deposition happened.*

Academic vocabulary:	Frames:
analyze consequences contrast cycle derived distinctive excluding interact link major maximum minimum minor modify reaction response shift similar vary	• _____ differs from/is similar to _____ in that. . . . • This event/response/action implies. . . . • _____ was a response/reaction to. . . . • The shift is the result of. . . . • _____ however/whereas/nevertheless. . . . • _____ on the other hand/on the contrary. . . .

FIGURE 3.4. Pairing language frames with academic vocabulary.

The more/less _____, the _____. *The more water that flows across the earth materials, the more erosion and deposition that occur.*

Middle school English teacher Amy Miles's students used language frames similar to those shown. When her students, many of whom were English learners, mentioned to their other teachers that they felt more comfortable orally conversing in class when they used these frames, teachers in the other disciplines elicited her support in developing frames for their disciplines. Amy developed the tool in Figure 3.5 to help students learn to master the syntax of discussion (and writing) in history and social studies classrooms. Because Amy's language frames tool for social studies was so successful, her science colleagues asked her to help them develop a similar tool for the sciences and health (see Figure 3.6).

These teachers reported that using language frames in their disciplines frames not only supported students' oral language, but they also felt their positive effects on students' written communication. These frames served as scaffolds that provided students a model of one way to state information. As students gain proficiency with academic language the frames become embedded in their communication discourses. Many students have little exposure to academic language before coming to school. By the time they are in middle and high school, their knowledge and use of both topical (the language of the discipline) and academic language are essential for success.

The examples of frames shown in this section are adapted from the following sources:

Geometry frames:
https://mathsentenceframes.wikispaces.com/Geometry

History frames:
http://ptgmedia.pearsoncmg.com/images/9780205627615/downloads/7368_Siop_Ch01_pp001-023. pdf

Literature frames:
www.lightsailed.com/wp-content/uploads/2016/05/Both-Sentence-Frames-onepager_2015_02_24.pdf (go to page 2 of PDF)

Science frames:
www.fossweb.com/delegate/ssi-wdf-ucm-webContent?dDocName=D567151

Purpose	Language Frames	Examples
Simultaneity (thing are happening at the same time)	1. While _____ was _____ (person or event) _____ (action, feeling, or event) _____ (something that happened during)	1. While looking at this map, I can see the route of Alexander's conquest.
	2. During _____ (event or situation) _____ (an event or situation that was happening at the same time)	2. During the time of Isaac Newton's scientific breakthroughs, new discoveries were made in physics, medicine, and chemistry.
Cause and Effect (something causes something else to happen)	1. Since _____ (person and action/fact/feeling or an event) _____ (what will happen or has happened because of that fact/action/feeling or event)	1. Since a globe is not flat, we should use this instead of a map in order to accurately follow a great circle route.
	2. Because _____ (person and action/fact/feeling or an event) _____ (something has happened/changed)	2. Because some documents and articles contain a point of view or bias, historians look at not only what is emphasized, but also what is left out.
	3. As a result of _____ (person and action/fact/feeling or an event) _____ (what happened because of that action/feeling or event)	3. As a result of the peasants' suffering, they decided to revolt against the nobles.

(continued)

FIGURE 3.5. Language frames that support academic discourse in history/social studies.

From *Literacy in the Disciplines: A Teacher's Guide for Grades 5–12* by Thomas DeVere Wolsey and Diane Lapp. Copyright © 2017 The Guilford Press. Permission to photocopy this material is granted to purchasers of this book for personal use or use with individual students (see copyright page for details). Purchasers can download enlarged versions of this material (see the box at the end of the table of contents).

Purpose	Language Frames	Examples
Before and After/ Sequence of Events (order in which event occurs)	1. After _____ (important event that happened first), _____ (important event that happened after). 2. Since _____ (important event/idea that happened first), _____ (important event/idea that happened after).	1. After Muhammad died in 632 C.E., a new leader was chosen to be caliph, or successor to the messenger of God. 2. Since the development of the American education system, many changes have taken place.
Contradiction (the opposite or denial of an idea, opinion or statement)	1. Although _____ (one important event or idea), _____ (a different event or idea that contradicts/denies the first). 2. While some people _____ (feel/believe/think/assume/say something), I _____ (fact that denies the first idea).	1. Although the Mayan people settled in a flat area called a Petén, *which had sinkholes,* they had a ready water supply from underground rivers. *Note:* Commas hug the extra information. 2. While some people may have thought that the commanding officers should have been chosen based on family ties, Genghis Khan chose them for their abilities.

You can also try these transitions:

- In fact,
- In addition,
- For instance,
- For example,
- Despite the fact that
- Even though
- In other words,
- Ultimately
- Therefore,
- Before
- Now that

FIGURE 3.5. *(continued)*

Purpose	Language Frames	Examples
Restating Comment or Summing It Up (using different words to get the same idea across)	1. In short (or summary), _____ . (restate your idea or fact using different language)	1. In short, when they are added together, a chemical reaction is created.

Transition in between statements:

A chemical change occurs when hydrogen and oxygen are added together. In short, a chemical reaction is occurring. |
| | 2. Previously stated, _____ . (restate your idea or fact using different language) | 2. Previously stated, people are influenced by the world in many ways.

Transition in between statements: |
| | 3. Thus, _____ . (restate your idea or fact using different language) | This public service announcement depicts how teens may be influenced by their peers both positively and negatively. Previously stated, people are influenced by the world in many ways. |
| | 4. In other words, _____ . (restate your idea or fact using different language) | |
| **Findings and Conclusions** (the opposite or denial of an idea, opinion or statement) | 1. Therefore, _____ . (what you are led to understand or find out) | 1. Therefore, if the volume is slightly increased, the temperature is slightly increased as well.

Transition in between statements: |
| | 2. Ultimately, _____ . (what you are led to understand or find out) | Charles law states that the volume is directly proportional to the temperature; therefore, if the volume is slightly increased, the temperature is slightly increased as well. |
| | 3. Furthermore, _____ . (what you are led to understand or find out) | The vertex point is (−4,0); consequently, the vertex lies on the x axis. |

FIGURE 3.6. Language frames that support academic communication in science and health.

LEARN MORE

About facilitating Socratic seminars from Learner.org:

www.learner.org/courses/readwrite/video-detail/facilitating-socratic-seminar.html

 To support you in implementing a Socratic seminar:

www.learner.org/courses/readwrite/video-detail/facilitating-socratic-seminar.html

About creating a culture of collaboration from Learner.org:

www.learner.org/courses/readwrite/video-detail/creating-culture-collaboration.html

CHAPTER 3 ACTIVITIES

1. What was the most successful discussion experience you can remember as a participant? What occurred among the discussion participants that made it productive? How might you adapt that experience based on your reading in this book and the videos we have provided to fit the needs of your students in your classroom?

2. Examine texts you use in your content area and develop five language frames that exemplify the syntax of language as it is used in your discipline.

Chapter 4

Choosing the Right Words

Instruction That Supports Academic Vocabulary Use in the Disciplines

Words, words, words!
I'm so sick of words
I get words all day through.

These famous words spoken by Eliza Doolittle in *My Fair Lady* may reflect the exasperation felt by students every period of the school day as they are bombarded with the words of each discipline. Words comprise their listening, speaking, reading, and writing vocabularies. Teachers are intent on ensuring that the language of each discipline is learned because they know that the right word matters. Indeed, the wrong word or the not quite right word can lead to misunderstandings and confusion. We are reminded of the power of just the right the word when we remember that after the atomic explosion of Hiroshima, the Japanese were encouraged to surrender. Their reply, which asked for a delay, was misinterpreted as a refusal. This language confusion caused Nagasaki to pay an extreme penalty. Being able to use precise language matters; most of us can recall an experience when not doing so resulted in miscommunication with negative consequences. Think about it: What should you have said?

Words convey ideas or they connect ideas. Let's use an example to illustrate. In a history class we might ask, What's the *difference* between one political candidate and another? The response to such a question would typically be a matter of opinion (one we hope is grounded in evidence!). However, in mathematics, the term *difference* conveys a very precise meaning that is specific to the field. Used this way, the term refers to subtraction, and it conveys the idea that an algorithm must be employed to find the desired result.

Vocabulary demands are indeed high as one studies information across the disciplines. In 1984, Nagy and Anderson estimated that students needed to have knowledge of approximately 88,500 words to be academically successful. They also estimated that the number of words known by high school students ranges from 17,000 to 50,000. This information was compiled decades ago, long before the advent of the Internet and technology, so think about the possible vocabulary increases that have occurred. It's also interesting that only about 5,000 to 7,000 of these words can be learned through engagement in everyday speech (Klein, 1988). So although collaborative conversations are important, they are not the only way that students can learn language. They must acquire vast quantities of vocabulary as word families through reading and being read to. As teachers share a text it is so important to think aloud in ways that illustrate how to unlock the meaning of words within the discipline. Blachowicz and Fisher (2000) also suggest that effective vocabulary instruction in any discipline must:

- Actively engage the learner in tasks that cause words to be learned.
- Invite the learner to make personal connection with words.
- Continually immerse learners in word learning (which means "so long" to the days of learners copying a list of words into their notebooks to be memorized for a quick quiz).
- Consolidate word meanings by using multiple information sources.

We have also found that there are many ways to increase one's vocabulary and to teach students to do the same. However, we believe vocabulary is best taught:

- In specific contexts and through word families.
- With repeated encounters.
  - Through reading and hearing the word used conversantly.
- With many opportunities to use the word in meaningful contexts.
  - Through speaking, listening, and presenting.
  - With specific feedback.
- And with knowledge of how words are used in the disciplines, including:
  - How words evolve and take on multiple meanings.
  - How words share similarities across languages and cultures.
  - How words pair with visual information.

Our intention is this chapter is to help you identify how to select the vocabulary you plan to teach and then to introduce you to a few instructional strategies that will help you teach vocabulary within your discipline.

SO MANY WORDS: THE THREE TIERS

Teachers need a way to think about vocabulary and what terms most need to be taught. That seems like a simple task, but it has challenged teachers, linguists, and students for a long time. Although several researchers have taken on the challenge, they seem to agree that words students need to know fall into three broad categories often referred to as Tier One, Tier Two, and Tier Three (Beck, McKeown, & Kucan, 2002)

Tier One words, in the Beck and colleagues (2002) model, are common or basic words requiring little or no instruction. While there are approximately 8,000 word families in this tier, and not every word in every family will be known equally well. While *cat* and *feline* are in the same family, *cat* is the more common word, and *cat* be used to teach the word *feline*. Tier One words are a part of our everyday vocabulary. These are words like *girl, boy, man, dog, red, three, tree, cookie,* and *shirt.* These are the sight words that are first learned in reading and are can be considered as common nouns, verbs, and adjectives. Tier Two words are high-utility words found across content or disciplinary lines and which are frequently used by mature users of the language. Tier Two words consisting of around 7,000 word families include words like *benevolent, ferocious, indignant,* and *maleficent.* Tier Two words support wide reading comprehension.

Tier Three words are found far less frequently and are limited to specific domains or disciplines. These approximately 400,000 words are unique to a particular hobby, sport, technology, occupation, or discipline. For example, in Chapter 1, we referred to an article that included words such as *eukaryote* and *microscopy.* These are terms that would only be encountered in a science context. Words that would be specific to the domain of skiing are *backcountry, Alpine skiing, bowl, basket,* and *bumps.* While several of these words seem familiar, they have specific meaning to skiers that may not be common to others. For example, a *bump* refers to an icy mound of snow also known as a *mogul,* and *basket,* which may be thought of as a container for carrying something, is a plastic piece as the end of a ski pole. You might recall that teacher Faith Bass-Sargent referred to words that are cognates, in the sense that they have multiple meanings in two different disciplines, in Chapter 2. *Mogul* is one such term. In skiing it has the meaning conveyed above, while in history, it refers to an important person, such as a magnate.

Now while it might be wonderful to know the meaning of all of these domain-specific words, it is not necessary unless one is required to participate in a community of speakers of this lexicon or language. Every profession, every discipline, and every community has domain-specific language, and it is only reasonable to conclude that success in a particular domain requires understanding the language. Most of us experience the feeling of not knowing domain-specific language each time new technology terms are introduced. We often feel that we have just grasped the meaning of a few and then new ones appear. Our experience with our own

growing language is that it is alive and continues to grow to accommodate communication within and across domains. Having wide and deep vocabulary knowledge
influences reading comprehension (Farley & Elmore, 1992) and performance in the
disciplines (Espin & Foegen, 1996).

There are many word lists, including the Academic Word List (Coxhead, 2000;
Massey University, 2004), which includes 570 word families and identifies the most
common word in each family and work across disciplines (Tier Two). An example
would be *clarity, clarification, clarified, clarifies, clarifying*—with *clarity* being identified as the most common. This list, developed based on a corpus of 3.5 million words
from university academic texts, includes words that exclude the most common in
the English language and those that are not specific to just one discipline (called
technical vocabulary in the Coxhead list). A premise of the academic word list is the
notion that instruction in words that students might encounter in academic texts is
likely to improve acquisition of those words as well as use in writing tasks.

SO MANY WORDS: WHICH DO I TEACH?

Flanigan and Greenwood's (2007) approach is that students' purposes for learning
specific vocabulary should be matched with instructional strategies that support
their learning the words; in other words, not just any vocabulary strategy will do. In
their framework, they propose four levels of vocabulary based loosely on the work
of Graves (2000), Beck and colleagues (2002), and others. Their four levels are (1)
critical words, (2) foot-in-the-door words, (3) critical "after" words, and (4) words
not to teach.

- *Critical words* are those that students must understand in order to comprehend text but are not fully supported in text. These words and the concepts
  they represent are necessary to understanding the text.
- *Foot-in-the-door words* are those that the gist of the word's meaning can be
  briefly introduced and in-text context (such as an appositive phrase containing a definition) provides enough support. For example, in *Wonder* it is
  more important to understand that Auggie has a facial deformity, which is a
  distortion of parts of his face, rather than to know all of the details of mandibulofacial dysostosis.
- *Critical "after" words* are those that add precision to the students' vocabularies, are high utility, or are well supported in text. Students who might be
  interested in Auggie's condition could learn more about the concept and the
  term that describes it: *mandibulofacial dysostosis*.
- *Words not to teach* suggests that teachers sometimes teach words simply
  because the teacher edition of the textbook identifies the words as vocabulary. Words not to teach include words students already know or words that

do not match the instructional purposes of the lesson. We also suggest that students need to grapple with word meaning, so some words not to teach include those with which students might struggle, but struggle successfully.

HOW DO I TEACH THE SELECTED VOCABULARY?

Once the vocabulary words that pertain to a lesson have been identified it's important to next determine which words you will teach directly and which ones the students will be able to indirectly learn from their reading, listening, and collaborative conversations. Making these determinations involves how much instructional time you have, the learners' age, the size of their language base, and the language they speak and read outside of school. If you feel that little academic reading and communication occur outside of school, then vocabulary learning should be a prominent dimension of your instruction. The following structures and routines promote vocabulary learning.

Creating a Vocabulary-Friendly Environment

When students are learning about the disciplines, they are also learning about what makes the vocabulary of each discipline different (see Shanahan, 2015) and how vocabulary works across disciplines (see Wolsey, Lapp, & Fisher, 2012). Shanahan asserts that vocabulary learning is pretty much the same across time and disciplines, and we agree. However, as knowledge increases, so does the need to understand how specific disciplines deal with vocabulary. Shanahan makes the case that scientists tend toward terms whose origins are in Greek or Latin. Social studies experts look more toward ideology in their choice of terms.

Whether you are promoting vocabulary acquisition in a second language or vocabulary acquisition specific to a discipline, we think that Graves, August, and Mancilla-Martinez (2013) have some good ideas about just what a vocabulary-friendly environment might look like. Language learning, and thus vocabulary acquisition, occurs through a combination of rich and literate environments, through purposeful instruction with individual terms, through instruction and mastery of word learning strategies, and by guiding students to be conscious of the words they encounter.

Vocabulary-Rich Environments

Vocabulary-rich environments in the disciplines are a matter of mind-set. Effective teachers recognize the power of creating environments that continually expose students to the language of their disciplines. They know that if students are to gain a respectable understanding of the discipline, they must see the words, hear the words, speak the words, and write the words.

Let's join Ms. Martinez in her social studies classroom. Students know they have to grasp difficult concepts such as federalism or diversity. Although students will see these terms in their readings, they often lack the experience in using the words conversantly and knowledgeably.

Ms. Martinez knows that her students' knowledge of the social studies vocabulary is developing, so she uses the terms she wants to teach when she speaks with her students. This modeling provides students with deepening nuances of the term. She also shows videos from the Internet that incorporate the concepts represented by the term. She keeps a file folder of news articles that relate to the topics being studied, which she often reads aloud to students and then poses conversational questions that students consider and discuss. Reading aloud from sophisticated texts followed by discussion guides students to develop deep word learning. In addition, students have a model of what effective texts in this discipline look like since they are provided by someone they trust and admire as an expert in the field: their teacher. She also invites students to add articles or identify topics they would like to have addressed. Ms. Martinez also begins with the reading and then has students write a response to a posed question, converse with a peer or table group, and revise their response before a whole-class discussion. For example, as they studied the economic structures of countries as compared with that of the United States, she shared article related to Greece's economic problems, the causes, and possible solutions. After reading one article students are also invited to find others that promote their positions. All responses must be based on documented information. In this classroom, students are exposed to the language of social studies topics through their viewing, reading, listening, writing, and discussions. Ms. Martinez's practices are applicable to other disciplines. Think about it—what features of your classroom routines will emphasize that language learning matters?

Purposeful Instruction with Individual Terms

Teaching vocabulary in meaningful contexts along with definitional information can make a big difference in language learning. Graves and colleagues wrote, "More lengthy and robust instruction that involves explicit teaching that includes both contextual and definitional information, multiple exposures to target words in varied contexts, and experiences that promote deep processing of words' meanings is likely to be more powerful than less time-consuming and less robust instruction" (2013, p. 23). We agree wholeheartedly. The principle is as true for English language learners as it is for vocabulary learners in the disciplines.

Mr. Turley knew the students in his science classes often struggled with the concepts presented in his astronomy units. The concepts, he knew, were often embedded in the vocabulary students needed to know. Recently, Mr. Turley read an article from the *Los Angeles Times* to his students about the fly-by of Pluto by the spacecraft *New Horizons*. The students had questioned why New Horizons did not simply orbit Pluto as many other spacecraft had done around nearer planets. To understand the principles, the students needed to be familiar with terms such as *Kuiper Belt, acceleration, deceleration, orbital physics,* and *gravitational pull.*

Fortunately, Mr. Turley knew his students needed to hear, speak, read, and write these terms often. Before reading the article, he pointed out the key terms that he believed would be "critical words." Because he understood the power of visuals, he drew brief, preplanned diagrams of each on the board. He used the terms frequently in all of his instruction, and, most important, he encouraged students to raise their hands and ask, "I think I heard this term before, but I can't remember exactly what it means. Would you remind me?" Mr. Turley knows that one or two exposures to a term usually is not enough, and he encouraged his students to ask for refreshers.

Later, he challenged his students to find three definitions that showed specifically how the terms were used in science and V-Tweet them to the rest of the class (you will learn more about how to do this—keep reading!).

In online documents, students used highlighting tools in PDFs to identify the terms in context. They used the annotation tools to note questions that arose about the terms and to clarify their earlier understandings.

Instruction and Mastery of Word-Learning Strategies

Because it is just not possible to teach all the words students might need to know, and because students will encounter new words on their own and after they leave school, they need approaches and strategies that will help them throughout their lives. Good readers encounter unfamiliar terms all the time, and they employ a range of tools when those words seem important. They view resources such as a glossary or a dictionary to look up words. They use context cues they find in the sentence containing the word or in other sentences in the passage. They employ knowledge of cognates or word families (e.g., *words, reword, wordy, wording, wordless, wordsmith*). They write notes digitally or on paper about the terms they encounter, ask colleagues about their encounters with the term, and look inside the word to examine the root word, prefix, or suffix for clues to the meaning. Less experienced readers don't know they should do these things, so they don't. It is very important that teachers show students how to approach unfamiliar words or words they know used in new ways. Thinking aloud about vocabulary is one useful way to do this.

Polysemy

As students' consciousness increases about words, they will notice that some words have multiple meanings. Sometimes those meanings are specific to a discipline. Teachers can help students avoid the tendency to overgeneralize from one definition to another when that is not appropriate. For example, Visual Thesaurus (2013)

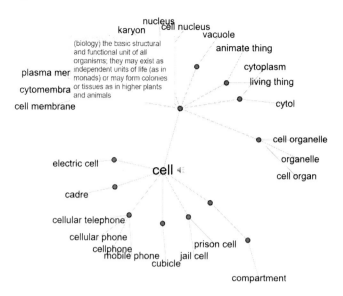

FIGURE 4.1. Visual Thesaurus display for the term *cell*. Reprinted with permission from Visual Thesaurus (*www.visualthesaurus.com*). Copyright © 1998–2016 Thinkmap, Inc. All rights reserved.

is a digital tool that clearly shows how many words are used in different disciplines. In Figure 4.1, a Visual Thesaurus display shows how the term *cell* is used in biology, and how it differs in the fields of electronics and technology, criminal justice, and in general.

Mathematics is loaded with polysemous words. *Angle* in everyday life means just to have a viewpoint, but in mathematics, it means something much more specific. We found this definition on Math Open Reference (2009): "A shape, formed by two lines or rays diverging from a common point (the vertex)" (n.p.).

We have found that pointing out the differences, often through think-aloud modeling, helps students understand the meaning of terms as they are used in specific disciplines, even if students are already familiar with the word in other contexts. Spending time teaching students how the term came to have a specific meaning in the discipline can also be helpful.

Word Consciousness

Play with words, notice how others play with words. Be intrigued with words and the nuances of how they are used in one context and not in another. These are the ideas behind word consciousness. What motivates students to want to learn words?

Word games, Internet memes (at times), and observing the joy the teacher finds in learning new words or new associations with known words all contribute to word consciousness among students. Diane and her teaching colleague Marisol

FIGURE 4.2. *Romeo and Juliet* visual meme.

Thayre asked 11th-grade English students to create memes of the characters in *Romeo and Juliet* (see Figure 4.2). As important, students who are conscious of the words in a discipline are more likely to be engaged with other aspects of the content. Motivation is hard to teach, but it is possible to encourage and promote.

ENGLISH LANGUAGE LEARNERS: COGNATES

What students know about words in one context can help them understand them in another. Cognate instruction recognizes that word roots tend to infuse multiple languages. For example, in social studies, the terms *abdication* and *abdicación* are cognates. Spanish speakers will quickly note the similarities between the English and Spanish versions of the word. In science, *atom* (English) and *atómico* (Spanish) share enough similarities that the meaning is quite clear. This is so in many of the Romance language (e.g., Italian, French), but also across some other languages. When students learn to associate words and word knowledge they have in one language with that of the language they are learning, it can be quite powerful.

For Spanish cognates, readers may wish to visit *http://spanishcognates.org,* and for more general information with helpful comparisons, check out *www.cognates.org.*

For a lesson and video that illustrates how to support students in learning the language of mathematics, visit *www.learner.org/courses/readwrite/video-detail/using-math-vocabulary-articulate-understanding.html.*

Word Walls

Okay, let's be honest. We love word walls. We love them in first grade when students are still learning foundational word patterns, and we especially love them in secondary schools when students are learning the vocabulary associated with a theme or unit of study. They do look a bit different in middle and high school, to be sure. However, there are few better opportunities for teachers to present words and help students revisit them often enough that they become conversant with them. You have seen how we use the word *conversant* throughout this book. It is important that students not only recognize words when they see them. It is not enough that they can grasp only the basic concepts behind the words when they see or hear them as they are appropriate to the discipline and age or grade level.

In secondary schools, teachers have the unique opportunity to display words that represent the content unique to their disciplines (or at least the words that are used uniquely in those disciplines!). Math teacher Faith Bass-Sargent uses word walls to support her students becoming conversant with key math terms. She created the word wall with the students by adding the mathematical terms they encountered and ones they thought they needed to see more often until they owned and used the word in their interactions. Ms. Bass-Sargent refers to the terms often, points them out to students to help them recall the term, and leaves them on the wall during periods of instruction critical to meeting standards and other instructional goals (see Figure 4.3).

She invites students to review the word wall and also to look to it if they are not sure what word to use in their reading or writing. Students need these opportunities to become conversant with the words (see Wolsey, Smetana, & Grisham, 2015). By

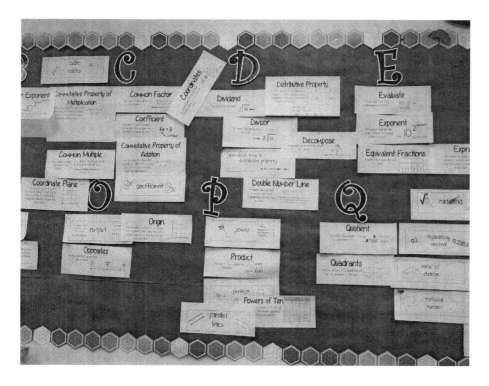

FIGURE 4.3. Word wall of math terms.

this we mean they need to develop the capacity to converse using terms they and their peers need to know well in order to comprehend and communicate in the discipline. Although this is an example of how a mathematics teacher uses word walls, this approach is certainly applicable to other disciplines.

Thinking Aloud with Academic Vocabulary

Thinking aloud invites listeners to view your inner cognitive dialogs. Because we can't see inside each other's brains or even our own to a degree, thinking aloud provides an opportunity for the teacher to demonstrate what is going on when a new word is encountered in written or spoken text. Thinking aloud also gives students the chance to clarify their thoughts as they grapple with new terms or terms used in unfamiliar ways. At the same time, as students think aloud, the teacher gets a glimpse into the student's thinking.

In a ninth-grade math class, we might hear this exchange which makes obvious the power of thinking aloud as a way to bring clarity to an unclear concept.

> MARICELA: I'm not sure I understand Cartesian coordinates.
>
> TEACHER: You know number lines, right? Well, Cartesian coordinates are just two number lines that intersect or cross each other. When I see the term in our math text, I think, "Okay, the x-axis or line runs across or horizontal and the y-axis runs up and down and is vertical." When the x- and y-axes are put together, they form quadrants. I know *quad* usually means "four." Cartesian coordinates are just a way to plot an equation on two number lines, one that is horizontal and one that is vertical. I think I'll draw a visual because that will help me to check my understanding.

Notice how often the teacher used the word *I*. This is a critical aspect of thinking aloud because you are not merely explaining, you also are inviting students to observe and listen to your cognitive processing. You are the expert, so spending time with you inside your mind is a very valuable experience for your students. Once you have modeled thinking aloud for your students, invite them to think aloud for a peer as they solve a problem, evaluate a thesis, or make conclusions about topics across the disciplines.

When students are asked to explain their thinking about a term, the teacher is able to pinpoint critical inaccuracies and provide feedback to guide the student to a more precise understanding. Baumann, Jones, and Seifert-Kessel (1993), suggested that think-alouds might improve reading comprehension, "require a reader to stop periodically, reflect on how a text is being processed and understood, and relate orally what reading strategies are being employed" (p. 185). We have applied the ideas of Baumann and colleagues to vocabulary learning. Thinking aloud permitted students to put various strategies into use through oral explanations of the reading strategies they were using. The same principle applies for vocabulary learning tasks (Wolsey & Lapp, in press).

VERBAL AND VISUAL WORD ASSOCIATION AND RELATED APPROACHES IN THE DISCIPLINES

Making word association connections is a primary way to grow word families or cognates. One way that experts and students who work with specific disciplines learn more about the domain is by exploring discipline-specific reference works. Fortunately, the Internet makes a wide variety of resources available.

Technical and Discipline-Specific Dictionaries and Encyclopedias Online

One effective way of learning vocabulary specific to a discipline is to use technical and discipline-specific reference sources. General dictionary entries are certainly useful, but dictionary and encyclopedic resources that provide information about science, social studies, and other topics are just the sort that experts use. The list below is not comprehensive, and anyone with suggestions to build this directory is encouraged to email me (DeVere) at *info@iaieus.com* message. I hope that the list will include references that are useful for students at any level who are novices with the stated discipline. Soon, I will put the resource on my blog for anyone who is interested to use with credit to anyone who contributes and share with everyone.

> *Criteria*
> - The resource must be fully accessible online.
> - The resource must be suitable for students in grades 6–12 and undergraduate (but not excluding those who are learning about the topic).
> - There is a reasonable probability that the resource will remain online for some time to come.
> - The resource presents accurate information that represents the field.

Mathematics

- *Illustrated mathematics dictionary*
  www.mathsisfun.com/definitions/index.html
  Easy navigation, intended for grades K–12.

- *Mathwords*
  www.mathwords.com
  Focuses on precision and readability. The site includes graphics to bolster the definitions.

- *Wolfram MathWorld*
  http://mathworld.wolfram.com
  Perhaps one of the most comprehensive resources for mathematics definitions on the web.

- *Encyclopedia of Mathematics*
  www.encyclopediaofmath.org/index.php/Main_Page
  An open-access resource with more than 8,000 entries.

- To view mathematical vocabulary being learned, go to the video and lesson plans at
  www.learner.org/courses/readwrite/video-detail/deconstructing-word-problems.html

  and
  www.learner.org/courses/readwrite/video-detail/annotating-word-problems.html

Social Studies

- *Ancient History Encyclopedia*
  www.ancient.eu/index
  Search alphabetically, by timeline, for images or for videos.

- *Online Dictionary of the Social Sciences*
  http://bitbucket.icaap.org
  A comprehensive dictionary, designed for undergraduates, by Athabasca University.

- *Catholic Online*
  www.catholic.org
  So many figures and ideas are associated with the Roman Catholic church that a reference work may be very helpful. This one is supported by ads that can be annoying.

- *Taegan Goddard's Political Dictionary*
  http://politicaldictionary.com

- *Geography Dictionary & Glossary*
  www.itseducation.asia/geography

- *Compilation of Architecture Dictionaries by Robert Beard*
  www.alphadictionary.com/directory/Specialty_Dictionaries/Architecture
  (Be sure to check out *www.alphadictionary.com/specialty.html* for many more specialty dictionary links. Some are better than others, but it's quite a collection.)

Science

- *The Science Dictionary*
  www.thesciencedictionary.com
  This is actually a search tool that aggregates search results specific to science.

- *Enchanted Learning*
  www.enchantedlearning.com/science/dictionary
  Links to several specialty dictionaries by Enchanted Learning for students (e.g.,
  botany, dinosaurs, land forms).

- *Geology Dictionary*
  http://geology.com/geology-dictionary.shtml
  Also, check out the map collections: *http://geology.com/state-map*

Technology

- *NetLingo*
  www.netlingo.com
  One of the first and best (in our opinion) dictionaries for those interested in
  technology- and Internet-related terms.

Physical Education

- *Sports Definitions*
  www.sportsdefinitions.com
  Searchable by type of sport or alphabetically.

Art

- *MOMA*
  www.moma.org/learn/moma_learning/glossary
  Search by artist, by theme, or alphabetically.

Music

- *Naxos.com*
  www.naxos.com/education/glossary.asp
  Search alphabetically.

Literature

- *Literature Dictionary*
  www.literature-dictionary.org
  Includes dictionaries of characters, dictionaries by author, and dictionaries of terms.

Business

- *Inc.com Encyclopedia*
  www.inc.com/encyclopedia
  Search many entries relevant to business and entrepreneurism.

Marzano (2009) suggests that several conditions apply to effective vocabulary learning.

- Provide a description, explanation, or example of the new term.
- Ask students to restate the description, explanation, or example in their own words.
- Ask students to construct a picture, pictograph, or symbolic representation of the term.
- Engage students periodically in activities that help them add to their knowledge of the terms in their vocabulary notebooks.
- Periodically ask students to discuss the terms with one another.
- Involve students periodically in games that enable them to play with terms.

The techniques we describe below blend all of these conditions and are adaptable to specific disciplines.

V-Tweets

Definitions are useful as long as they are understood. With V-Tweets, we ask students to consult at least three dictionary definitions they find online, including at least one that is specific to the discipline. They work with a partner to synthesize a definition from the three or more definitions they have found that meets the demands of the discipline. Here are the steps:

- The teacher scans the reading assignment and selects Tier Two and Tier Three words for critical after-reading study.
- Student pairs are assigned words to investigate (Internet, dictionaries, background knowledge) and must consult at least three sources for the Tweet and an image or visual (may be drawn and scanned or photographed; or use Google Images with teacher approval).
- Students must identify the sources of their definitions/explanations of the words.
- Students combine the sources, discussing and drafting a 120-character "Tweet" for the classroom website. Wait, 120 characters? Stay tuned.
- Students then share their V-Tweets with each other prior to reading, and they are available as students read the text.
- Use hashtags and Twitter handles to encourage conversation. For example, Ms. Hernandez might ask her period 1 students to use the hashtag #Hern1 to encourage Twitter conversation among her students in that class period. A handle, such as @thernandez can ensure that the teacher receives the Tweet.
- Because Tweets can only have 140 characters, it is important to make room for the hashtag or handle and the image, all of which take up some of the characters allotted. We suggest about 120 characters.
- Students will negotiate how best to define their assigned term within the character limitations.
- In addition, students can carry on the conversation as they use hashtags to expand or elaborate on each others' posts.

In this example, the Tweet is developed from three online definitions, composed to fit the Twitter format, and posted:

TDWolsey
@TDWolsey

Consciously think about your feelings and thoughts-look inside yourself, which is called introspection. #ilavoc

Vocabulary Self-Collection Strategy Plus

One very adaptable instructional routine is rooted in a time-tested approach from the 1980s (Haggard, 1985; Ruddell, & Shearer, 2002). Wolsey and colleagues

(2015b) adapted it as a strategy using 21st-century tools they call Vocabulary Self-Collection Strategy Plus (VSS+). The strength of this routine is that students are asked to work together, combine visuals and text, and refer to texts to reinforce their understanding.

Students attempting to understand the term *Anthropocene,* a proposed new epoch to be added to the geologic time scale for Earth, used VSS+ to fully explore the term and all the related concepts in an article they chose to read on the topic (Stromberg, 2013). Attending to discipline-specific resources, students create a dictionary entry for their class or that can be shared publicly that includes the following elements:

- The word and a definition relevant to the reading.
- Image.
- Rationale recorded as an audio podcast.
- Semantic web (see the online resources in Figure 4.4).

 Students then link their dictionary entries to a class resource that all can refer to later. We used a wiki, but other formats can serve the purpose just as well. Read more at *http://literacybeat.com/tag/vss.*

LEARN MORE

Learn more about using Prezi to create an online Frayer model vocabulary-building experience for your students:

 http://literacybeat.com/2015/08/30/zooming-in-on-vocabulary-prezi-and-the-frayer-model

---

Wordsift:
    http://wordsift.com

Visual Thesaurus:
    www.visualthesaurus.com

Wordflex for iPad®:
    www.graphite.org/app/wordflex-touch-dictionary-for-ipad

FIGURE 4.4. Visual representations of words and ideas online.

CHAPTER 4 ACTIVITY

Consider how terms are used in everyday life or in other disciplines and what they mean specifically in mathematics or another discipline. What are the differences? How would you teach students to use and understand these terms: *area, table, domain, degree, power*? What words in your discipline might students confuse with their everyday use or with how the word is used in other disciplines?

Chapter 5

Arguing It Well

Instruction That Supports Communication in the Disciplines

This chapter is about how to teach students the art of argumentation, one of the more gripping challenges of our time as teachers. First, we have to put our views in context of our own experiences; then we have to embrace something that is new to us as teachers. Persuasion has been part of the teaching landscape, especially for English-language arts teachers, for years. Argumentation is different, though.

While we are getting started, it is worth a minute of our time to point out that argumentation reaches across the language arts. While it is certainly important that students be able to construct an argument in writing, they must also be able to present arguments with multimedia and in speaking, discuss them with other students and even in public, and recognize the merits of an argument in speech or in the works they read.

While persuasion tends to admit any sort of tactic that might achieve the objective of persuading the reader, argumentation depends on critical analysis of the argument and the foundations on which the argument rests. Argumentation requires a level of examination that persuasion, taken as a whole, does not. In short, a solid argument is always based on evidence. In one approach to standards, opinions based on evidence lead to more formal arguments (e.g., NGA & CCSSO, 2010). Formal argumentation involves making an argument with organized claims, presented with supporting data and reasons or warrants (Toulmin, 2003) that document relationships between the claims and the data.

Aristotle, in *Rhetoric*, stated that persuasive writing (or speaking) involves use of one or several rhetorical appeals that include

- *Logos*: An appeal to facts and numerical data.
- *Ethos*: An appeal to credibility (e.g., an author might be a credible and recognized expert on a topic).
- *Pathos*: An appeal to the emotions of the audience (e.g., do this because your children's health is at stake).
- *Kairos*: An appeal to urgency (e.g., if we don't do this now, the opportunity will be gone for good).

Persuasion, in general, does not qualify how the above appeals are achieved. The author of the persuasive piece is permitted to choose the evidence that is most beneficial to the goal of getting the audience to go along with the author. Argumentation, on the other hand, asks that the author support the claims in a systematic way using evidence, backed with warrants. More sophisticated arguments consider qualifications to the argument.

FALLACIES

Fallacies are integral to understanding just what an argument is and what it is not. While there is not space in this book to explore all that a fallacy entails, it is important to keep in mind that errors of logic or critical thinking are easy traps. The time teachers ask students to spend in looking at errors of logic is well worth the investment.

A fallacy is simply a failure to address the argument or a flaw in an argument that might make that argument invalid. For example, a person might state that many people purchase and smoke cigarettes; therefore, cigarettes must be okay to smoke. The argument is invalid because it assumes that popular opinion is sound evidence in support of an argument to smoke cigarettes. Another fallacy is to mistake a correlation (an instance where one event tends to happen consistently with another event) as a cause. A classic correlation is that ice cream sales tend to go up in the summer, and murders do as well. However, it would be a fallacy to assume that ice cream causes people to commit murder. Parents might be familiar with ad hominem attacks, a logical fallacy that goes after the person rather than the argument: "Mom and Dad, I received a 'C' on the assignment because the teacher hates me." See the sidebar for a variety of online resources on logical fallacies and argumentation.

ONLINE RESOURCES FOR ARGUMENTATION AND LOGICAL FALLACIES

General Resources

- The Online Writing Lab at Purdue University has a wealth of resources for writers in schools and universities. Although this one is intended for university students, it is accessible for high school students as well.
  https://owl.english.purdue.edu/owl/resource/685/05
- The WebEnglishTeacher has compiled a number of resources for teachers to use as they and their students work with opinions and arguments, including suggested prompts from the *New York Times*.
  www.webenglishteacher.com/argument.html
- The Utah Education Network (UEN) offers many resources for teachers and students, as well. The resources include lessons, explanatory material (such as a handout on the differences between argumentation, persuasion, and propaganda from ReadWriteThink), and graphic organizers.
  www.uen.org/core/languagearts/writing/argumentative.shtml
- Writing samples of argument and opinion writing for various grade levels are available in Appendix C of the CCSS (scroll down the right side to find the link for Appendix C):
  www.corestandards.org/ELA-Literacy
  and at Achieve the Core:
  http://achievethecore.org/page/507/in-common-effective-writing-for-all-students

Discipline-Specific Resources

- Science: Lessons and resources for argumentation in science classes are excerpted here from The Science Teacher.
  www.indiana.edu/~ensiweb/Sci.Argumentation.html
- Social studies: This game from iCivics.org allows students to argue real U.S. Supreme Court cases.
  www.icivics.org/games/argument-wars
- Social studies: TeachingHistory.org offers some tips for writing in history using evidence with links to guides for high school and middle school teachers along with guides for teaching students to annotate documents and read them closely.
  http://teachinghistory.org/issues-and-research/research-brief/24487
- Mathematics: *Making the Case: Mathematical Argumentation* is a video from WGBH Education that explores arguments in math.
  https://youtu.be/pVdH91NkEzM

DEFINING AN ARGUMENT

Now that we have an idea of how argumentation fits with persuasion, we can more fully explore just what an argument is. Although arguments are intended to persuade, they always rely on evidence or data to establish the claim. Generally, we will just use the term *evidence* from now on, even though data inform what will become evidence. As important, the evidence used to establish the claim must be linked to the claim in a logical manner. That link is called a warrant, and it explains why the evidence is worthwhile. We can think of this simple argument as

$$\text{Claim} = \text{Evidence} + \text{Warrant}$$

This looks pretty good, but for 21st-century students, it is only a starting point. In fact (did you see what we did here? Is the following statement a fact or evidence in support of the claim you will read in just a moment?), students need to develop the capacity to work with abstractions that are the backing for the warrants themselves. That is to say, there must be reasons that support why Lujana's *claim* ("He stole my backpack") is supported by *evidence* ("It was here and now it's not") with a *warrant* ("Bob was the only other person in the area of my backpack") and backing (it is generally accepted that if it is a fact that no one else was in the area, the person who stole the backpack had to be nearby). *Backing* for a warrant is the reason that shows why the warrant is appropriate for the type of argument, the evidence, and the claim. Backing provides further support for the warrant.

That seems like a slam-dunk case, doesn't it? Bob obviously purloined the backpack. But there could be more. Bob's advocates might say that just because Lujana did not see anyone else near the backpack may not mean someone else was not close enough to swipe it. Maybe she was distracted. Or maybe she didn't see John sneak in from behind the wall. That's a *rebuttal* or counterargument.

In an upcoming chapter we explore graphic organizers in more detail, but you probably know from your own experience that graphic organizers help make what is complex more comprehensible, so Figure 5.1, a graphic organizer, should help. You

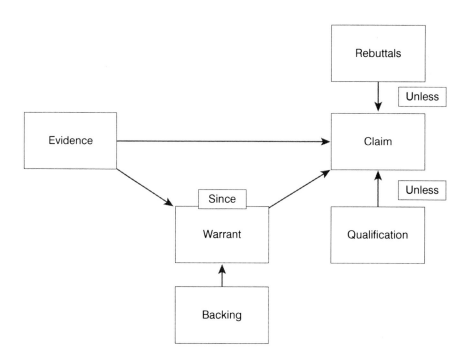

FIGURE 5.1. Toulmin's theory of argument adapted.

can literally plug simple arguments right into the organizer. More complex arguments might need something a little more flexible. Now that you've had a chance to look over the organizer, you probably noticed that there is one box we haven't discussed: *qualification.*

In Toulmin's theory, he placed the qualification directly between the evidence and the claim when qualifications were necessary. We agree with Hillocks (2011) and in our figure have moved it to the bottom of the claim for clarity. A qualification is how an argument addresses probability. In the next section, we provide an example from science to demonstrate what we mean. Bear with us for now, when we say it is not a hypothesis in science if you cannot disprove or falsify it in some way. Most argumentation schemes in other disciplines are the same. A word experts in argumentation and rhetoric use to describe this condition is *defeasible,* that is, they are subject to revision and further clarification. Statistical analyses are used to establish probability. When statistics don't fit the evidence, we might use qualifying phrases such as *likely, in general,* and so on.

PROVE IT OR REFUTE IT?

The first thing we need to know is what a claim actually is. At its most basic, it is an assertion that something is probably so. Now, that seems reasonable, but declaring something to be true is problematic most of the time; notice that we included the word *probably.* For example, the public tends to believe that what scientists do is prove this hypothesis or that theory. The reverse is actually the case; scientists look to disprove or refute a hypothesis, and any scientific hypothesis must be testable. Peterson (2005), a scientist at the University of Montana, shows us how something most people take as proven is actually a collection of studies that failed to disprove their existence:

> We know that electrons exist, but here's the rub: Science can never prove that electrons exist. Hypotheses about the existence of electrons have been supported after countless tests using the scientific method. *In other words, they have not been refuted* [emphasis added]. Knowledge of the precise nature of electrons will always be undergoing refinement, but the weight of scientific evidence clearly supports the existence of electrons. (¶ 5)

By now, you can see where we are going here. Argumentation in science and in other disciplines relies on healthy debate that constantly tests a hypothesis—a form of argument—relies on the possibility that the hypothesis is falsifiable. If a hypothesis isn't falsifiable, it is not science. There are several forms or schemes in argumentation, and it is well beyond the scope of this book to lay them all out. Moreover, it probably would not serve students or their teachers if we tried. Walton, Reed, and Macagno (2008) provide a compendium of 60 different argumentation schemes some with several subschemes. Fortunately, they propose a general classification with only three major categories (see Figure 5.2).

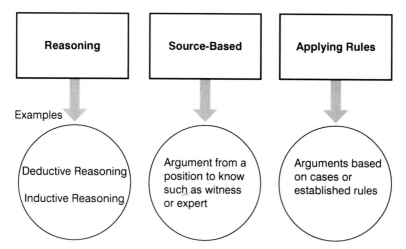

FIGURE 5.2. Proposed classification system for argumentation schemes. Based on Walton et al. (2008).

Pretty nifty, isn't it? That simple organization is something we can handle and that will inform how we approach teaching our students about arguments and also how to construct them. Right away, you will probably recognize the example arguments in each broad category. Mathematicians (but not only mathematicians) use deductive reasoning in the construction of mathematical proofs. Professionals in the social sciences rely very heavily on arguments from a position to know (such as a witness who was at a historical event). Literary judgements drawn from reading literature are a source-based argument. Arguments made by applying rules are found in appeals courts and in some of the sciences (medicine, for example, often relies on the use of case studies).

Hillocks (2011), like Walton and colleagues (2008), found it helpful to describe arguments using three designations based on the ideas of Aristotle. He explained arguments, as they might be taught to secondary school writers, as arguments of fact, of judgment, and of policy. Each must be approached somewhat differently, even as they follow the general Toulmin framework you saw in Figure 5.1. You might notice that there are some similarities between Hillocks's system and Walton's, as well. For example, Hillocks's arguments from judgment share some features with Walton's source-based arguments.

GETTING STARTED WITH ARGUMENTS

The idea of an argument as something students are supposed to do in school takes a little training and experience on their part. Some guides to simple argument construction using language frames (see Chapter 3) and graphic organizers (see Chapter 9) are good ways to help students get going with guidance from you, their teacher.

View these videos with demonstrations and lesson plans of teaching arguments:

 www.learner.org/courses/readwrite/video-detail/teaching-argumentation-skills.html

www.learner.org/courses/readwrite/video-detail/supporting-claims-evidence-and-reasoning.html

 www.learner.org/courses/readwrite/video-detail/citing-evidence-primary-sources-support-arguments.html

Diane and her colleague Amy Miles developed the organizer with language frames in Figure 5.3 to help students analyze an argument they encounter in an article they have been given. By reading arguments and marking out the elements of the argument (or noting the lack of an argument), students start to acquire the skills necessary to recognize thoughtful arguments and construct their own. They ask students to use Educreations (*www.educreations.com*) to record their critique of the article and then share it with classmates.

Students who need more practice can use the sample worksheet in Figure 5.4 to expand their knowledge of claims, evidence, and warrants. You might want to extend this for more advanced students to include backing as well.

When students understand the concept of argument, they can begin to build their own. Once again, language frames are very helpful. Amy and Diane use the ones in Figure 5.5 to get students started. Notice how these language frames have been adapted to promote thinking about science.

As students become increasingly proficient, they can use guides for their writing. Normally, we don't prefer to use essay formats based on a specified number of paragraphs, but here we feel that students need the safety of knowing they need not construct an essay that will go on for many pages. The format in Figure 5.6 gets them started. Instead of underlining and circling, your students may prefer to use colored highlighters. At Health Science High, students choose essential questions that guide them throughout the school year. This year, students wondered about the essential character of the human being. Are humans essentially good, evil, or something else?

In the disciplines, the unique details of each can become more complicated. As we move deeper into the caverns of what makes a good argument, keep in mind the basic structures we discussed above. Your students will need your guidance. Later, in the final chapter, we also share a rubric you can adapt for working with arguments and providing feedback to students as they construct their own arguments.

Examine the student essay at your table. The essay is missing the coding for the claim, evidence, warrant, and counterclaim. Take a picture or scan of the essay and, using Educreations, record a critique. Use the following sentence starters and chart to plan what you will say and underline in your recording.

	Possible Language Frames	Which sentence will you underline/highlight?
Claim (underline)	In this essay the writer is making the claim that _____. I can tell because _____.	
Evidence (circle)	The evidence used to support the claim is _____ _____. The writer uses language like _____ that lets me know it is evidence. Additional evidence is _____ that lets me know that _____.	
Warrant (draw a square)	The warrant for this evidence is _____ _____, and it supports the claim because _____. Another warrant is _____ and supports the claim because _____.	
Counterclaim (use a squiggly underline)	The counterclaim is _____. The writer uses words like _____. Another counterclaim is _____.	
Additional comments you could say	This person forgot to add the _____. One thing that is incomplete is _____. I like how this essay _____. I agree with this person's claim that _____ because _____.	

FIGURE 5.3. Argumentative Critique Planning Guide.

Introduction: As we've discussed in class, a claim is an assertion made in an argument, and evidence is support for the claim. In addition, all arguments are based on unstated beliefs or ideas, called warrants. This exercise is designed to help you understand and identify these concepts.

Instructions: Identify the claim and evidence in each of the following sentences, and then explain the unstated assumptions, or warrants.

    Example: The family was justified in killing the wrens because wrens are pests.

        Claim: The family was justified in killing the wrens.

        Evidence: Wrens are pests.

        Warrant: It is ethically justifiable to kill pests.

Cocaine and heroin should be legalized because legalizing drugs will keep the government out of people's lives.

    Claim:

    Evidence:

    Warrant(s):

Note to the teacher: These are possible responses for **Warrant(s)**: The government doesn't belong in people's lives. Drug use is a private, not public, issue. Drug enforcement is the chief evidence for government intrusion into private lives.

FIGURE 5.4. Worksheet for argumentation practice.

The **three reasons** for selecting _____ **as** an efficient source of

energy are _____, _____, _____.

While some people might say that there are disadvantages to using _____

such as _____, **I believe that** _____ **is still**

the best because _____.

I selected _____ **as an efficient** source of energy **because**

_____.

The **three reasons** for selecting _____ **as** an efficient source of

energy are _____, _____, _____.

While some people might say that there are disadvantages to using _____

such as _____, **I believe that** _____ **is still**

efficient because _____.

FIGURE 5.5. Argument language frames.

100 Point Essential Essay #2
Due: Wednesday, Jan. 22 (Jan. 21 for 5 extra points)
Teachers: Amy Miles and Diane Lapp

QUESTION: Do humans tend toward good or toward evil?

ESSAY: 4 paragraphs

KEY COMPONENTS: Identify the main components of argumentative writing in the text using this key.
- Claim (underline the appropriate part of the text)
- Evidence (circle)
- Warrant (square)
- Counterclaim (squiggly line)

STRUCTURE:
Introductory paragraph:
Include a hook

Include a thesis statement (CLAIM) about the nature of humans as good, evil, or something else.

My thesis statement (CLAIM):

Second paragraph:
Restate claim as related to *Stuck in Neutral* by Terry Trueman.

Includes details and support (EVIDENCE) for the thesis statement related to a character from the book.

Character's name: _____

Good, evil, something else?: _____

Why is this person an example of good or evil?

What are the actions of this person that makes him/her good or evil?

Provide examples from the book when your character represented good or evil.

Include a WARRANT to support your evidence and claim.

Include a COUNTERCLAIM that contradicts your evidence.

(continued)

FIGURE 5.6. Writing a response to an essential question.

Third paragraph:
Restate claim in relation to a famous or historical person.

Includes details and support (EVIDENCE) for the thesis statement related to a famous or historical person.

Person's name: _____

Good or evil: _____

Why is this person an example of good or evil?

What are the actions of this person that makes him/her good or evil?

Provide examples from this person's life to support your thesis.

Include a WARRANT to support your evidence and claim.

Include a COUNTERCLAIM that contradicts your evidence.

Conclusion:
Include a brief summary of your essay's main points.

Restate your thesis statement in another way.

Ask a provocative question, use a quotation, end with a warning, describe a vivid image, etc.

REMEMBER: Work and share this essay with your English teacher in Google Docs! Title this, for example: Period 1 Essential Essay #2 First Name Last Name

Times New Roman, size 12	Paragraph #2 describes *Stuck in Neutral* character as good or evil
Double spaced	
Heading single spaced: 　Name 　Date 　Period	Paragraph #3 describes a *famous or historical person* as good or evil
	Conclusion restates the thesis statement
Clever title	
Indent each paragraph	Check spelling
Hook in the introduction	Check grammar
Thesis statement that can be argued	Share essay with Dr. Johnson and Ms. Tricaso ONLY WHEN FINISHED in Google Docs
Use the key, above: claim, evidence, warrant, and counterclaim	

FIGURE 5.6. *(continued)*

HOW TO ARGUE FACTS: SCIENCE

We asked Dave Scales (personal communication, August 11 and 12, 2015), whom you met in Chapter 2, to comment on the scientific hypothesis as an argument in a Facebook thread. You will find the conversation interesting (Dave is interesting, not so much DeVere), and we have included it here:

DAVE: If properly done, any hypothesis is, by definition, a type of argument. Remember that science is merely the combination of empiricism and rationalism, and that rationalistic component is the argument itself. The prediction that is made in the hypothesis is an extension of the theory you're (1) operating under, (2) the one you're trying to test to see whether it holds water, or (3) both. In order for that to work, an argument must be presented in some form.

DEVERE: So, it's also that rationalist side that says we need to look at probabilities and insist that a scientific hypothesis has to be falsifiable?

DAVE: Almost. Those are two separate yet highly correlated ideas, and neither includes the empirical component. Popper's (1963) principle of falsifiability is predicated on the assumption that we cannot prove anything to be true—the best we can do is to prove something false (or, in social science/ education research, so unlikely that there's no way it could have occurred by chance, indicating that there's something systematic going on). Rationalism in itself is merely the argument put forth, but in its purest sense is a triumph of form over content—argument via logistic syllogism in which the content is irrelevant as long as the premises lead to the conclusion.

Example with three premises: 1. God is love. 2. Love is blind. 3. Ray Charles is blind. Therefore, Ray Charles is God. Neither 1 nor 2 can be proven, but under the rules of rationalism it doesn't matter—the conclusion is inescapable based on the three premises and the rules of logical deduction.

Enter empiricism. The argument above doesn't work in any real-world sense for the simple reason is that there is no physical, tangible evidence via the five senses that God is love or that love is blind. Science demands empirical evidence, but empiricism itself is a collection of facts with no order, like a bag of M&M's—content without form. So, we take the good parts of both rationalism and empiricism (an argument that leads to a single conclusion based solely on the empirical evidence at hand) and call it the scientific method.

In order for it to work, we now invoke the principle of falsifiability. Popper says we can't prove anything to be true, but it's the easiest thing to prove something false. The usual textbook example is the statement "All swans are white." It's impossible to prove it true because of all the swans on Earth at any given time, and the difficulties in accounting for them all simultaneously. However, finding one black swan proves the statement false. Our statements and arguments need to be set up in such a way that they can be proven false. This is why we only test the null hypothesis; if the statement that begins "There is no difference . . ." is false, then its opposite that begins "There *is* a difference . . ." must be true, and 99% of the time that's the statement we want to be true in the first place anyway because that provides evidence in favor of our theory.

DEVERE: Dave, I love M&Ms.

Porter, Sullivan, and Johnson-Eilola (2009) remind us that arguments of fact respond to some of these questions:

- Is there a problem?
- What is the problem?
- How would you define it?
- How large or severe is the problem?
- Where is the problem located?
- When did the problem begin?
- Who has reacted to the problem so far, and in what ways? (Arguments of fact, ¶ 1).

HOW TO ARGUE JUDGMENTS: LITERATURE

While fact-based arguments tend to be of the type "Did Professor Plum kill Mr. Boddy in the conservatory with a wrench?" (from the board game Clue), in literature, most arguments tend to be questions of judgment. Hillocks (2011) argues that understanding literature comes from conceptual work that goes beyond merely assigning a great many works to be read, including the work itself, background information, and explanatory material. Rather, teachers can help students make judgments and inferences. Both require criteria. Sometimes the students develop the criteria themselves, and sometimes the criteria are derived from other sources. You will see that there is some overlap in the three broad categories: arguments of fact, judgment, and policy.

In an essay some time ago, comedian Steve Allen (1985) wrote about his love of classic literature and how one can learn to enjoy classic literature, a daunting task for some students and some adults, too. He offered many suggestions that included reading what the author of the book read and read about the author's life and times. We think there is an important distinction that both Hillocks and Allen are getting at here. It is one thing to simply assign many texts to students and quite another to go after understanding the work by exploring the criteria that others use and that they can develop themselves. The themes of literature (here we mean the type of literature that fit in the broad category of fiction) are hard to understand without some initial guidance.

It is just as important that students learn to develop criteria for making judgments about literature based on their ever-increasing knowledge of the universe of literature, or the part of it that they have come to know well on their own and with the thoughtful guidance of a teacher. According to Hillocks (2011), this takes shape using a conceptual unit that focuses on a human quality or characteristic.

The key to Hillocks's approach is selecting a concept using these guiding questions:

1. Does it have generative power? That is, is the concept of sufficient richness that many discussions, more reading, and multiple writing opportunities arise because students want to explore the concept more thoroughly?
2. Will students be able to apply the concept to multiple reading and life experiences? Making connections that teachers often refer to as text-to-text, text-to-world, and text-to-self (Harvey & Goudvis, 2000) are important aspects of understanding and creating arguments of judgment. Harvey and Goudvis remind us, however, that tangential connections that do little to advance understanding of the text present some difficulties. We return to that idea in Chapter 7.
3. Will students find the concept interesting? We have long believed that it is not so much of what interests students as it is a question of whether we teachers can interest them in the topic.

Then teachers and students select works that in some way incorporate the concept or characteristic. These could become a text set (see Short & Harste, 1996) that students can read in class, at home, during independent study periods, and so on. The idea is that kids become student experts on the topic; they become conversant with their own insights to share. Through discussion of the works they read and the experiences they can bring to the class, students develop their own warrants and backing for the arguments to which they respond. They also learn to listen to each other and build on the available data, as well as the arguments of others.

At Health Science High and Middle College in San Diego, these themes are often infused through the use of essential questions (Wiggins & McTighe, 2005), as we mentioned earlier, developed by the students with guidance from their teachers. In the past, they have asked themselves, "If we can, should we?" The essential questions permeate their work in social studies, science, literature, and mathematics.

HOW TO ARGUE POLICY: SOCIAL STUDIES

Arguments of policy are central to the social sciences. Although arguments of fact and of judgment are also common to the social sciences, policies present to students many opportunities to engage in useful argument. Often, students are asked to write persuasive pieces that might be about topics that concern them, but ultimately are not within their control. For example, it might be fun to ask whether students should wear uniforms at school, and students might care about the topic. However, if their voices ultimately will not be heard, why ask them to participate in the conversation?

Often students are asked to respond to the same tired policy questions: Should students wear uniforms? Should homework be abolished or curtailed? Unless there is a realistic opportunity for students to be heard on the topic, and that the teacher will actually facilitate making those students' voices heard, questions like these are better off not asked. On the other hand, Hillocks (2011) wrote about a group of students who chose to take on the gum-chewing policy at their school. They found that the evidence for the policy was rather compelling—students did stick a lot of gum under desk tops and other places. But, based on their research, they speculated that students often put spent gum under the desk because of the fear of getting caught. They argued to the principal that if gum were allowed, there would be less gum placed under the desks and school custodial resources could be put to better uses than removing wads of gum.

We think that students who make a sound argument should have an audience that can act on what they have to say. At the time we were writing this book, a policy argument was occurring right before our students' eyes.

In matters of law, as we mentioned earlier, policy arguments tend to revolve around the greater good of society or some segment of it (see Swift, 2004). The reverse, in matters of law, is an argument of equity; that is, an argument for the equal treatment of the individual.

Porter and colleagues (2009) suggested:

> Arguments of policy often build on arguments of fact to answer the question "What should be done?"
>
> - What potential responses could we have to this problem?
> - What criteria for responses do we need to establish?
> - Which of the criteria are more important to the organization? Which are less important?
> - How should we act? (Arguments of policy, ¶ 1)

Even if the facts are not in question, and sometimes they are, what should be done if indeed there is a difficult problem? In the social sciences, mock trials are often employed as a tool to help students understand the tenor of the times under study and the context surrounding court decisions.

In the 1857 United States Supreme Court decision *Dred Scott v. Sandford,* the court affirmed that Mr. Scott, an individual who had been a slave but had lived in a free state for several years, not only remained a slave but also had no standing to sue in federal courts. The ruling reached far beyond that. DeVere's students participated in mock trial reenactments to try to understand this complicated ruling and the people and the facts that led to it. Students often noted that facts, as they were presented in the case, were actually only opinions that were not based on evidence as we understand it today. They did walk away with an understanding of the time when some U.S. citizens believed that slavery was a fully justifiable, if peculiar, practice.

We can see the reverberations of this policy and Supreme Court decision today as arguments when citizens in the 21st century maintain that slavery had little to do with the Civil War and its causes or that states had a right to determine who might or might not be enslaved. If you would like to view a well-argued position that slavery was "the single most important cause of the Civil War" (Seidule, August 10, 2015, time index 0:23), watch the following video: *www.facebook.com/prageru/videos/923232114386312.*

Colonel Seidule (see Figure 5.7) uses facts in support of a policy argument that responds to the question "Was the Civil War fought because of slavery?" The West Point Military History Professor (yes, we just appealed to expertise and authority with cause) makes the case in a model of policy arguments.

FIGURE 5.7. Screenshot from Colonel Seidule's video. Reprinted with permission from Colonel Seidule.

A FEW WORDS ABOUT SOURCES

The term *sources* is used in different ways in argumentation schemes, but we should explore the idea of sources here. A useful tool to get students started thinking about sources is found in Figure 5.8. Our main point is that whatever sources are appropriate for your discipline, students should learn to be accurate. To do that, they can take the approach to Read Up, Ask Around, and Double-Check (Wolsey, 2014). This is not a strategy in which students simply follow the steps and, presto, they have good sources. Rather, the idea is that students read and listen to many sources from an inquiry stance. They ask for help and guidance when they recognize they need it, and they double-check sources to be sure they are accurate. The basics of Read Up, Ask Around, and Double-Check are as follows:

- Read up includes reading widely to become familiar with the most salient ideas surrounding a topic, and students read up to look for specific information.
- Asking around means knowing when to ask peers who are also writing, speaking, or otherwise composing media about a topic. It also means consulting with experts, often using electronic communications to connect with those who are in a position to know.
- Double-checking is just what it says, a check for accuracy. Students reread, cite their sources, and use the notion of reading up and asking around to make sure that the information they provide is accurate.

CHAPTER 5 ACTIVITIES

1. Find the op-ed section of a major newspaper and choose a column that interests you. Use highlighters or colored pens to identify the claims, evidence or data, warrants, and perhaps backing for any arguments introduced. What did you learn? Next, find a document that makes a claim specific to your field or discipline. Do the same as you did above. What did you learn?

2. Building on the practicality of using sentence frames, Diane and Amy constructed a bookmark for their students to use. Make copies of the bookmark in Figure 5.9 or design your own!

Research Question: _____
From the sources you have reviewed, summarize major arguments that support and major arguments that oppose.

For each of the arguments, cite at least one source that supports this fact or point of view.

Argument/facts in favor of . . .	Source supporting this argument:
1.	
2.	
3.	
Argument/facts in opposition to . . .	Source supporting this argument:
1.	
2.	
3.	

Evaluate the credibility of the arguments and evidence presented by these sources. Which sources are more trustworthy and why? Which sources warrant some skepticism because of bias or insufficient evidence?

FIGURE 5.8. Worksheet for thinking about sources.

CLAIM	I will argue that _____ _____.
	This paper will show that _____ _____.
EVIDENCE	One piece of evidence is _____ _____.
	Another piece of evidence to support my claim is _____ _____
	Additional evidence is _____ _____.
	To support the claim that _____, _____.
WARRANT	As a rule, _____ _____.
	Generally speaking, _____ _____.
	Most people would agree that _____ _____.
	It is the accepted belief that _____ _____.
	Some may argue that _____ _____.
	The truth is _____ _____.
COUNTERCLAIM AND COUNTER TO COUNTERCLAIM	There are those who would claim _____ _____, however, _____.
	Some people think _____ _____.
	But in reality, _____ _____.
	It is possible to argue that _____ _____.
	Upon closer inspection, however, _____ _____.

FIGURE 5.9. Sentence frames to support crafting an argument.

Chapter 6

Reading It Carefully

Instruction That Supports Reading in the Disciplines

"I am not a teacher of reading!"

The preceding sentence is one that every middle and high school practicing teacher or preservice teacher has either thought or said. We totally agree, most of you did not go to college to become a reading specialist, and therefore you do not have the skills to be a teacher of reading. Rather, your role as an expert in your discipline is to expose students to your content information in ways that make them want to study it and become so excited about it that they choose a related profession as a career path. One way to accomplish this is by helping them acquire the literacy skills they need to be able to gain information from texts in your discipline. A component of being literate in a discipline is reading, and being able to read means that students can access information from printed text materials across the disciplines.

How and when students read within a class period may differ by discipline. For example, many science teachers would never introduce a science concept by first asking students to read about it. Most want students to initially and actively engage in experimentation as a way to gain information and then to eventually compare their newly acquired insights with the expert voices of other sciences that have researched and published on the topic. As noted in Chapter 2, through the voices of experts working across the disciplines, reading also takes many forms in social studies, art, music, and physical education as students read or view various artifacts, documents, scores, paintings, and maneuvers. Printed text is often secondary to these first explorations. Our intent in this chapter is not to convince you to discontinue your tried and true disciplinary practices, but rather to introduce you to three practices that will engage your students with print. These include *read-alouds, shared reading,* and *reciprocal teaching.* You will notice that we have embedded other powerful practices like *ReQuest* and *QAR* within this discussion because proficient readers use both of these practices to help them draw meaning from a text.

READ-ALOUDS

A read-aloud, which is usually conducted by the teacher, is done to focus attention on a passage or text. The students are engaged as listeners, if they are motivated enough to do so. Reading aloud a poem or portion of a text has often been thought of as an experience that happens after lunch in elementary classrooms. While this remembrance may conjure memories of wonderful early-grade experiences, many adolescents also share these same memories. In fact, Erickson (1996) noted that being read aloud to is also very motivating for adolescents, and Ivey and Broaddus (2001), after surveying more than 1,700 adolescents, found that more than 62% identified being read to by a teacher as a favorite activity.

There are however, reasons other than motivation for reading aloud to your students. It also works well for introducing complex information, making connections among various complex ideas being studied, activating prior knowledge that can support learning the new information, and getting students excited about a new topic (Worthy, 2002). It also supports students who have difficulty reading the textbook because they lack the necessary background knowledge, language, and reading skills. While the idea of reading aloud is a way to get students involved with a topic, all of the reading cannot be done by the teacher, and what is read aloud will not eliminate students' reading problems. Some students may need to have access to a reading specialist and they may also need to acquire a textbook that has an audio component, if one exists. Once students who lack proficient reading skills get beyond third grade, their problems are exacerbated without support from a trained reading specialist. Our goal in this discussion is not to teach you to take on this role, but rather to share how you might use the strategy of reading aloud to promote engagement and foster critical thinking about topics in your discipline, since read-alouds have been found to have very positive learning effects in mathematics (Richardson & Gross, 1997), social studies (Irvin, Lunstrum, Lynch-Brown, & Shepard, 1995) foreign language, and many other disciplines. A read-aloud can be shared in any discipline and with any type of text that is being used to convey written information.

Give It a Try!

If you're looking for terrific resources on the specifics of how to conduct the read-aloud strategy, you might want to get a copy of *The Read-Aloud Handbook* (Trelease,

2006), which contains many types of texts and ideas for sharing, and *Read It Aloud!* (Richardson, 2000), which contains texts for reading aloud across the disciplines. Let's look at the following YouTube video to get you started: *www.youtube.com/watch?v=qnTFjAGYs2Y.*

Did you notice that the professor advised the student to select a passage that connected to his students and the topic being studied? In addition to selecting a relevant passage, she also advised that the read-aloud be conducted interactively to engage students and also to give them a foundation to support additional learning. The more opportunities students have to interact with the teacher and peers during the read-aloud, the more opportunities they have to take ownership of the topic being studied and its related vocabulary.

As you prepare to conduct a read-aloud, let's expand these suggestions and consider the following criteria that were identified by Fisher, Flood, Lapp, and Frey (2004) as ones that were used by teachers identified by their principals as excellent at integrating interactive read-alouds into their lessons. Use the planning guide in Figure 6.1 to plan, share, and assess your read-aloud.

As you plan your read-aloud(s), continually think about the ways that you can promote your students' interaction with the text, whether it is a section of a textbook, a poem, a chart, a news article, or any other print material. The props, questions, discussions, and extensions should all serve to familiarize your students with the topical language and concepts and to make them more comfortable reading independently.

For example, if you were reading aloud a text on earthquakes, your purpose may be for students to learn how plate tectonics can cause earthquakes. As you read, students take notes in their note-taking guide about information that supports how plate tectonics cause earthquakes. You might decide to read the first three paragraphs and ask students after you read to talk to a partner, use their notes, and describe the differences between extensional, transform, and compressional plate tectonic environments.

After partner and whole-class share-out, you may read the next four paragraphs aloud, asking students to attend to how the lithosphere slides over the lubricating asthenosphere. Sketching a picture or diagram in their notes might help students make meaning of the text being read aloud. Finally, you may conclude the read-aloud by reading the final three paragraphs and asking students to attend to the types of earthquake faults. As you read, students could fill in a four-column chart in their notes, writing down components of each type of fault. Students should share notes with one another and then a whole-group share-out could occur.

After the read-aloud, students could use the information from their notes and discussions to write a paragraph about how plate tectonics cause earthquakes. This is your formative assessment to see how much your students learned and what, if any, information needs to be retaught in the future.

PLANNING

1. **Look at standards.** Be mindful of the standards you are planning to address.

2. **Purpose.** Decide on a lesson purpose. What do you want your students to pay attention to as you read? What do you want students to learn?

3. **Select a reading** that is appropriate to the content being studied, and students' emotional and social development and interests.

   • Name the selected text

   • How does this selection relate to the topic of study? Think back to your lesson purpose.

4. **Chunk the text.** Decide on stopping points in the text and the questions you will ask. Ask questions that evoke thinking and discussion rather than yes/no responses.

5. **Practice the selection.** Your first time reading the text can't be when you are presenting it to your students. You need to be prepared. Practicing the text helps you to decide when to use voice inflection, reading rate, and tone. With practice you will be better able to emphasize the connections you feel are needed to support students' understanding the topic and motivation to listen to you read. You need to sound like a fluent reader.

6. **Plan student and text interactions.** Decide how students will interact with the text. Will there be partner talk at stopping points during the reading? Will students be taking notes? Will there be a whole-group discussion at the conclusion of the reading? Will there be an extension task that involves related reading or writing?

DURING THE READ-ALOUD

1. **Read it.** This is a chance for your students to hear how a proficient reader sounds when reading complex texts. For students who are not fluent readers and those who are learning English as an additional language, your modeling of proficient oral reading may be what they need to gain confidence as both readers and with the information you are reading.

2. **Engage students and connect them to the text.** Students can be motivated to listen to the read-aloud if it is introduced with intriguing pictures, props, diagrams, charts, illustrations, and manipulations. If the reading is taken from your text, be sure to select some related visuals that you might use to introduce it. Any type of anticipation that can be created hooks the students.

   What supporting materials can you use to support interest in the text you've selected?

3. **Stop periodically to ask questions.** Appropriately spaced interactions with students during the reading breaks up the text and maintains engagement. Asking questions provides the perfect opportunity for students to reflect on what is being read. Be sure to ask questions that cause them to think deeply about the reading. Why do you believe that character [name] is acting this way? Why do you think the author wrote this text? Your

(continued)

FIGURE 6.1. Read-Aloud Planning Guide.

questions should not be easy-to-answer, literal questions. They should require the reader to listen. You might even want to pose a question to get the reading started. A question like "As I'm reading, listen to determine what factors really caused the South to enter the Civil War' is one that causes the reader to focus on the entire selection in order to be able to answer. Before beginning, chunk your text into big-idea areas and then ask a question about each chunk, or ask a question that causes students to make connections across chunks.

How will you chunk your text and what questions will you ask?

4. **Engage students in discussion.** The selected read-aloud and questions being discussed should promote additional discussion and connections to other texts. Identify additional texts that can support topical connections to the text you have selected for your read-aloud. This is an opportunity to encourage your struggling readers to connect to texts on the same topic that are not written at such a complex level. Once they begin to develop the language and topical concepts they will be better able to read the more complex passage. Your goal should be to provide the scaffolds needed to ensure that all of your students are able to grow in their abilities to read increasingly complex texts.

What are some less difficult texts on this topic that your students can easily access?

What are additional texts on the same topic that are more challenging than the one you have chosen to read aloud?

5. **Make direct connections to students' independent reading and writing.** At the conclusion of the read-aloud, there should be related activities that the students do to use the information they have just finished listening to and discussing. If the selection was an entire text, students might be asked to write a summary of what has been read and then to pose next questions for investigation. If the selection was a chunk of a longer text that is to be continued, ask students to make predictions about what they believe will happen next. Be sure to ask them to support their thinking with information they have just heard and discussed. What will be the next steps for students at the conclusion of the close reading?

6. **Assess throughout the planning, sharing, and extension activities.** What will you use to determine whether your students accomplished the lesson purpose? Will you collect their response journals, exit slips, etc.?

FIGURE 6.1. *(continued)*

SHARED READING

Shared reading is a strategy that is similar to a read-aloud. Both ease students into independent reading as teachers do the oral reading and thus provide students with a model of proficient, fluent reading. This model of proficiency as a reader can be viewed as a scaffold that supports students in developing the behaviors of independent readers. Guided practice with the text can also be provided as students listen, discuss, and view the text as the teacher points out important concepts, vocabulary, and structures. These are also scaffolds that support students gaining the skills and comfort to eventually read related material independently.

The primary difference between a read-aloud and shared reading is that during a shared reading the students are not just listening to the teacher reading aloud;

they are also viewing the text. Their viewing of the text as it is read enables them to see a written representation of the topical language and information. Teachers might decide to hook students into a topic with an interactive read-aloud, and once they are familiar with the topic and language, they will be more comfortable and able to read and study independently. Teachers can then visually share a viewed copy of the text. There is, however, no sequence that must occur. Teachers can begin with the shared reading experience and some teachers prefer using only a shared reading experience. The choice is yours and it should be made based on the purpose of the lesson.

Modeling and Guided Practice

Modeling and guided practice, features of both read-alouds and shared reading, are components of the gradual release of responsibility model of instruction (GRR; Pearson & Gallagher, 1983) that many teachers use as their instructional frame. The theory that supports GRR was introduced in the 1930s by Russian psychologist Lev Vygotsky (1978) as the zone of proximal development (ZPD). His theory of ZPD, which became much more established in the 1970s, defined the zone as the difference between the level at which the learner can independently problem solve and the level at which he or she can independently do so with guidance from knowing others. Scaffolds support the learner moving to independence.

 To understand how a math teacher incorporates a shared reading and think-aloud to help students solve a math problem, view *www.learner.org/courses/readwrite/video-detail/using-gradual-release-responsibility.html*. The instructional frame guiding this lesson is the GRR model.

Scaffolding theory was introduced by Bruner (1960) in the late 1950s, and the term *scaffolds* was coined by Wood, Bruner, and Ross (1976), who shared many of the same beliefs as Vygotsky. Scaffolds describe the resources and instruction students need to receive from experts to support their learning and become independent at a new task. Brush and Saye (2002) noted that there are both hard and soft scaffolds. Hard scaffolds can be determined prior to teaching the lesson as the teacher thinks about what is to be taught and the skills of those who will be learning it. Interactive read-alouds and shared reading experiences can serve as hard scaffolds that move the entire class to independence. Soft or contingent scaffolds are offered to individuals when the teacher assesses that they need additional support to accomplish the learning goals. Soft or contingent scaffolds can be shared as the teacher circulates the room and listens to a peer conversation and determines that asking an additional question can move students to independence. Contingent scaffolds can also be shared with a smaller group of students at the conclusion of a lesson. Here again a read-aloud or a shared reading could occur.

Give It a Try!

During shared reading, teachers often model how they use comprehension strategies (Fisher, Frey, & Lapp, 2008) to support their comprehension. While teachers might also do this during a read-aloud, doing so during shared reading allows students to view the sections of the text that are being emphasized as the teacher changes pitch, inflection, and tone. It also allows the student viewer to see the text features, language (including new vocabulary) and the punctuation that is accenting the reading. The following considerations will help you prepare and present a shared reading.

1. *How will the text be chosen?* While read-alouds are often shared as a way to build interest and background knowledge with a topic, texts chosen for shared reading should contain opportunities to teach comprehension strategies, language structures, or text features the teacher is attempting to highlight. A shared reading is often coupled with a think-aloud. During the think-aloud the teacher can emphasize whatever feature or skill she has identified.

2. *How will the text be displayed?* Since students will be viewing the text, the first decision is to determine how this will occur. Will students have paper copies or will the text be displayed on a whiteboard, or through some other means? Even if students have individual paper copies we have found that it is more effective to also have an enlarged version so that students can view any notations being made by the teacher. As they watch the teacher interacting with the text, students begin to have a model of how reading involves interaction between the reader and the text (Wade & Moje, 2000).

3. *What exactly is a think-aloud, and how does it work with a shared reading?* A think-aloud is a process that involves an expert, often the teacher, thinking out loud about a problem he or she is solving or a passage he or she is reading or analyzing. This allows the students to hear what is going on in the mind of an expert. Teachers often use the think-aloud to provide explicit modeling about information or text they want students to learn or figure out (Davey, 1983). When you use this strategy some key points to remember are:

- Use only a short text or a chunk of a text in your discipline. Brief think-alouds work well because you can keep them focused and you can also keep the students engaged. If think-alouds are too long or happen too often they may become less effective.
- Be sure the text contains the features or the information you want to share. Make notes on your copy to be sure you emphasize the comprehension strategy, text structure, language, and information you intend.
- Practice before thinking aloud; this will help you to sound authentic. Include annotations on your copy so you can be concise, precise, and authentic.

Into the Classroom

In Mr. Jackson's eighth-grade social studies class, students are studying the economic growth and decline among American workers. Let's observe him presenting a shared reading coupled with a think-aloud. One topic of study in this class was the New York Conspiracy of 1741. To make this event more present in the students' lives Mr. Jackson presented, as a shared reading, the primary document *Horsmanden's Conclusion to the Case*. This was published in *A Journal of the Proceedings in the Detection of the Conspiracy Formed by Some White People, in Conjunction with Negro and Other Slaves* (1744). This text was chosen because it supported the topic of study and also contained the features of a legal document.

Mr. Jackson wanted to familiarize students with both the language, topic, and text layout structure. This was successfully accomplished as students viewed the text with him and listened as he thought aloud about these features.

> "As I look at this document I wonder if it is the cover of a journal or if this is how a court document is titled. I notice its interesting structure and the fact that it uses a couple of different font types and sizes. I wonder if this is done for emphasis. Since it isn't familiar to me I need to look carefully at each section."

After reading the first section, he continues:

> "Seems the first section briefly identifies what happened and why. The next section has the title 'Containing,' which I bet identifies the three sections that will follow. Finally I notice that it says, 'By the Recorder of the City of New York.' Since it was recorded I know it is a legal document. I am also surprised that the language seems so familiar since it is a legal document that was written over 200 years ago."

In this shared reading Mr. Jackson was thinking aloud about the structure of the text. Teachers also often share a reading coupled with a think-aloud to model how they interrogate a text by applying various reading strategies. We explain six possible strategies below, including *inferring, summarizing, self-monitoring and self-questioning, identifying text structures, attending to text features*, and *interpreting visual representations*.

Inferring

Making an inference occurs by paying attention to every clue the author gives. For example, in Chapter 1, "A Most Terrible Sea," of *The Longitude Prize* (Dash, 2000), we see the power of the inference-making in the few lines when Dash illustrates that by attending to the word *reckoning*, we can infer in the seaman's account that he and his mates were off course and as a result their ship was destroyed.

At six in the morning I was awaked by a great shock, and a confused noise of the men on deck. I ran up, thinking some ship had run afoul of us, for by my own reckoning, and that of every other person in the ship, we were at least thirty-five leagues distant from land. (p. 3)

Making an inference involves the reader figuring something out from the clues that are given.

Summarizing

Being able to summarize involves being able to condense a large piece of text into a smaller one that maintains the most significant features. This can occur throughout the reading. In fact, proficient readers often then synthesize the chunks of information they have summarized. Synthesizing involves combining new and previously learned information.

Self-Monitoring and Self-Questioning

Proficient readers often question themselves to be sure they are comprehending. If they are not comprehending, they often return to the text to question it. One practice that supports readers learning to question themselves by questing the text is ReQuest (Manzo, 1969).

Notice in the following video that students in Mrs. Miles's class are working as partners as they use ReQuest to question the text:

www.youtube.com/watch?v=KxvRvWDvDt8

Before they begin, Mrs. Miles and her colleague, Diane Lapp, model the process for them. We have found that modeling any strategy helps students better understand how to independently proceed.

What's Involved in Teaching ReQuest?

You'll notice in the ReQuest video that these teachers made this process a challenge between pairs of students. The majority of students love a challenge, and this was definitely true in this classroom. After partner teams were identified, they tasked the teams to interrogate the text. To begin, the teachers identified a section for the students to read. Both students were to read the same section but with a different lens. Partner 1 was charged with reading the identified section and while doing so craft a few challenging questions to ask his partner. He was cautioned not to quote from the passage, but rather to use his own words to convey the questions. Partner 2 was charged with reading the same section and thinking about possible questions that Partner 1 might ask. When finished they were asked to change roles. They were encouraged to repeat this two or three times.

To be sure that students are asking questions that capture the significant ideas of a passage you can practice with them. To begin, have them all read the same text and then ask them several significant questions. For example, in a 10th-grade English class, Mr. Jacobs introduced his students to ReQuest as they read *The Melting Pot* by Anna Quindlen. After reading, he asked, "What is being described? What is America being compared to? What does the narrator mean by mongrel nation? What is the author's tone? What is the author's point of view and how does she support it?" Answering these questions helped his students move from a very basic understanding of the text to a much deeper meaning because of the analysis that was involved in deriving an answer. If at first they were unable to answer a question, he asked them to return to the text for the answer or for the justification for their answer.

ReQuest is a strategy that, once learned, students can use independently to support their comprehension. Questioning the text helps them develop their metacognition, or awareness of how well they are comprehending the passage.

What's Involved in Teaching QAR?

Another strategy that involves questioning the text and also results in enhancing comprehension is *Question–Answer Relationship* (QAR). Designed by Raphael (1984, 1986), this strategy involves the reader asking four types of questions identified as *Right There, Think and Search, Author and You,* and *On Your Own.* QAR question types are based on the earlier work of Pearson and Johnson (1978), who classified questions as *text explicit* (those that can be answered from information that is literally stated in the text), *text implicit* (those that are implied within the text and involve the reader synthesizing several segments of the text in order to answer), and *script implicit* (those that involve the reader blending text information and prior knowledge and experiences). The key to using QAR to support one's comprehension is being able to identify what type of questions have been asked. This level of awareness then helps the reader understand what he or she is doing with the text and his or her experiences to answer the question. Figure 6.2 helps to explain the four QAR questions types.

In order to become proficient using QAR, students need to see models of each type of question being asked and answered and they also need lots of practice asking each type. You may want to create a chart similar to Figure 6.2 that contains example questions and responses from your text or discipline. During a shared reading that you couple with a think-aloud, you can ask yourself questions that call for each type of response. After modeling the asking and answering of each, allow time for students to practice. Continually remind them that reading any text involves an interaction between the information in the text and the reader's background knowledge and experience.

Question Type?	How Identified?	What's the Plan?	Example?
Right There	Explicitly in text.	Use words taken from the text that can be answered by restating words directly in the text. Answers usually address who, what, when, and where questions.	Q: What are the three types of rocks? A: The three types of rocks are sedimentary, metamorphic, and igneous. Answer is explicitly stated in the text on p. 8.
Think and Search	Implied in the text.	Words from the text can be used to ask the question, but the reader must search the text and synthesize information in order to answer. Answering think and search questions involves the reader in describing the character, mood, setting, or symbolism, comparing/contrasting, and inferring.	Q: What are Romeo's character traits? A: The answer is in the text, but the reader must read several sections.
Author and You	Implied in the text and coupled with one's knowledge about the topic.	The question relates to the topic. The answer blends the text information that is implied with the experiences of the reader. The reader does the blending.	Q: Using the height you determined earlier in the problem, what is the volume in cubic inches of the pyramid shown in the picture? A: In order to answer this question, the reader must use her mathematical computation skills and information shown in the text picture to arrive at the answer.
On Your Own	Based on one's experiences.	The question may relate to the topic, but the answer comes from the reader's experiences rather than from what is found in the text.	Q: How would you feel if . . . ? A: The response comes from the reader's own experience or feelings.

FIGURE 6.2. QAR question types.

Identifying Text Structures

Being able to identify various text structures is another comprehension strategy that is empowering to readers. By the time students reach the middle and high school years they are confronted with multiple organizational structures across the disciplines and also often within the same text. The structures that are most common are cause–effect, compare–contrast, problem–solution, sequence, chronology, and description. Figure 6.3 is a chart showing some of the words that signal that a

Text Structure	Signal Words
Cause–effect	*because, if, when, reason, cause, then, so, which, effect*
Compare–contrast	*same, at the same time, like, still, some, others, different, however, rather, yet, but, or*
Problem–solution	*problem, trouble, challenge, difficulty, puzzling, question, doubt, answer, discovery, improve, solution, overcome, reply, response, resolve*
Temporal sequence and chronology	*first, second, third, last, next, finally, then, now, since, soon, meanwhile, in the meantime, at the same time, following, not long after*
Description	*such as, characteristic of, to illustrate, to demonstrate, an example*

FIGURE 6.3. Signal words denoting text structures.

particular structure is being used in the text. You may wish to create such a chart and encourage your students to add to it as they read within your discipline.

Attending to Text Features

When readers attend to text features, they support their comprehension. Text features include headings, subheads, captions, and direction. During a shared reading be sure to model how carefully you read directions and also the possible errors that might have occurred for you if you had skipped them.

Interpreting Visual Representations

This is a comprehension strategy that is used by the reader to understand information presented in charts, graphs, and diagrams. It's important not to skip over these graphics and also not to assume that students know how to read them. Teaching students how to read graphic information can happen easily if you plan to address it as a shared reading coupled with a think-aloud.

Different disciplines attend to visual information in unique ways. In Chapter 2, we saw how scientists and medical personnel attend to visual information such as charts, figures, and tables. This is a good time to take a look at how historians might approach visual information by visiting the National Archives and Records Administration website for teachers. On the right, you will find a number of resources for different types of primary source documents: *www.archives.gov/education/lessons*.

Additional information that will support weaving literacy into history can be viewed at *www.learner.org/courses/readwrite/video-detail/reading-and-writing-history.html*. As you watch this video, Reading and Writing in History, consider how you might also teach students to read and write historical documents.

Have you noticed that these six comprehension strategies can be taught within the context of every discipline? If you decide to teach text structures, inferring, or any other strategy, be sure you do so in the section of your text that contains examples of each. Remember the following tips as you plan to introduce these strategies.

- Select a text that contains the features.
- Teach them when they naturally occur in the text and in the lesson.
- Be sure that teaching these strategies aligns with your lesson purpose.
- Consider presenting each during a shared reading, coupled with a think-aloud.
- Be sure the students know the intended purpose and why this strategy is worth learning.
- Don't assume the strategy has been learned after being shared only once. Incorporate it into multiple lessons.
- Provide lots of time for students to practice each strategy and remind them often to use these.

Now you understand the power of incorporating read-alouds and shared readings coupled with think-alouds into your instruction to teach comprehension strategies. Next we look at a powerful instructional strategy known as Reciprocal Teaching.

RECIPROCAL TEACHING

Reciprocal Teaching is an instructional strategy that tasks four students with a cooperative investigation of a text (Palinscar & Brown, 1986) as they assume the roles of a *questioner, summarizer, predictor,* and *clarifier.* Once students learn the details of the roles, they can enact their roles independently. What results is that they take ownership of their comprehension of a text. This student-centered activity, which is used widely across the disciplines, was found to be a very effective strategy for learning (Rosenshine & Meister, 1994) and motivation (Palinscar & Herrenkohl, 2002).

Give It a Try!

To prepare a text to be used during Reciprocal Teaching, the teacher begins by first chunking the text into smaller segments. This alerts students to interact with smaller units of text and to assess their understanding of the information more frequently as they talk about segments of the text. In order to learn how to interact with the text while assuming each of the roles, the teacher must first model how to act in each. However, when students independently engage in a Reciprocal Teaching activity, they will only assume one role. Their roles should, however, change as they use this strategy throughout the school year because proficiency in each supports their individual abilities to interrogate a text when they are tasked to read it alone. Across the disciplines, proficient readers question the text, summarize it, clarify information, and make predictions. An ultimate goal for a teacher, after much guided practice with students, might be to remove role assignments, with the caveat that students use the reciprocal teaching strategies to talk about texts. In other words, each student is expected to freely engage in conversations in which they predict, question, clarify, and summarize together with peers in small-group conversations centered on chunked pieces of the text.

Let's look more specifically at each role in Figure 6.4. As you attempt to introduce the four roles to your students you might find that cards containing a few tips about each role are a terrific support. We have found that literally holding the task card helps students better assume their roles.

The strength of this approach is the collaboration that occurs among the four students. Of course, before they can become good at applying reciprocal teaching they must learn the process. As you begin you will need to model each role until students learn it. This involves presenting several lessons where you model an identified role.

For example, you might present several texts where you model how to ask questions. During each lesson you can invite students to also ask questions of a chunk of the text. Remember to model "how-to" question at all levels of depth of knowledge (DOK). Model questioning during Reciprocal Teaching just as you modeled questioning during ReQuest and QAR. Once students are proficient at questioning a text you are ready to move to introducing another role.

For example, in an eighth-grade history class Ms. Martinez had chunked the text *Blood, Toil, Tears and Sweat*, which was Winston Churchill's 1940 speech to Parliament as the new Prime Minister. After she read the first chunk she asked, "What had Churchill been doing since assuming the role of Prime Minister?" She then modeled how she would reread the first three paragraphs and gather evidence for her answer. She then continued, reading the next three paragraphs of the text, which was the next chunk she had identified. After reading, still playing the role of the questioner, she said, "What exactly is Churchill asking the house in his resolution?" To answer she then read the resolution, which was stated in paragraph 4. Now feeling that the students were beginning to understand the role of the questioner, she invited them to read the final four-paragraph chunk. When they finished she asked, "What is the mood of this speech? Please show language that supports your thinking." Over the next few days Ms. Martinez also modeled how to perform the other roles and engaged students in guided practice, doing so until she felt they had achieved an understanding of the role of questioner.

QUESTIONER

The questioner asks questions about information in the text. The questions should help readers find information that builds their understanding of the text. Being able to answer these questions helps readers assess whether they understand the information.

Tips:
- Ask main idea questions.
- Ask questions about facts. These are *who, what, when,* and *where* questions.
- Ask questions that PROMPT interpretation of information. These are questions that answer *how* and *why*.
- Ask questions that PROMPT readers to find additional sources, experts, or information for the answers. These questions might involve statements like "Have you wondered if . . . ?" or "Have you considered why . . . ?"

CLARIFIER

The clarifier has the role of helping to clear up any confusion that occurs during the reading. To begin, the clarifier has to pay attention to any words or ideas that cause him confusion while reading. Once areas of confusion are identified, you might need to consult an expert, look up the information on the internet, in a dictionary, or in the text glossary. The clarifier needs to get prepared to clear up any confusion the other students have when they are reading. Sometimes the clarifier identifies the areas of confusion but may not be able to figure them out alone. This may need to occur through collaboration with the other students.

Tips:
- List information or words that are confusing to you.
- Next, decide how you will clear up the confusion.
- Then be ready to share information to alleviate confusion.

What is confusing?	How will I solve this?	What new information clears this up?

SUMMARIZER

Throughout the reading of each chunk of the text, the summarizer recaps and condenses what has been learned so far.

Tips:
- After reading a chunk of information, say it in your own words.
- Check yourself to be sure you included the significant information.
  - Did I list the big ideas and concepts?
  - Did I include key locations, places, or items?
  - Do I have the key words?
  - Put it all together to check yourself.
  - Say it out loud to be sure you have included all of the key information.

(continued)

FIGURE 6.4. Reciprocal Teaching role cards.

PREDICTOR

Based on what has been read and discussed, the predictor identifies what will probably be information that appears next in the text.

Tips:
- Look at the graphics on the next pages for clues about what the next section will be about.
- Survey the next headings to predict what information can be expected in the next section.
- Think about the topic and what you have learned so far or what you already know about it. Based on this, what might a reader expect would be the next section?

FIGURE 6.4. *(continued)*

Let's Make a Prediction

For example, when modeling how to be the predictor Ms. Martinez showed the students how she would think about what she already knew about the topic; what she observed from the pictures, charts, and graphs included in the text; and, most important, how she drew information from any clues she gained from the subheadings. She introduced her predictions with phrases like the following:

> I think _____.
>
> Based on the next subheading, I predict _____.
>
> By looking at the photo on page _____, I predict _____.
>
> As a result of what we've learned so far, I believe _____.

Ms. Martinez modeled how to predict, using academic language and accountable talk. This means that the speaker provides evidence for her predictions using scholarly language or "school talk."

Allow Me to Clarify

When Ms. Martinez modeled how to assume the role of the clarifier, she reminded students that being confused when reading is okay as long as you try to help yourself gain an understanding of the information and continue to persist in your reading. She modeled how she used thinking frames like the following to help her make sense of confusing parts of a text:

> _____ is a word that I don't know, and without it I couldn't understand, so I looked it up in the glossary or dictionary.
>
> At first the section on page _____ didn't make sense to me, so I slowed down and re-read it, and now I know that it means _____.

I was confused when I got to the section on _____ because I
thought it meant _____. I looked it up on the Internet and found
out _____. Now I understand that _____.

At first I didn't understand _____, but after I read further I was able
to clarify that _____.

She wanted her students to understand that when texts get confusing, good
readers have strategies for helping themselves gain understanding. She suggested
that the clarifier is like a detective who keeps searching for clarifying clues.

Let Me Summarize

Finally Ms. Martinez taught the students how to summarize each chunk of a text as
a way to get a deeper understanding. She modeled how to keep a summary concise
by including the main ideas, not the unnecessary details. While she read she modeled how to highlight or underline key words and phrases, and how to make notes
in the margins about main ideas and events. She also modeled how to circle words
like *therefore, in conclusion,* or *in summary* that signal or transition the reader to
organizational patterns. Then she modeled how to verbally summarize the text to
someone. At the conclusion of her modeling she reread the text and wrote a summary paragraph.

Into the Classroom

Let's next visit 10th-grade science teacher Dr. Grant as she models how to engage
in all four aspects of Reciprocal Teaching: predicting, clarifying, questioning, and
summarizing. To do this, Ms. Grant conducts a think-aloud in which she articulates
her thinking about the text. She plays all four roles and shares aloud the thinking
that goes on in her head as she is the *modeler,* the *clarifier,* the *questioner,* and the
predictor. As she models, students make notes on a Reciprocal Teaching note guide.
They indicate how Dr. Grant plays each role and they document what she notices.
Following this and a brief debrief of the think-aloud, Dr. Grant asks students to
participate in a "fishbowl." Be sure to check back to Chapter 3 to review the fishbowl approach as we described it with Socratic seminar. Fishbowl is a strategy in
which some students have the role of practicing newly learned activities (the fish
inside the bowl) and others have the role of observing how it's done (those looking
into the fishbowl). To do this, Dr. Grant has four students come up front to play
the roles of predictor, clarifier, questioner, and summarizer. She provides them with
individual sentence starter cue cards, as described above.

The rest of the class is given a blank note-taking guide, with the task of documenting how each student in the fishbowl plays his/her role. Everyone in class has

a job and all have a copy of the chunked text, which is about the science of cloning cats. Students inside the fishbowl take turns reading the chunks aloud to each other. While reading, each of the "fish" plays their role. The *predictor* starts out by predicting what the text will be about. He uses titles and pictures to make his prediction. The *clarifier* notes confusing terms and phrases and then uses strategies to mediate the confusions. The *questioner* asks questions of the text and provides answers when she can. Finally, the *summarizer* notes key ideas in a short conclusion statement.

They continue to engage in this way as they read the text. As students in the fishbowl try Reciprocal Teaching out, Dr. Grant prompts, cues, and questions to keep them on the right track. At one point, she gestures to the clarifier, Elena, "Does anything need to be clarified?" The clarifier, unsure because she is just trying this out for the first time responds, "No, I don't think so." Dr. Grant adds, "Sometimes there is nothing to clarify. Let's keep going." As they continue on to the next chunk, Elena articulates her confusion about a section of the text: "I don't know which cat they are talking about. There are so many cats in this article." Dr. Grant prompts her to think about it as Elena begins to reread—a clarification strategy the class had discussed previously. After rereading, Elena sorts out her own confusion, as Dr. Grant notes that Elena has answered her own clarification question by rereading.

After the fishbowl, all students get a chance to try Reciprocal Teaching with another article. Dr. Grant moves throughout the room guiding students, prompting, cueing, and supporting their acquisition of this strategy's elements. Students in Dr. Grant's class will use Reciprocal Teaching to discuss and analyze texts at least once every week or two. Dr. Grant knows that as their proficiency increases, students will be able to tackle more complex texts because they are engaged in academic discourse that allows them to share with and teach each other. She also knows that students will begin to acquire and *own* the academic language from the cue cards. She's already heard Elena say, "I just want to clarify. . . ." Eventually, Dr. Grant will take away the roles and will allow students to predict, clarify, question, and summarize as they discuss a complex text in a less constrained conversation. Dr. Grant starts with scaffolds, but then removes them as students gain proficiency.

To observe Dr. Grant teaching her students to use reciprocal teaching to support their comprehension of science texts, visit the following YouTube sites: Reciprocal Teaching—Introduction, *http://bit.ly/reciprocalteaching1* and Reciprocal Teaching— Guiding the Learning, *http://bit.ly/reciprocalteaching2*.

Like the teachers in these scenarios, you are a specialist who is intent on teaching your students many things about your discipline so that they can use and expand information. One very important thing you must teach them is to be independent learners. The reading practices shared in this chapter will help them develop this independence and pride in learning.

CHAPTER 6 ACTIVITIES

1. *Read-Aloud*: Select a text that you are planning to use for a lesson you'll be teaching soon. Prepare to use it as a read-aloud. Be sure to identify your instructional purpose. For example, will your reading of the text provide you with a forum for introducing background content knowledge, preview vocabulary, or the organizational structure of the text? Or will your intention be to model fluent reading, or motivate additional reading on this topic? Once you have identified your purpose, note your stopping points and the questions you will ask students, and then practice reading the text aloud. Remember your questions should relate closely to the intended purpose.

2. *Shared reading with think-aloud*: Select a text that supports accomplishing the lesson purpose. Read it and plan your stopping points. Until you become familiar thinking aloud you will also want to script exactly what you are going to say—just in case you get nervous as you model for students exactly how you are thinking your way through the text. Be sure to use "I-statements": "When I look at this word I think . . . ," "When I consider the actions of this character, I wonder if . . ." "I am inferring that the tone of this article is . . . , which is making me think the author's purpose might be . . . I need to read further to see if there is additional evidence to confirm or alter my thinking." Remember, you are not asking these questions of students or stopping to hear their thinking. You are instead reading and talking aloud, and they are reading along and observing you reading.

3. *QAR, ReQuest, and Reciprocal Teaching*: Teaching your students to question the text supports their learning how to become independent readers of your discipline. To begin, select a text and identify the instructional purpose. Remember that a small segment of a larger text will work just fine. Review the instructional procedures we've outlined in the chapter for using QAR, ReQuest, and Reciprocal Teaching. Decide which will work best for the selected text. Over time, you will want to use all three of these strategies so that students learn various ways of interacting with a text. Plan how you will model the strategy for your students, then allow students time to practice before you ask them to apply it independently.

Chapter 7

Reading It Closely

Instruction That Supports Close Reading in the Disciplines

Every day in middle and secondary classrooms, teachers ask their students to closely read documents, chapters, poems, stories, charts, musical scores, problems, data, and many other written texts. They expect their students to comprehend the information well and be able to use what they learn to support their work within their discipline. One approach to reading that supports this deep analysis is close reading, which Brown and Kappes (2012) describe as

> an investigation of a short piece of text, with multiple readings done over multiple instructional lessons. Through text-based questions and discussion, students are guided to deeply analyze and appreciate various aspects of the text, such as key vocabulary and how its meaning is shaped by context; attention to form, tone, imagery and/or rhetorical devices; the significance of word choice and syntax; and the discovery of different levels of meaning as passages are read multiple times. (p. 2)

Before we share examples and ideas to help you think about how to teach your students to closely read and analyze an array of complex texts, let's begin by assessing your foundational understanding of close reading. Please respond to each of the true/false statements in Figure 7.1 and check your responses. Assessment always helps us know where we need to focus our attention as we think about every topic affecting our work as teachers. Either during or at the conclusion of closely reading this chapter, please return and reassess your knowledge. Our own answers to the true/false assessment in Figure 7.1 appear at the end of the chapter.

Belief or Claim	True	False	Why Do You Think This?	Reassessed Response: True or False?	I Found This Information on p. ___, para. ___.
1. Close reading is a teaching technique.					
2. The best assessment of a student's success with close reading is his or her ability to summarize the text					
3. Close reading always involves rereading.					
4. Close reading is the same as leisure reading for skilled readers.					
5. The goal of close reading is to understand the author's intention, how it is being accomplished, and what it means.					
6. Prior knowledge should never be activated or shared prior to a close reading.					

(continued)

FIGURE 7.1. Self-assessment of close reading knowledge.

Belief or Claim	True	False	Why Do You Think This?	Reassessed Response: True or False?	I Found This Information on p. ____, para. ____.
7. Teachers should not share a purpose for close reading because doing so tells too much about the text.					
8. The criteria for selecting a text for close reading should be more focused on stretching the cognitive and linguistic growth of students than on matching the text to their instructional levels.					
9. It's okay for students to preview the text before beginning a close reading.					
10. There is no specific sequence or plan that needs to occur during a close reading.					
11. Questions asked by teachers during close reading should serve as scaffolds for readers.					
12. The first reading of a close reading should invite the reader to evaluate the deep meaning and value of the text by making connections with other texts.					

FIGURE 7.1. (*continued*)

Before continuing the chapter, we encourage you to watch the following video of sixth-grade science teacher Amy Miles supporting her students as they closely read a text about rocks: *www.learner.org/courses/ readwrite/video-detail/fostering-close-reading.html.*

CLOSE READING

Now with a shared vision of a close reading, let's consider the answers to a few often-asked questions about close reading and also look closely at a few examples that are intended to help you to design close reading experiences for your students.

What Type of Text Should Be Selected for Close Reading?

The text should be complex. When identifying text complexity you will need to consider both quantitative and qualitative features. *Quantitative* features are ones you can count such as numbers of words, the syllables, word frequency, and the length of the sentences. These calculations often generate a grade-level equivalent, such as "7.5" (7th grade, 5th month). A text's readability level is identified by a lexile level. The Common Core State Standards (CCSS; National Governors Association Center for Best Practices & Council of Chief State School Officers, 2010) have developed Appendix B, which contains examples of narrative and informational texts and their designated lexiles. A lexile is arrived at by counting the same features as previous readability formulae (e.g., Fry, Dale–Chall; Accelerated Readers). However, instead of rating the texts with grade-level equivalents (7.5), a number is generated that can range from 0 to above 1300. The number appears in front of the letter *L* for lexile. There is no set correspondence between grade level and lexile levels. As shown in Figure 7.2, a student in a designated grade-band should be able to comfortably read the texts within the identified lexile level.

Grade	Midyear lexile levels of middle 50% of students	Text demand of the Common Core recommended "stretch-level" texts
6	665L–1000L	
7	735L–1065L	925L–1185L
8	805L–1100L	
9	855L–1165L	
10	905L–1195L	1050L–1335L
11–12	940L–1210L	1185L–1385L

FIGURE 7.2. Lexile levels and corresponding stretch-level texts.

As you will notice in Appendix B, a text like Elie Wiesel's *Night* has a 590L that places it in a grade-band for students in second or third grade. If you examine this text, you will quickly realize that the complex language and themes in this text are too sophisticated for primary-grade students. We mention this to highlight the fact that lexiles or the quantitative features of a text are only the starting place for identifying the complexity of a text. Short sentences and one- or two-syllable words do not provide insights about the content of the texts. To determine text complexity, you must also consider the *qualitative* features of the text and the language, sophistication, and knowledge of the readers of the text and the tasks you'll be assigning.

Qualitative dimensions of texts focus on features that are not quantifiable. These features include structure, coherence, and audience appropriateness (Fisher, Frey, & Lapp, 2012). Structures are often signaled by editorial cues such as headings and diagrams and authored cues such as key word identifying problem–solution, sequence, cause–effect, and other relationships. In narrative texts, qualitative features offer clues that help the reader follow the development of a character or unlock the deepest structure of the plot. Text coherence addresses how logically and plausibly the text or narrative is connected across paragraphs or chapters. Coherent texts make explicit connections, use familiar language, repeat concepts, and make pronoun referents clear. Coherent texts are considerate of the reader. A coherent narrative text uses literacy devices such as flashbacks, imagery, and metaphor to support reader engagement and understanding.

The level of text complexity also depends on the knowledge and related experiences of the reader.

To help you understand these features, we have included two rubrics in Figure 7.3. Select a text for your discipline and use these rubrics to determine the text's areas of complexity. Think about your students as you conduct the analysis. They will be the ones who are reading the text, so when you are considering features such as if the vocabulary is familiar, you need to be conducting the analyses with them in mind.

Use these rubrics to determine the complex features of the text you have selected. As you look at each feature noted on the rubric identified in the column "Dimensions and Considerations," think about the students who will be reading the text as you consider each question. For example, notice that the question addressing a narrative text organization asks if it follows a typical chronological plot pattern, or if it is more unconventional. Once you answer this question, think about your students and their experiences reading similar texts. Thinking about your students helps to determine if this text is an Easy or Comfortable, Moderate or Grade Level, or a Challenging or Stretch text. With these insights, you'll be prepared to craft questions that will help them to focus on the complex features. Select a text from Appendix B and give it a try.

A short piece of text works well for close reading because students need to read either the whole text or parts of it more than once in order to deeply analyze its meaning, structure, and language. Close reading involves more than summarizing a text as readers analyze the author's message and the craft used to share the information. A shorter piece of text always allows time to annotate the text, answer teacher-directed questions about it, and also have time to engage with peers in collaborative conversations about it.

The selected text can be a subsection of a science or social studies chapter, a primary document, a news article, a speech, a problem, a musical score, a poem, a narrative, or numerous other sources that are related to study occurring within the discipline. At the conclusion of a close reading, students should be able to understand the text well enough to use what they have learned to make comparisons with other texts on the same topic. The criteria for selecting a text for close reading should be focused more on stretching students' cognitive and linguistic growth than on matching the text to students' instructional levels.

Is It Necessary to Reread the Text during Close Reading?

It is not necessary to reread all texts, especially those read for leisure. Those chosen for close reading, however, need to be complex enough to warrant multiple rereadings. Close reading always involves rereading with the intent being to analyze what the author is saying and how he is doing so. Questions teachers ask should send students back to the whole text or to sections of it to reread as a way to learn more about the author's language choices, the organizational structure of the text, and the intended message. Most but not all of the rereadings need to be done independently by each student. If students are seated at tables, one student may volunteer to provide one of the readings. If a speech is being analyzed, students might also listen to a recording during one of their readings. The teacher might provide a second or third reading of the text, especially if it contains dialogue or complex language that students need to hear being pronounced fluently. While the teacher may serve as the reader, the cognitive analysis must be done by the students, for if we are to become independent learners, "we must know how to make books teach us well" (Adler & Van Doren, 1940/1972, p. 15). To be fully literate, we must know how to read for deep understanding rather than for mere identification of facts. Rereading is required to accomplish this.

Should the Text Be Annotated during Close Reading?

Most of us mark a text that we are deeply engaged in reading. We write notes and questions in margins, and highlight or underline ideas or words we want to remember. A reader is usually paying close attention to a text that he can be involved with

Dimension & Consideration	Questions	Scoring = 1 Easy or Comfortable Text	Scoring = 2 Moderate or Grade-Level Text	Scoring = 3 Challenging or Stretch Text
Text Structure: Organization	• Does the text follow a typical chronological plot pattern, or is it more elaborate and unconventional, incorporating multiple storylines, shifts in time (flashbacks, flash forwards), shifts in point of view, and other devices?	☐ The text follows a simple conventional chronological plot pattern, with few or no shifts in point of view or time; plot is highly predictable.	☐ The text organization is somewhat unconventional; may have two or more storylines and some shifts in time and point of view; plot is sometimes hard to predict.	☐ The text organization is intricate and unconventional, with multiple subplots and shifts in time and point of view; plot is unpredictable.
Notes on Organization				
Text Structure: Visual Support and Layout	• Is text placement consistent, or is there variability in placement, with multiple columns? • Are visuals compatible/consistent with the storyline?	☐ Text placement is consistent throughout the text and uses a large readable font. ☐ Illustrations directly support text content.	☐ Text placement may include columns, text interrupted by illustrations, or other variations; uses a smaller font size. ☐ Illustrations support the text directly but may include images that require synthesis of text.	☐ Text placement includes columns and many inconsistencies as well as very small font size. ☐ Few illustrations that support the text directly; most require deep analysis and synthesis.
Notes on Visual Support and Layout				

FIGURE 7.3. Qualitative scoring rubric for narrative text/literature. From Moss, Lapp, Grant, and Johnson (2016, pp. 26–31). Copyright 2016 by ASCD. Reprinted by permission.

Text Structure: Relationships Among Ideas	• Are relationships among ideas or characters obvious or fairly subtle?	☐ Relationships among ideas or characters are clear and obvious.	☐ Relationships among ideas or characters are subtle and complex.	☐ Relationships among ideas or characters are complex, are embedded, and must be inferred.
Notes on Relationships Among Ideas			
Language Features: Author's Style	• Is it easy or difficult for the reader to identify the author's style? • Is the language used simple or more intricate, with complex sentence structures and subtle figurative language?	☐ The style of the text is explicit and easy to comprehend. ☐ The language of the text is conversational and straightforward, with simple sentence structures.	☐ The style of the text combines explicit with complex meanings. ☐ The language of the text is complex, may be somewhat unfamiliar, and includes some subtle figurative or literary language and complex sentence structures.	☐ The style of the text is abstract, and the language is ambiguous and generally unfamiliar. ☐ The text includes a great deal of sophisticated figurative language (e.g., metaphors, similes, literary allusions) and complex sentences combining multiple concepts.
Notes on Author's Style			
Language Features: Vocabulary	• Are the author's word choices simple or complex? • How demanding is the vocabulary load? • Can word meanings be determined through context clues or not?	☐ Vocabulary is accessible, familiar, and can be determined through context clues.	☐ Vocabulary combines familiar terms with academic vocabulary appropriate to the grade level.	☐ Vocabulary includes extensive academic vocabulary, including many unfamiliar terms.
Notes on Vocabulary			

Continued →

FIGURE 7.3. (*continued*)

Dimension & Consideration	Questions	Scoring = 1 Easy or Comfortable Text	Scoring = 2 Moderate or Grade-Level Text	Scoring = 3 Challenging or Stretch Text
Meaning	• Is the text meaning simple or rich with complex ideas that must be inferred?	☐ The text contains simple ideas with one level of meaning conveyed through obvious literary devices.	☐ The text contains some complex ideas with more than one level of meaning conveyed through subtle literary devices.	☐ The text includes substantial ideas with several levels of inferred meaning conveyed through highly sophisticated literary devices.
Notes on Meaning				
Author's Purpose	• Is the author's purpose evident or implied/ambiguous?	☐ The purpose of the text is simple, clear, concrete, and easy to identify.	☐ The purpose of the text is somewhat subtle, requires interpretation, or is abstract.	☐ The purpose of the text is abstract, implicit, or ambiguous, and is revealed through the totality of the text.
Notes on Author's Purpose				
Knowledge Demands	• How much and what kinds of background knowledge are needed to comprehend this text? • Do my students have the background knowledge to comprehend this text?	☐ Experiences portrayed are common life experiences; everyday cultural or literary knowledge is required.	☐ Experiences portrayed include both common and less common experiences; some cultural, historical, or literary background knowledge is required.	☐ Experiences portrayed are unfamiliar to most readers. The text requires extensive depth of cultural, historical, or literary background knowledge.
Notes on Knowledge Demands				

FIGURE 7.3. (*continued*)

Dimension & Consideration	Questions	Scoring = 1 Easy or Comfortable Text	Scoring = 2 Moderate or Grade-Level Text	Scoring = 3 Challenging or Stretch Text
Text Structure: Organization	• Is the pattern of the text clearly identifiable as descriptive, sequential, problem/solution, compare/contrast, or cause/effect? • Are signal words used to alert readers to these structures? • Are multiple structures used in combination?	☐ The text adheres primarily to a single expository text structure and focuses on facts.	☐ The text employs multiple expository text structures, includes facts and/or a thesis, and demonstrates characteristics common to a particular discipline.	☐ The text organization is intricate, may combine multiple structures or genres, is highly abstract, includes multiple theses, and demonstrates sophisticated organization appropriate to a particular discipline.
Notes on Organization				
Text Structure: Visual Support and Layout	• Is the text placement consistent, or is there variability in placement with multiple columns? • Are visuals essential to understanding the text without explanation? • Are visuals accompanying the text simple or complex? Do they require literal understanding or synthesis and analysis?	☐ The text placement is consistent throughout the text and uses a large readable font. ☐ Simple charts, graphs, photos, tables, and diagrams directly support the text and are easy to understand.	☐ The text placement may include columns, text interrupted by illustrations or other variations, and a smaller font size. ☐ Complex charts, graphs, photos, tables and diagrams support the text but require interpretation.	☐ The text placement includes columns and many inconsistencies, as well as very small font size. ☐ Intricate charts, graphs, photos, tables, and diagrams are not supported by the text and require inference and synthesis of information.
Notes on Visual Support and Layout				

Continued ➔

FIGURE 7.3. (*continued*)

Dimension & Consideration	Questions	Scoring = 1 Easy or Comfortable Text	Scoring = 2 Moderate or Grade-Level Text	Scoring = 3 Challenging or Stretch Text
Text Structure: Relationships Among Ideas	• Are relationships among ideas simple or challenging?	☐ Relationships among concepts, processes, or events are clear and explicitly stated.	☐ Relationships among some concepts, processes, or events may be implicit and subtle.	☐ Relationships among concepts, processes, and events are intricate, deep, and subtle.
Notes on Relationships Among Ideas				
Language Features: Author's Style	• What point of view does the author take toward the material? • Is the author's style conversational or academic and formal?	☐ The style is simple and conversational, and it may incorporate narrative elements, with simple sentences containing a few concepts.	☐ Style is objective, contains passive constructions with highly factual content, and features some nominalization and some compound or complex sentences.	☐ Style is specialized to a discipline, contains dense concepts and high nominalization, and features compound and complex sentences.
Notes on Author's Style				
Language Features: Vocabulary	• How extensive is the author's use of technical vocabulary? • Can students determine word meanings through context clues?	☐ Some vocabulary is subject-specific, but the text includes many terms familiar to students that are supported by context clues.	☐ The vocabulary is subject-specific, includes many unfamiliar terms, and provides limited support through context clues.	☐ The vocabulary is highly academic, subject-specific, demanding, nuanced, and very context dependent.
Notes on Vocabulary				

FIGURE 7.3. (*continued*)

Meaning	• Is the amount and complexity of information conveyed through data sophisticated or not?	☐ The information is clear, and concepts are concretely explained.	☐ The information includes complex, abstract ideas and extensive details.	☐ The information is abstract, intricate, and may be highly theoretical.
Notes on Meaning			
Author's Purpose	• Is the author's purpose evident or implied/ambiguous?	☐ The purpose of the text is simple, clear, concrete, and easy to identify.	☐ The purpose of the text is somewhat subtle or abstract and requires interpretation.	☐ The purpose of the text is abstract, implicit, or ambiguous, and is revealed through the totality of the text.
Notes on Author's Purpose			
Knowledge Demands	• How much and what kinds of background knowledge are required to comprehend this text?	☐ The content addresses common information familiar to students.	☐ The content addresses somewhat technical information that requires some background knowledge to understand fully.	☐ The content is highly technical and contains specific information that requires deep background knowledge to understand fully.
Notes on Knowledge Demands			

FIGURE 7.3. (continued)

137

this intensely. Adler and Van Doren (1940/1972) offer the following rationale for text annotating:

> Why is marking a book indispensable to reading it? First, it keeps you awake—not merely conscious, but wide awake. Second, reading, if active, is thinking, and thinking tends to express itself in words, spoken or written. The person who says he knows what he thinks but cannot express it usually does not know what he thinks. Third, writing your reactions down helps you remember the thoughts of the author. (p. 49)

Adler and Van Doren also note what these annotations might include:

- *Underlining* of major points or forceful statements.
- *Vertical lines in the margin* to emphasize already underlined statements or to identify statements too long to be underlined.
- *Star, asterisk, or other doodad in the margin*—use sparingly to emphasize the ten or dozen most important statements. You may want to fold a corner of each page on which you make such a mark or place a slip of paper between the pages so you can easily find these references.
- *Numbers in the margin* to indicate a sequence of points made by the author in development of an argument.
- *Numbers of other pages in the margin* to indicate where else in the book the author makes the same points.
- *Circling of key words or phrases* to serve much the same function as underlining.
- *Writing in the margin, or at the top or bottom of the page* to record questions (and perhaps answers) which a passage raises in your mind. (pp. 49–50)

Teachers often create annotation charts similar to the one shown as Figure 7.4. As this chart illustrates, it is so important to encourage your students to write notes in the margins so that they will be able to identify what their annotations meant when they return to them later. Using a similar structure, CUBES, which was designed by math teacher Staci Benak, asks students to think through problems in mathematics. They:

- Circle the mathematical information (words and numbers).
- Underline the problem.
- Box the mathematical terms (especially those that are confusing).
- Evaluate the information.
- Solve and explain the solution.

Then, a sentence frame gets them started: "I found that . . ." (see Figure 7.5).

Figure 7.6 shows examples of texts that were annotated by two eighth-grade students during a close reading of a slightly modified version of *The Myth of the Street Gang as a "Family Substitute"* by Stanton E. Samenow (2007). Their teacher, Ms. Thomas, had selected it as a partner text to accompany the reading of *The Outsiders* by S. E. Hinton that was being shared as a whole-class reading.

Don't forget to make notes in the margins.

Underline or highlight major points.
Circle unfamiliar words and phrases.
Draw arrows to show connections to main ideas.——————→
☆ Star text you find interesting.
? Use a question mark near parts you find confusing or that inspire a question.

FIGURE 7.4. Annotation symbols.

Ms. Thomas taught these students how to annotate a text, and together they had created a chart similar to the one shown in Figure 7.4, which was posted in their classroom. As she asked each question during the close reading, she encouraged students to write it on their papers. She also encouraged them to annotate with colored pens that corresponded to the color of pen they used to write each question. She no longer has students use highlighters because they were having trouble writing with them. They used colored pens and pencils so they could write notes in the margins of their copies. She felt this helped the students to identify what their annotations referred to when they returned to the text. She also asked

FIGURE 7.5. CUBES chart with sentence frame.

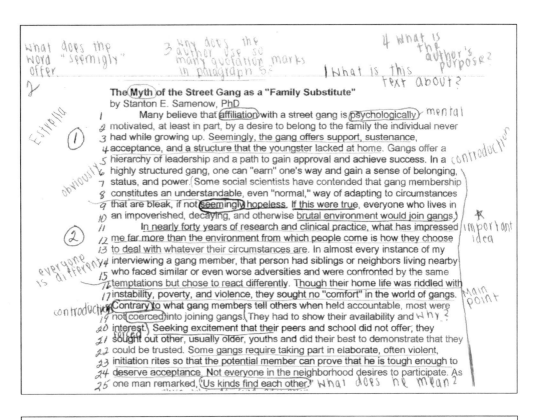

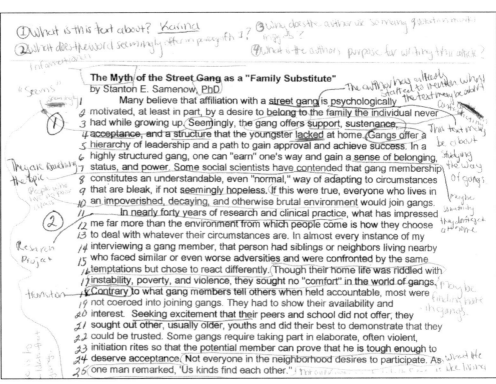

FIGURE 7.6. Examples of student-annotated texts for "The Myth of the Street Gang as a 'Family Substitute.'"

140

the students to number the paragraphs and the lines in the text for ease of reference during partner talk.

During this close reading Ms. Thomas posed four questions:

1. "What is this text about?"
2. "What does the word *seemingly* offer to our understanding of the text?"
3. "Why does the author use so many quotation marks in paragraph 5?"
4. "What was the author's purpose in writing this text?"

Notice that the questions asked during the close reading did not always call for a rereading of the entire text. Between each reading the students engaged in partner talk, and during rereadings 2 and 4 they engaged in whole-class discussion. While students are always engaged in partner talk after each reading and annotating, Ms. Thomas invites whole-class discussion only if she assesses that students need additional conversational scaffolds to support their deep analysis. It's interesting that in both annotations students drew lines between ideas they felt were connected and one starred points she felt were important. These annotated texts illustrate the deep analysis that these students engaged in during this close reading. This teacher encouraged students to make notes to themselves in the margins so that when they returned to these texts for a later discussion or to complete an extension assignment, they would remember what their annotations addressed.

What Types of Questions Scaffold Students' Thinking during Close Reading?

Once you've selected a text that you think has sufficiently complex ideas and language to promote analytic thinking, challenge, and support collaborative talk among your students, test it further by designing questions that you believe will push students to think about it in ways that, depending on the genre, cause them to analyze the author's propositions, arguments, and language.

Questions teachers ask during close reading should serve as scaffolds causing readers to critique the text as they comprehend the issues, ideas, motivations, plots, and themes. Although many questions are designed before the close reading, additional questions can be asked if the teacher determines that a particular area of the text needs additional scaffolding.

Questions That Support Analysis of *What the Text Says*

To craft questions that move students to this point of comprehension, you will of course need to read the text carefully and prepare your questions in advance. The questions should initially cause students to think about *what is being said in the text.* These questions should help students to gain a general understanding about the key ideas, details, and big problems the author is laying out. Constructing answers should allow students to identify facts that support their hypothesizing what the text is literally about. Developing this initial understanding or gist regarding what the text is generally about lays the foundation needed to move beyond a surface level of understanding. This initial understanding will deepen as students engage in additional analysis of other text features. Let's look into two classrooms to better understand the types of questions that might be asked to push readers toward a general understanding of the text they are reading. This knowledge increases the potential of acquiring the deeper text meaning.

SEVENTH-GRADE SHORT STORY

To further understand the power of asking key detail questions as a way to lay the informational base students need to acquire a general understanding of the text and also to build the foundation needed to eventually comprehend the deepest levels of text, let's consider questions seventh-grade teacher Mr. Kelly asked as his students engaged in a close reading of Sandra Cisneros's *Eleven*. This short story describes how an embarrassing moment at school complicated 11-year-old Rachel's birthday. Notice how the questions, while addressing key details, lay the foundation for readers to go from a literal surface-level understanding to a deep understanding of external and internal conflict within the character. Figure 7.7 contrasts significant and nonsignificant text-dependent questions to demonstrate the precision needed to ask significant questions that will enable the reader to acquire meaningful information needed to begin deeply comprehending even from the initial reading.

Did you notice a primary difference between the text-significant and non-text-significant key detail questions? Both sets caused the reader to return to the text, but only the text-significant questions pushed the reader to critically identify information that would eventually enable understanding the complex meaning of the text. These key detail questions got the process of deep analysis started in the reader's mind. By identifying key details through answering the text-significant questions,

	Significant Text-Dependent Questions	Nonsignificant Text-Dependent Questions
General Understanding	• What happens on Rachel's birthday?	
Key Details	• Whose birthday is it? • What details in the story help you understand how Rachel feels about her sweater? • Why does the narrator wish she were 102 years old?	• What is the name of the girl who tells the class the sweater belongs to Rachel? • How old does the narrator say you are when you say something stupid? • How old are you when you sit on your mama's lap?

FIGURE 7.7. Seventh-grade English: Narrative—general understanding and key detail questions.

the reader gained a deeper understanding of the text. The less significant questions also caused the reader to extract some specific bits of information. While these facts might be interesting, they will never take the reader into Rachel's conversations with herself and the realization the author is pushing us toward; the realization that, "like a layered onion," we carry the facets of our life stories from one year to the next.

11TH-GRADE PHYSICS

Now let's visit 11th grade-physics teacher Ms. Williams and her students, who are studying the topic of mechanics, including motion and forces. Students are investigating elements of mechanics within a context of engineering and design. As a part of their investigation, Ms. Williams is having students learn about innovations that improved devices we use in our everyday world. She knows that bringing real-world engineering into the classroom helps to make science more meaningful and relevant. It also helps students understand the need for being scientifically literate. After students learn more about technological breakthroughs and design, they will apply their knowledge to a design project that involves building a mousetrap car that can go forward and then reverse, while documenting the iterative design process. As part of their work, Ms. Williams shared a *Scientific American* article, "Electronic Stability Control" by Mark Fischetti, as a close reading text. The first two paragraphs of this article can be found at *www.scientificamerican.com/article/electronic-stability-cont*.

Again, notice the contrast between the significant and nonsignificant questions noted in Figure 7.8. While they all cause the reader to return to the text, the significant questions ask the reader to identify information that will support a deeper analysis of the text's meaning, which is that continued improvement in brake stability ensures better safety for motorists.

To get you started practicing how to craft questions that cause the reader to analyze what the text says, select a short, complex text that relates to a topic you are planning to explore with your students. You can find a sample passage in Appendix B of the CCSS: *www.corestandards.org/assets/Appendix_B.pdf*.

	Significant Text-Dependent Questions	Nonsignificant Text-Dependent Questions
General Understanding	• How are automakers promoting better brake stability?	
Key Details	• What causes antilock brakes to be safer? • What happens when a driver slacks on the antilock brakes? • What words or phrases indicate this is a developing process?	• Do more or fewer cars have antilock brakes? • How long ago did automakers begin to build antilock brakes? • Are antilock brakes safe?

FIGURE 7.8. Eleventh-grade physics: Informational—general understanding and key detail questions.

Text Name, Author, Reference: _____

Lesson Purpose: _____

General Understanding Questions

Question	Possible Response	Found in Text Chunk

Key Details

FIGURE 7.9. Questions: What the text says.

From *Literacy in the Disciplines: A Teacher's Guide for Grades 5–12* by Thomas DeVere Wolsey and Diane Lapp. Copyright © 2017 The Guilford Press. Permission to photocopy this material is granted to purchasers of this book for personal use or use with individual students (see copyright page for details). Purchasers can download enlarged versions of this material (see the box at the end of the table of contents).

Use Figure 7.9 to practice writing a few questions that support students in gaining a general understanding of what the text says. If you selected a narrative text, ask key detail questions about the characters and their relationships and conflicts, plot, time frame, and setting. If your text is informational, ask questions about the central idea or message, location, time period, point of view, purpose, and graphics. You only need to ask enough questions to help students gain a general understanding of what the author is trying to say.

Questions That Cause Analysis of *How the Text Works*

Once students have a literal understanding of the key ideas and details to support what the text is generally saying, you will want to next encourage an analysis of how the text works. Understanding the workings of the text can occur by analyzing the vocabulary, the organizational structure, and techniques the author used to craft the text. These questions should push students to analyze:

- How the author used vocabulary words and phrases to create mood, tone, flashback, and foreshadowing.
- How language was shared to support inference making about the theme, create an argument, and persuade.

- The text structure to identify if the text is narrative, informational, persuasive, or technical.
- The text structure(s) that were used to organize the text. In narrative, was a simple story structure shared, or were elements of drama conveyed? In informational texts, what signal words were used and what meaning did they convey?
- The text structure to identify whether it is a descriptive passage, a problem–solution, a compare–contrast, a sequence of time or information, or a cause–effect.
- The author's craft (what techniques the author is using).
  o Language devices in a narrative (simile, metaphor, personification, parallel structures).
  o Point of view, presentation of problems and issues, solutions.

As readers begin to understand the author's intentions by analyzing the vocabulary choices, the selected text structure(s), and the crafting techniques used to tell the story or convey the information, they have moved beyond a surface level of understanding. They are developing a foundation for unaided independent analysis. Let's again consider the questions that some teachers asked as they attempted to teach students what to consider in their analysis of how the text works.

SEVENTH-GRADE SHORT STORY

As Mr. Kelly's students read Cisneros's *Eleven,* notice how his next questions invited analysis beyond a surface-level interrogation of the text. He designed questions to push students beyond understanding what the text said by focusing on the language and craft the author used. Mr. Kelly's questions focused on the literary devices Cisneros used. He knew he had so many possibilities, but since his purpose was to support the understanding that each person is a composite of all of his or her life experiences, he asked the questions shown in Figure 7.10.

Vocabulary	• What words are used to describe the sweater? • What is the purpose of using the figurative language phrase "I wish I didn't have eleven years rattling inside me like pennies in a tin Band-Aid box"?
Structure	• What is the structure of this story? • What descriptions phrases are used? • Why are so many descriptive phrases used?
Author's Craft	• What is the tone of the passage? • What similes did the author use to make this experience believable?

FIGURE 7.10. Questions that support analysis of how the text works.

Did you notice how Mr. Kelly's questions caused students to look deeply at the author's craft? He knew that focusing on this writer's style and techniques would add to his students understanding of the text and also provide them with ideas about writing techniques they could use in their own writing.

EIGHTH-GRADE SCIENCE

Ms. Companza selected the text "Geology" from the *U*X*L Encyclopedia of Science,* edited by Rob Nagel, from page 98 of Appendix B of the CCSS: *www.corestandards. org/assets/Appendix_B.pdf.*

She and her students had been studying the planet Earth and related topics such as energy, water, and mineral resources. Her purpose was to promote learning that helped her students to understand what role they played in affecting their environment. She believed that by understanding earth's geologic processes and the dynamics related to plate tectonics, and natural hazards like landslides, volcanoes, earthquakes, and floods, they would be better prepared to analyze their relationship to their environment.

The article she selected introduced the students to two broad categories of geological study: physical geology and historical geology. Ms. Companza felt that this foundational understanding would help them begin to realize what role they could actually play in their world. To accomplish this, Ms. Companza prepared the questions shown in Figure 7.11. She knew she may not need to ask all of these, but she wanted to be ready with questions that would push her students to analyze how this text worked.

Ms. Companza asked questions that focused the intent of the reading. Before students began, she reminded them to annotate as needed and to be sure to write

Vocabulary	• What is meant in paragraph 1 when the author says, "Each of these are all the domain of the geologist"? • What's the difference between physical geology and historical geology? • What descriptive words help you know the difference? Which science words give you an indication of the differences?
Vocabulary and Author's Craft	• How does the author inform you of what certain words mean—*fossils,* for example?
Structure	• What type of organizational structure is the author using to share this information? • What type of text is this? • How does the author structure his writing to help you understand the roles played by different kinds of geologists (volcanologist, seismologist)?
Author's Craft	• What does the author want you to know? How do the examples he shares support this?

FIGURE 7.11. Questions that support analysis of how the text works.

their questions in the margins. When the students concluded each reading, she engaged them in partner talk as a way to share and extend their ideas. She sometimes also conducted a whole-class discussion. As her students independently read, annotated, and then engaged in partner talk she moved among them, listening in to determine how well they were understanding the text and what next questions she should ask to support them further. She didn't always ask them to reread the entire text; often she just asked them to read one of the paragraphs or a few lines that were essential to unlocking the needed information.

Let's now use Figure 7.12 to practice writing a few questions that support students in gaining a general understanding of how the text works. Use the text you chose when you prepared questions that prompted students to consider what the text says. As you prepare questions that address the workings of the text, you need to think about what will cause students to examine the vocabulary, the organizational structures, and the techniques the author used to convey information or tell the story.

Questions That Support Analysis of *What the Text Means*

The intention of close reading is to ferret out information and meaning that is not explicitly stated in the text. To gain this deep meaning, readers must identify the author's purpose for writing the text, even when it is not explicitly stated. They must detect information that helps them grasp the implied meaning. Sometimes the total meaning may not be contained in just one text written by an author. Students who are left with unanswered questions need to be taught that by reading other texts by the same author or other texts on the same topic they can expand their understanding and informational base. To understand the deepest meaning of a text the reader must investigate the author's purpose as well as intertextual connections.

SEVENTH-GRADE SHORT STORY

Let's return again to Mr. Kelly's class to study the questions he asked his students to push them to a deep analysis of *Eleven* by Cisneros. As we return to the story, consider how much more deeply a reader would understand the author's intent by contrasting a few of her other works, such as *Salvador Late or Early, House on Mango Street,* and *Bad Boys,* to realize the causes of emotional turmoil and inner resolve felt by her characters. Intertextual connections made across authors or themes cause readers to make inferences and consolidate ideas and concepts as they move to a conclusion about the text they are reading.

The questions Mr. Kelly asked (see Figure 7.13) supported his students' understanding of a dimension of author craft, which involved Cisneros's revealing of a deeper analysis of the character through her actions and thoughts.

Text Name, Author, Reference: _____

Lesson Purpose: _____

Vocabulary

Question	Possible Response	Found in Text Chunk

Structure

Question	Possible Response	Found in Text Chunk

Author's Craft

Question	Possible Response	Found in Text Chunk

FIGURE 7.12. Questions—How the text works.

Author's Purpose	• What is the author's purpose for giving readers so much information about what it means to be 11? • What point is she trying to make?
Inferences	• What do the narrator's self-description and speech tell you about her personality?
Opinions/Arguments, Intertextual Connections	• Think about Rachel's struggle in this story. What is stronger, an internal or external conflict?

FIGURE 7.13. Question that support analysis of what the text means.

When students are challenged with these thought-provoking questions, they have no choice but to delve into the inner and external conflict that the main character is experiencing. This analysis occurs through the careful, detailed attention of many facets of the text. Readers give the time and attention needed for this analysis when they return to the text for purposeful rereadings.

EIGHTH-GRADE SCIENCE

In Ms. Companza's eighth-grade class, she offered questions that prompted inference and intertextual connections as the students continued their study of Earth. For example, she asked students to go back to the text as they considered these questions:

> "How does the author help you to understand the dynamic nature of Earth and the resultant implications for humans on the planet? What is his intent in sharing this information?"

When Ms. Companza wanted to guide students to connect this text to another they had read about volcanoes, she told them:

> "Recall our recent reading in the *National Geographic* article 'Ol Doinyo Lengai' (*http://ngm.nationalgeographic.com/ngm/0301/feature2/fulltext.html*). How does the vivid description of the Ol Doinyo Lengai volcanic eruption help you to understand the geology excerpt?"

Both questions were intended to help students conceive of Earth as a changing place, with landmasses sliding, moving, and colliding. This foundation supports students' understanding that we must learn to live on a planet that is not stagnant, but is instead dynamic and powerful.

Each of these teachers asked questions that caused their students to scrutinize the author's purpose for writing the text as well as the intertextual connections among topically related texts. Now, return again to your selected text and add questions that would support readers identifying, analyzing, and evaluating the deepest meaning of the text you selected (see Figure 7.14).

 To practice reading and annotating texts, go to *www.learner. org/courses/readwrite/interactive/close-reading-activity.html* (left) or *www.learner.org/courses/readwrite/media-index.html* (right).

Author's Purpose	
Inferences	
Opinions/Arguments, Intertextual Connections	

FIGURE 7.14. Deeper analysis chart.

HOW DOES TALKING ABOUT THE TEXT DEEPEN UNDERSTANDING?

In each of the preceding scenarios, students were engaged in very purposeful conversations. Talking with peers and the teacher about the text being closely read supports students' developing an understanding of the information. These interactions provide opportunities for students to share their ideas, clarify them, and expand them. Conversation during a close reading episode should occur after each rereading. Teacher modeling of academic language, as well as the sharing of language through the use of language frames, support student talk.

Language Frames

A major component of a close reading is providing students with occasions to discuss the text. Conversations with peers provide opportunities to use academic and topical language and concepts. Teachers often post language frames on classroom walls, on desks, and in notebooks to be easily used by students during oral discussion and also when writing. Having examples of academic language observable at all times easily weaves this more formal register of language into students' language patterns. Some common language frames that support conversation during close reading are:

I think _____ because on page _____ it says _____.

On page _____ the author said _____.

I agree with _____ because _____.

Language frames, whether they are sentences or paragraphs, offer students the language support to share their ideas. For example, if students are closely reading an article about planets they might be asked to compare two planets. A frame like the following could support their presentation.

> I read on page _____ that _____ has _____, but on page _____ it says that _____ has _____.

This frame invites the reader to share a comparison of information about the selected planets.

We first explored language frames in Chapter 3. Here, we use them as scaffolds for close reading and the related discussions that ensue. As students engage in collaborative conversations during a close reading, they have opportunities to try out their thinking in a safe environment. They are also able to hear what others think in response to the teacher-posed question. During the close reading students reread sections of the text and converse about it multiple times. Many students initially need support to engage in academic conversation about a text. To support them, teachers use language frames as one type of scaffold to get them started with these conversations.

Students at this middle school gained such confidence because of the support they felt from language frames that they asked their teachers in science, health, social studies, and math to prepare language frames too. In Chapter 3 we shared examples of the language frames Amy Miles helped to develop with her social studies colleagues (Figure 3.5) and her science and health colleagues (Figure 3.6). Amy and her colleagues have found that as students view academic language displayed in sentence or paragraph frames, they become very comfortable adding this more formal register of language to their everyday language.

> Some terms we have encountered that are similar to language frames include *sentence frames* and *sentence starters*. We view *language frames* as inclusive of *sentence frames* and *sentence starters*.

Math teachers also use language frames. In Figure 7.15, a math teacher created a chart to remind students of the social, content, and language purposes of talk and written work in her classroom, and then in Figure 7.16 she created a chart with example sentence starters or frames to help the students get started using language to more thoroughly understand the mathematics.

You may now with to watch several teachers engage their students in close reading:

Middle school science
www.learner.org/courses/readwrite/video-detail/fostering-close-reading.html

Ninth-grade English
www.learner.org/courses/readwrite/video-detail/identifying-theme-through-close-reading.html

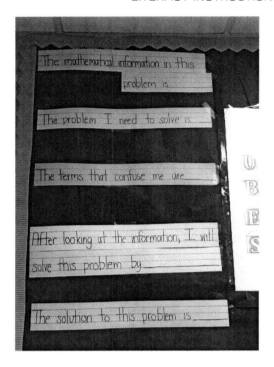

FIGURE 7.15. Chart on the purposes of talk and writing in a math classroom.

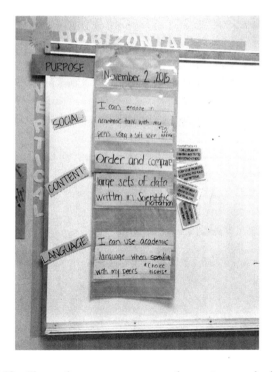

FIGURE 7.16. Chart of sentence starters or frames in a math classroom.

Ninth-grade social studies
www.learner.org/courses/readwrite/video-detail/close-reading-primary-source.html

 Eleventh-grade history
www.learner.org/courses/readwrite/video-detail/reading-historian.html"

A CLOSE READING PLAN

Plans for close reading will still benefit from a developing research base. Still, we believe that students do well when there is some recognized structure to their learning experiences. Although the texts, questions, and extension activities change, Lapp, Moss, Grant, and Johnson (2015) and Moss, Lapp, Grant, and Johnson (2016) have found that the following sequence supports teachers as they plan close reading experiences, and students as they closely read texts across the grades and disciplines.

Select the Text That Relates to the Instructional Purpose

You will want to select a text that helps students gain knowledge that relates to a well-established instructional purpose. The text should stretch the reader's cognitive and linguistic knowledge and should not move you away from the instruction. For example .if you are studying the topic of planets in a science class and your purpose is to have your students understand the unique features of each planet so that they can determine whether there could be more than one planet where humans could live, you could select a subsection from the science basal to use for a close reading investigation. If you are reading a novel as a whole class you can also use a few paragraphs in the novel for a close reading. When you select the text for close reading, stay aligned with the instructional purpose.

Prepare the Text-Dependent Questions

As we've noted in the earlier sections of this chapter, it is important to be prepared with questions that make your students consider multiple dimensions of the text. You may not have to ask all of these. Your continuous assessment of your students' growing understanding of the text will help you determine which questions to ask, or whether you need to create additional ones. The questions you initially design should be created with your students and the text in mind. If, for example, you decide that most of the vocabulary used in the text is familiar to your students, you may have a greater focus on an area that your students might need to analyze more closely. The author's craft as a writer or purpose for writing are often areas that call for additional questions and discussion. For example in the speech "On Women's Right to Vote" by Susan B. Anthony, the questions you ask might focus more on the persuasive techniques and the uses of evidence in the speech rather than on the vocabulary. These decisions will depend on a consideration of the text and students.

Introduce and Model the Process of Close Reading

Before you can expect your students to know how to closely read a text you will need to explain that close reading is an approach to analyzing a text that involves the reader sifting through layers of meaning with the intent of uncovering the deepest levels of meaning. You will need to model how you closely analyze a text, how you ask yourself questions while reading, and how you annotate to keep track of your insights, ideas, and questions. You'll need to show that the questions you ask are ones they can also easily ask when they are independently engaging in a close reading. Using a think-aloud to model how you closely read a text supports becoming independent close readers of texts.

Questions like "What information is being shared?"; "What words are new or difficult for me?"; "What does the author want me to think?"; "What techniques does the author use to convey this message?" prompt returns to the text for deeper analysis. Explain that questioning yourself while reading helps you to stay focused on the information, and it ends with you understanding what you read and also what words or ideas you still find perplexing. After you finish the close reading model how to revisit the information again and ask, "What was the main message of this text?"; "Do I want or need to read more about this?"; "What do I think about what I just read? How can I use this information?" Explain that this final self-questioning helps you to do more than just summarize the author's message. It enables you to identify the inferences you have made as well as the next steps for you as a reader of this topic. Do you need to add to your initial base of information in order to more fully understand this topic, or are you ready to fold this information into your own thinking as you critique the author's position, ask new questions, or take action? Your goal is to teach your students how to closely read a text and then give them lots of opportunities to own the approach.

 Listen to ninth-grade teacher Kelly Johnson discuss the strategies she uses to support her students closely reading a text at *www.learner.org/ courses/readwrite/video-detail/collaborating-and-writing-components-close-reading.html.*

Share the Purpose without Unnecessary Frontloading

Be careful when you share the lesson purpose not to preteach or frontload key information that the reader can independently, and with the support of scaffolds, infer. The questions you ask should invite the reader to look at the language, structure, and meaning in order to comprehend the textual information. However, this doesn't mean that students can't independently preview the text before they begin the close reading. It also doesn't mean that you can never offer the meaning of a word that cannot be figured by context or build background knowledge students cannot obtain from the reading itself.

Tenth-grade teacher Ms. Heather Anderson and her class were reading *Mein Kampf*. During her preparation, Ms. Anderson realized that the students would not be able to figure out the word *succumb* because there were very limited contextual clues and many of her students were English learners. Before they began their first reading she called their attention to the sentence containing the word, gave the definition, and then began the close reading. She used her professional judgment because she realized that her students needed to know this word in order to make sense of the text. She knew that her English learners would shut down and probably be unwilling to read the passage more deeply. If she had not seen this word as a major roadblock to their deeper analysis, she would have set the purpose for the reading, asked a question that would have motivated them to delve in, and then observed them as they worked. She would never have begun by divulging information they could have ferreted out on their own. After all, the investigation that occurs during a close reading is often what causes students to rub their heads at the end and say, "Wow, I feel so smart." Ms. Anderson could also have begun the first reading and then, if she had seen that their comprehension was stopped, she could have defined the word before the second reading.

We encourage you to remember that you know your students well; use your professional judgment to make decisions regarding possible roadblocks to their comprehension. Your purpose for engaging them in close text reading is not to cause them to fail or become discouraged but rather to ask motivating questions and encourage collegial dialogue that promotes text scrutiny at the deepest of analysis.

Number the Passage

Identify the text and ask students to number the lines or paragraphs of the text. If they are working in a text that cannot be written on you should supply Post-it Notes so they can add the numbers. It is difficult to have a follow-up conversation unless all students are able to identify the lines of the text being cited by the speaker. You can also show the text on a document camera that has a numbered passage. It is fine for students to preview the text before the first reading. You shouldn't preview it for them, but encouraging them to do so gives them the context for the information they'll be reading.

First Reading: Independent

While there is no specific sequence of questioning that must occur, you may often ask a first question that is designed to establish a general understanding. As students read, keep an eye on specific students who may need more assistance with making meaning of the text. Encourage all students to make notes to themselves about the major events, and observe their silent reading closely as you watch for signs of difficulty. Encourage them to circle or underline words, phrases, or sentences that are unclear to them. The first reading should invite the reader to gain a general understanding of the text—to stay with it to determine what it is about.

First Discussion: Partner Talk to Support Understanding

After students have finished the initial reading, ask them to turn to a partner to share the information they gleaned from the text that addresses the question you asked. Encourage them to use their language frames to share their responses.

> I believe this text is about _____ because on page _____ the authors talk about_____.
>
> Because on pages _____ and _____ the author talks so much about _____, I think this text is mostly about that.
>
> It appears that this is a story about _____, because _____.

Ask students to write their response and their partner's in their notes. You may want to have a few responses shared with the whole class. This ensures that everyone has a general understanding of the text.

Second Reading:
Options—Independent, Student-, or Teacher-Led Reading

To focus the next reading, ask a question that invites students to analyze how the text was written, how it works. You may need to do the oral reading or you might invite students seated in smaller groups to select one of them as the reader. Who is doing the reading is not the primary feature of significance. The important point is that each student is engaging in his or her own analysis. Be sure that everyone is reading along. Depending on the complexity of the passage, you may need to ask additional questions about the workings of the text.

Next Discussion

Again invite table discussions. It is through these discussions that students learn to share their text-based inferences. As they converse about ideas, they expand their understanding of the topic as well as their insights about themselves as readers and conversing participants. They are deepening their knowledge of the content and their view of themselves participating in an academic conversation. They learn the give and take of conversation. As they talk about segments of the text, they scaffold their understanding of the entire text.

Additional Readings

While there is no exact number of readings that need to occur, a complex text will usually need more than two readings. On the third reread, students may still need to focus on additional features regarding how the text works or they may be ready to analyze the message the author is sharing. As you watch your readers you will be able to determine the next type of question to ask. Keep in mind that the purposes of text-dependent questions are to prompt rereading, encourage the use of textual evidence to support answers, and to deepen comprehension using analytic processes.

Additional Discussions

You may decide that a discussion is warranted after each reading. Extremely complex texts become more comprehensible through discussions that begin by addressing a related targeted question. The intent of the questions and the discussions is to scaffold knowledge, so be careful not to stop the process of conversational analysis before all students have succeeded in understanding the text.

Extend What You Know

At the conclusion of a close reading, new knowledge needs to be integrated into the reader's existing base of knowledge. This can occur by inviting students to use the information they have learned by sharing it with others through critiques, presentations, blogs, debates, argumentative writing, calls for action, and new questions and investigations that might have been triggered.

CLOSE READING IN ACTION

Let's look at the following examples of close reading. Each of these teachers began by selecting a text that related to a unit of study in which their students were engaged. They analyzed each text to determine the areas that would be complex for their students and then designed text-based questions to promote deep analysis and potential extensions of the information. They had previously modeled for their students how to closely read and analyze a text.

Close Reading in Middle School

Select the Text

Sixth-grade English teacher Mrs. Garcia chose R. J. Palacio's book *Wonder* to support her students' understanding of how the choices and actions of characters reveal who they are as people. Because *Wonder* is told from many different character perspectives, Mrs. Garcia knew it would help support students' comparing and contrasting characters and events. *Wonder* is a story about a fifth-grade boy (August) who, after years of being home-schooled because of a facial deformity, attends public school for the first time. Each section of the book is told from the perspective of a different character, including August's friends and family members. Mrs. Garcia decided that while most of the text would be read as a shared reading experience, close reading of some sections might be warranted.

Identify Area(s) of Focus

Mrs. Garcia spent time before the lesson assessing the chapter titled "Jack Will, Julian, and Charlotte," to identify a section that would be complex enough to call for a close reading. She first decided that the structure of the text, language, and knowledge demands were not going to cause much confusion for her students. That is, the narrative structure was simple, explicit, and chronological; the language was contemporary, familiar, and conversational in tone; and the life experiences that were portrayed were somewhat common to Mrs. Garcia's diverse group of students. She also identified within the chapter areas where her students would need some instructional scaffolding. She decided that pages 21–22 would be perfect for a close reading because the meaning of this section of the chapter was somewhat complex. Mrs. Garcia was certain that her students would wrestle with identifying how particular actions helped to shape a reader's understanding of a character. Mrs. Garcia knew that having her students closely read these two pages of the text would give them a better understanding of how characters' action and choices reveal their complexity and personality.

Share the Purpose

Mrs. Garcia began her lesson by telling students that readers build impressions or theories about characters and find evidence to support their ideas. She made this idea relevant to students by telling them that we "read" people all the time. She said"

> "We 'read' people and make theories about people based on a lot of different
>   things: the way people dress, the way people talk, the way people act, etc. If

several people walked into this classroom right now wearing suits and ties and speaking with a thick accent, you may have a theory that they are visitors to our school, perhaps from another country."

To further share and contextualize the purpose, Mrs. Garcia encouraged students to read closely and pay attention to the characters' actions, words, and choices in order to understand them more deeply. She said:

> "So as you read these pages and also as you closely read other texts, pay attention to the actions and choices of the characters and think about what their actions reveal about them as people. Okay, let's begin."

Mrs. Garcia read the beginning of the chapter aloud while students followed along.

First Reading

When Mrs. Garcia finished reading the first two pages of the chapter, she asked students to "take a turn." She asked them to read the next two pages and annotate as they read. She tasked them to identify what was happening in these next pages. Mrs. Garcia had made copies of these pages so students could mark them as needed. She reminded students to "talk to the text," that is, underline words, circle phrases, draw arrows among words and write comments in the margins about their thinking. As they read she mingled among them addressing their understanding by observing their annotations and margin notes. After several minutes, Mrs. Garcia began a whole-group discussion. She often had students initially engage in partner chats before beginning a whole-class chat, but since the class was also sharing and talking about this text as a whole, and because of their annotations, Mrs. Garcia began with the following questions:

> "What is happening here?"
> "What did author R. J. Palacio spend two pages writing about?"

These questions were intended to give students a general understanding of the close reading passage and also, from the student's responses, help Mrs. Garcia make informed decisions about her next instructional moves. When Mrs. Garcia heard the following conversation, she knew she was ready to move on to deepen her students' understanding.

> MORIA: It's Auggie's first day at school. Well, not his first actual day. More like a tour day. An orientation day . . . but a private one.
>
> JALEN: Yeah, and some kids from the school are there to show him around.

HAZELYN: Sounds like they are going to take him to homeroom, science labs, library and . . .

STEWART: The music room—even though Auggie doesn't play an instrument.

Second Reading and Talking about the Text

Now Mrs. Garcia was ready to have students go back to the text and deepen their understanding by focusing their attention on the characters and their actions.

"This time when you look at these pages, I want you to put a star by anything that Auggie does or says. Pay attention to the language the author uses to paint a picture of what Auggie is like."

Since students had a general understanding of the text, they were ready to move on to deepen their understanding about language and structure. Students returned to the text and most put a star next to the phrase *looking down*. Most students noticing what the other characters were doing and saying put stars next to Jack Will's, Julian's, and Charlotte's actions. They did, however, have some difficulty identifying the language the author was using to write about August.

Mrs. Garcia knew additional text-dependent questions were needed to scaffold the reading after she observed what students were annotating and sharing. By carefully posing her next questions, students were able to locate evidence needed to more fully understand August.

MRS. GARCIA: Let's look again at page 21. Where does the author give us clues about August?

CARLY: Oh, right here—at the top of the page. He grows his bangs out. It says, "It helps me block out the things I don't want to see."

MRS. GARCIA: Great! Can you find other parts in the section that tell about August's actions or choices?

GRANT: He said he didn't want to meet anyone right here, on page 21. We should put a star next to that.

By listening carefully to responses to the questions she asked to scaffold students' analysis, Mrs. Garcia knew her students were ready for deeper analysis. Next she asked them to examine what some of August's actions and what they indicated about his character. Based on what she was observing from her students' annotations and hearing from their conversations, she knew that students were comprehending the clues the author shared regarding how one's actions offer insights about one's character.

Third Reading and Talking about the Text

Mrs. Garcia guided students to revisit their annotated copies of the text to attend to the layered meanings behind some of the words and phrases they had starred.

> "Okay, now I would like you to just go back to the parts you starred. Knowing what the author has written and the language she has used to describe August's actions and choices, what does it mean? In other words, what do those actions and choices that August made tell you about him? How do they help you to describe him?"

Students eagerly returned to the text. They had gained confidence with this reading and felt supported enough to return to the reading again and again because of their success with understanding its complex meaning. After several minutes of again walking around the room noticing what students were marking and noting in their margin comments, Mrs. Garcia asked them to turn to a partner to share some of their annotations. She directed them to fold a piece of paper in half, making a T-chart. On one side of the T-chart students wrote the actions or choices August made. On the other side, students wrote what this told them about his character (see Figure 7.17).

After several minutes of collaboratively working on a T-chart, two students joined another pair and created a "quad pod." These quad pods shared ideas, expanded original ideas, and came to a more thorough understanding of what August was like as a character.

Writing Extension

Satisfied that her students had a better understanding of August as a character, Mrs. Garcia knew that she was just touching the surface. Several other characters needed close examination. Likewise, she wanted students to identify that August's character was initially dynamic but would change from these early chapters to those

August's choices and actions	What this tells me
"I looked down. . . ."	August is shy, embarrassed, uncomfortable.
"I grew my hair long. . . ."	Doesn't want to see the world, doesn't want the world to see him; is in hiding.
"My heart literally started beating. . . ."	He's nervous—nervous around kids, not adults.

FIGURE 7.17. T-chart for *Wonder.*

at the end. To accomplish this, students needed to transfer the skills of investigating a character that they learned in this close reading lesson. They needed to apply them for further analysis of all characters. In order to archive the students' hard work and thinking, Mrs. Garcia asked them to go to Padlet.com (*https://padlet.com*) and write a sentence or two about what they knew at this point about August, and how they know it. Padlet.com is an online bulletin board that allows students to construct responses for the entire class to see.

To help them get started, Mrs. Garcia posted sentence frames for those who needed some additional support:

> August is _____. I know this because _____.
>
> The author writes that _____. This tells me that August is _____.

Within minutes, an entire online bulletin board was filled with students' thinking about what they knew about August with text-based evidence to support their claims. Mrs. Garcia concluded this lesson by pointing to her white board and revisiting her purpose:

> "Let's see, remember boys and girls, today we set out to pay attention to what the characters were doing and saying, and the choices they made in order to understand them more deeply. Let's look at our online bulletin board together and read some of your responses. [Students read responses chorally.] Do you think you have a clearer picture of who August is?"

Mrs. Garcia heard a resounding "YES!" from her students but also saw the evidence of their learning on the interactive white board.

Although Mrs. Garcia had the students return to these two pages three times for close reading, annotating, and conversation, that is not always the number of times they reread a passage. While three times is a common number, students often read a text additional times during a close reading, and also on additional days. Mrs. Garcia believes that each time her students reread they gain deepened insights.

Close Reading in 11th Grade

In an 11th-grade journalism class, Mr. Nolan wanted to begin exposing his students to complex texts worthy of a close reading. He was certain that his students were examining texts closely in English, history, and science. Close reading was something new for him and his colleagues in the arts, sports, and other technical subjects. Mr. Nolan knew the first task was to find a text worthy of being closely read and discussed.

Select the Text

Mr. Nolan selected an online article about his school from a local newspaper. The article reported the recent fights at the school and showcased the school in a very poor light, albeit subtly. Mr. Nolan thought that the article would be a perfect way to introduce tone and bias using a highly motivating informational text. The close reading lesson would help support students' understanding of author's point of view and purpose.

Identify Area(s) of Focus

Mr. Nolan did not plan to have his students read the entire article using a close reading approach. Rather, he planned to distribute the article and read some of it aloud using a shared reading method. While he was planning for the lesson, he was looking for complex parts of the article that might cause his students some struggle. He determined that the last three paragraphs of the article were full of tricky language that would be difficult for students without a more careful examination. He knew that the text-dependent questions he was preparing must scaffold students toward uncovering the meaning of the words that were used in the article and the effect the words would have on the reader. He felt this would be a perfect lesson for enabling students to identify written bias and tone.

Share the Purpose

Mr. Nolan began the lesson by asking what novel the students were reading in English. The students eagerly told Mr. Nolan that they were almost finished reading *Of Mice and Men.* Mr. Nolan continued asking about the novel, although students were quite puzzled as to why their journalism teacher was asking about another class.

> "John Steinbeck, right? What's the tone of the book? What was the author's attitude?"

Mr. Nolan questioned the students who chimed in with words like *sympathetic, honest, dismal,* and when Mr. Nolan asked how they knew the tone, the students had a hard time explaining more than "It's just a feeling we got when we read it."

Bingo! A perfect opportunity to introduce tone in journalism. Mr. Nolan told students that authors have an attitude about a topic and often write the way they do to persuade readers to feel the same way.

> "Today our purpose for reading this article is to examine how the author used words and phrases to help us interpret the tone."

Mr. Nolan continued:

> "When you read today, pay close attention to the words and phrases the author
> used so you can interpret and understand how he feels about a particular topic.
> And in this case, the topic is our very own Marenview High School."

With little frontloading, Mr. Nolan had connected his students and the text.

First Reading: Independent Reading and Talking about the Text

When Mr. Nolan finished reading the first page of the article, he asked students
to closely read the rest of the article, paying attention to what the author's attitude
was about their school. Students were used to annotating in other classes and began
immediately circling, underlining, and writing notes in the margins and between
paragraphs to capture questions, connections, and clarifications. While students
read and annotated during the first reading of this section of the article, Mr. Nolan
circulated around the room, assisting some students who were struggling to decode
some of the multisyllabic words that could not be defined by the context. He was
also recording some of the annotations his students were making so he knew which
text-dependent questions to ask first. After students had completed their first reading, Mr. Nolan asked, "What is the author writing about?" to assess students' general understanding of the text.

The following whole-class conversation occurred after Mr. Nolan' initial question:

> SARAI: He's writing about our school.
>
> JAMAL: Yeah, about all the fights we've been having.
>
> KAI: I didn't even know we had those fights.
>
> MR. NOLAN: What else is the author writing about?
>
> KEITH: He gives some statistics about how many we've had and how some
> parents feel about it.

Second and Third Readings: Talking about the Text

Confident that his students had a general understanding of the article, Mr. Nolan
wanted to draw their attention to some of the key details, since this information
would help them better understand the tone. For the second reading, Mr. Nolan
asked the students to pay attention to some of the key details in the article. He
asked them to put a box around the details that seemed interesting and to note
in the margins what was interesting about the detail and how it made them feel.
After students had read for a second time and shared with their tablemates some of

their insights, Mr. Nolan felt that he needed to push them even further to address specific areas of the text in order to really understand how carefully authors make word choices that support readers' inferring the intended tone. He prompted them to do so by saying:

> "Look again at the eighth paragraph. What does the author say about suspension rates? How does the author describe the students on campus? Who is quoted in paragraph 9?"

Notice how these questions pushed students back to the text for a third time. They did not reread the entire passage again. Not every reread must involve rereading the entire selected passage or be followed by conversation if it is apparent to the teacher that an additional question will promote continued analysis. Mr. Nolan knew from listening to his students' conversations that they needed to be directed toward a specific section. In response, students again shared some of the key details with their tablemates and then with the whole class:

> JON: He's reporting a lot of statistics. Those are high percentages of fights and suspensions.
>
> AMARION: He is interviewing the school police a lot.
>
> STEPHANIE: And some community members.
>
> MR. NOLAN: Does anyone else get interviewed? (Students scan their articles.)
>
> MIKE: No. (*after a long pause*) Hey, why not? How come he didn't interview us?
>
> STEPHANIE: I bet he doesn't want to hear what we have to say. He didn't interview teachers either.

Mr. Nolan knew that by attending to the key details that previously were overlooked, the students were beginning to hear the bias in the article and the tone was becoming clearer. He feared, however, that if he didn't ask the next right text-dependent questions and have students return to the text for a fourth reading, they would miss the purpose of the lesson and the deepest meaning of the article.

Fourth Reading: Talking about the Text

Mr. Nolan complimented the student journalists on their deep thinking and pushed them further into the text. He wanted them to pay attention to the language the author used and interpret what tone was being conveyed. He said:

> "This time when you read these last few paragraphs, revisit what key details you have put boxes around and see if there are any words surrounding those key

details that make you have a certain feeling or tell you what the writer might be feeling."

Students got right to work, but not so silently because by now they knew the text fairly well. At one table, Mr. Nolan heard students talking about the text. It seemed that what they were discovering was that the article was filled with words that made them angry.

KURT: He writes this statistic and then the word *shockingly*.

JIM: And when he interviews the community member he uses the word *outrageous*.

LIN: Why is he using the word *dangerous* so many times? This school isn't *dangerous*!

KOSAME: Where does he use that word?

LIN: (*pointing to paragraphs 7, 8, and 9*) Right here, here, and here.

KOSAME: That's just what *he* wrote, though. That's his opinion. He didn't even ask any of us what we thought.

Mr. Nolan knew he could walk away from this small-group discussion because these students are well on their way to uncovering the tone and bias of the article. They were identifying specific words that helped interpret the writer's attitude about their school. They also inferred that the key details were described only by the writer himself and outside community members rather than those on the inside of the school, namely teachers and students. At this point the students' papers were filled with annotations and commentaries in the margins. During a whole-class discussion students shared some of the words the reporter used and what tone those words suggested.

Collaborative Conversation and Writing Extensions

Mr. Nolan likes to incorporate technology into lessons to strengthen understanding so he invited students to retrieve their laptops and go to Voki.com (*www.voki.com*). Then he instructed students to collaborate as a group to gain consensus about the tone of the article. This collaborative conversation involved students sharing ideas and supporting their chosen tone words with text-based evidence. Once groups of students had come to consensus, each student created an avatar using Voki.com. They wrote from the perspective of the author, explaining how he felt about Marenview High School. By writing from the perspective of the author and using some of the tone-rich words from the article, students deepened their understandings about how a writer's words influence the tone of the article.

Students uploaded avatars to the class website. As they viewed each others' avatars they gained an even deeper understanding of how student journalists in their class viewed the tone of this article and the language and insinuations made by the author that caused these interpretations. To conclude, Mr. Nolan invited students to modify their own avatar with new insights gained from peers.

CONCLUSION

As these lesson examples suggest, teachers can involve students in close reading experiences as a way to engage them in deep text analysis. As students become skilled with this approach, they will be able to access increasingly complex text with their peers and independently. As we have argued earlier in this book, teaching students to read and understand complex texts begins with an understanding of what makes a text complex. Teachers, not computers, need to analyze texts and determine the instructional match between the texts and their students. Thankfully, there are a number of resources available for teachers, including quantitative readability formulas and qualitative assessment tools that can be used in these analyses. In addition, teachers need to consider the reader him- or herself as well as the task students will be expected to complete with the text before making a final selection.

Teachers play a key role in teaching students to stick with a text as they learn to read closely. Notice in the video *Tackling a Scientific Text* at *www. learner.org/courses/readwrite/video-detail/tackling-a-scientific-text.html* all of the encouragement being offered by 12th-grade science teacher Tracy Tran.

We must commit to our students and help them read increasingly complex texts, and read those texts well. We hope the examples we have shared also free you to craft the close reading experiences that support your students' accomplishing each lesson purpose. While limited frontloading of information by the teacher should occur during close reading, we hope these examples help you to realize that the close reading path takes many directions, although all are designed to ensure that students gain competency in knowing how to independently analyze a text. There is no set way that this must happen. Revisit the examples that we've shared and you'll realize that every decision the teachers made about the features that needed to be analyzed, the questions that needed to be asked, and the number of times the text needed to be reread were dependent on the developing competencies of their students as readers who could deeply analyze a text.

In the past, our profession may have been a bit complacent, waiting for students to develop their literacy skills. That time is over. If we can put a person on the moon, we can ensure that students can read about it. If we can create the Internet, we have the responsibility to ensure that all students can access and evaluate the information contained therein. And if we expect to solve the problems present in the world today, problems our ancestors could not have imagined, then we must ensure that students can think deeply, look for evidence, and justify their ideas and proclamations.

TRUE/FALSE ANSWERS

Just in case you are still wondering about some of the answers to the true/false initial assessment we shared at the start of this chapter, here's what we think.

1. Close reading is a teaching technique.

   False. It is an approach to reading that skilled readers use to deeply analyze a complex text.

2. The best assessment of a student's success with close reading is being able to summarize the text.

   False. When one closely reads a text he or she goes beyond summarizing to analyze the author's main ideas and craft in sharing them.

3. Close reading always involves rereading.

   True. If the deepest meaning of a text can be comprehended with one reading, then the text ideas and language are not complex enough to warrant a close reading.

4. Close reading is the same as leisure reading for skilled readers.

   False. Close reading never involves a leisure read; these are very different approaches to reading. Skilled readers employ each, but for different purposes.

5. The goal of close reading is to understand the author's intention, how it is being accomplished, and what it means.

   True. The goal is to objectively analyze what the author is saying and how he is doing so.

6. Prior knowledge should never be activated or shared prior to a close reading.

   False. While this is primarily true, the final decision remains with the teacher. There are no hard and fast rules in close reading because the teacher should be very much in control of the situation. If the teacher has assessed that a key vocabulary term needs to be defined because there is no content in the passage that will support readers in unlocking the meaning, then the teacher should share the meaning. If the teacher has analyzed the passage and determined that the questions she'll ask will provide the needed scaffolds, then there is no need to preteach or frontload any information. Just share the purpose, the initial question, and let the students begin to closely read the text. If you aren't sure, let them have an initial try at the text. They may do quite well. If not, you can always ask a question that will direct them to an area of the text that will support them. The important point is not to jump in and save them when indeed they may be able to succeed with just a few well-designed and strategically interjected question scaffolds.

7. Teachers should not share a purpose for close reading because doing so tells too much about the text.

False. Giving students a purpose for reading gives them a context or a roadmap (read to find out the differences between rocks and minerals, or read to find out how this character overcomes obstacles) that kick-starts their developing analysis of the text. Be careful when sharing the purpose not to reveal too much information about the text or you will interfere with your students' joy in unraveling the text.

8. The criteria for selecting a text for close reading should be more focused on stretching the cognitive and linguistic growth of students than on matching the text to their instructional levels.

True. As promoted by the College and Career Readiness Standards for Reading, all students must be able to comprehend texts of steadily increasing complexity as they progress through school.

9. It's okay for students to preview the text before beginning a close reading.

True. Students should be encouraged to look over any text they are about to read. When preparing for a close reading the teacher should not do the previewing, but it is okay for students to look it over. This allows them to have a context for what it to come.

10. There is no specific sequence or plan that needs to occur during a close reading.

True. The plan you develop should depend on the complexity of the text, strengths and needs of your students, and your instructional purpose.

11. Questions asked by teachers during close reading should serve as scaffolds for readers.

True. Although many are designed before the close reading, the teacher may ask additional questions if he or she determines that a particular area of the text needs additional scaffolding.

12. The first reading of a close reading should invite the reader to evaluate the deep meaning and value of the text by making connections with other texts.

False. The first reading should invite the reader to gain a general understanding of the text—to stay with it to determine what it is about.

Chapter 8

Writing It Down

Instruction That Supports Writing in the Disciplines

Have you noticed that schools are asking students more often to do worthwhile things? Not just take things in, but to learn by doing, creating, or making? As we discussed in Chapter 7, reading is immensely important; however, having read about a topic, we now ask students more and more to create something or write something. This chapter is about writing something, and that something should help them learn and understand your discipline in a way that is increasingly like that of experts in the field.

WHY WRITE?

It is very easy to think that writing is just evidence of having done required reading or a way to monitor students' understanding of any topic. In this chapter, we take the view that writing is a keystone in the architecture of learning just about anything. The role it plays varies depending on the demands of the discipline, but in every discipline we can think of, writing is a way to construct knowledge about that discipline.

Perhaps we could take a look at what seems that most unlikely of pairs, mathematics and writing. "Ms. Bass" (whom you met in Chapter 2), you can hear her students say, "This is math, not English class." But she knows and understands that writing informs the most basic of mathematical work. Mathematicians, and students of math, are trained to look at the accuracy of the proof, with less consideration for who wrote it (e.g., Siebert & Draper, 2012). Proofs may be relatively short, a few sentences, but they represent a great deal of thinking and preparation.

Proofs consist of a theorem and the proof itself. It often rests on certain assumption or it is an assumption, for example: *There are infinitely many prime numbers.* Straightforward enough, right? It stands to reason. Okay, prove it. Well, many mathematicians have done exactly that. That is where the proof comes in, but it is only valuable if it is accurate. The few sentences that describe the proof are not long, but the thinking that went into this is deep and beautiful.

Suppose there are only finitely many primes, let's say n of them. We denote them by $p_1, p_2, \ldots, p_n$. Now construct a new number

$$p = p_1 \times p_2 \times p_3 \times \ldots \times p_n + 1$$

Clearly, p is larger than any of the primes, so it doesn't equal one of them. Since $p_1, p_2, \ldots, p_n$ constitute *all* primes p can't be prime. Thus it must be divisible by at least one of our finitely many primes, say p_n (with $1 \leq n \leq n$). But when we divide p by p_n we get a remainder 1. That's a contradiction, so our original assumption that there are finitely many primes must be false. Thus there are infinitely many primes. (Euclid, circa 400 B.C.E.)

Now, you are likely thinking, this sounds like arguments that we discussed in Chapter 5. And if you are thinking that, you are absolutely right. A proof in mathematics is an argument, and it is deductive in its construction. As you learned in Chapter 5, not all arguments are deductive, but in mathematics, the deductive nature of thinking is often paramount (although it is more complicated than that, as any mathematician will tell you). Writing it out in a clear and elegant manner is where the argument meets the words and symbols that are the foundation for communication in that discipline.

 Watch how students learned to write proofs in an eighth-grade math class at *www.learner.org/courses/readwrite/video-detail/real-world-mathematics-collaboration.html*.

Writing in mathematics serves other purposes, as well. Burns (2004) describes her own learning about the important role that writing plays in mathematics. She found that students who could write about what they learned and how they learned it improved their mathematical thinking. Similarly, what students wrote provided her and her students with a window into how they came to their understandings of math, what they misconstrued, and how they felt about the topics and their own learning of math. Even in math, perhaps especially in math, how students feel about the topic is useful information for the teacher and for the students.

Watch how a 10th-grade teacher uses formative assessment to assess students' understanding and engagement at *www.learner.org/courses/readwrite/video-detail/writing-deepen-mathematical-understanding.html*.

WRITING IN OTHER DISCIPLINES

While some types or formats of writing seem predetermined to land in the realm of each discipline, there is much more to it than that. The important thing to consider is the value of the writing tasks we ask of students. If we ask math students to write out a word problem, then we must ask ourselves, "What are they learning as they write?" Are they learning something worthwhile about mathematics and are they learning to use words to help them understand math? If so, we are on the right path. If we are only asking students to write because someone told us kids need to write, that is probably not good enough.

Thinking about genres, we might consider typical assignments in the disciplines. Students in science might be asked to write a lab report detailing what they learned as a result of an experiment. In social studies, they might be asked to write a report on a particular era, event, or important person. However, we think writing in the disciplines involves more than just genre.

DIVING INTO THE DISCIPLINES

We think that a focus on a type of writing is a good start—the report, the essay, and so on. However, thinking about what is important in each type of writing might provide a clearer vision of what writing in the disciplines means. For this, we draw from the ideas of Bazerman (1995, 2010), who described writing based on the sources used to inform the written work and the time from which the sources originated. Much of the remainder of this chapter is drawn from his work, and we encourage our readers to consult his books for details. This helps teachers think about writing across the disciplines, and it helps writers think about the sources they might consult as they write and before they write. Look at Table 8.1 and notice how the disciplines don't line up exactly by the larger content area. Rather, they are interwoven depending on what is being studied and when it occurred.

If we proceed with this framework, we now have a means of thinking about what to write and what sources are appropriate to consult. Here we will add that Bazerman also offered a fourth category of writing that included working with theory. Certainly, some students are capable of this kind of work, but it does require extensive background in the field where the theory applies. Thus we will leave this to another volume for another time.

Although there are times when disciplines overlap or are intertwined, let's look at each of the three categories:

1. Writing about events from the past.
2. Writing about events as they occur.
3. Writing about experimental events.

TABLE 8.1. Writing in the Disciplines, by Time and Source

When	Example sources	Example disciplines
Past events	Artifacts (a clay pot, a rock, a fossil), written accounts from the time of the event, and other written records, human creations from the fields of architecture, literature, music.	Reconstructive disciplines, such as history, geology, archaeology, and interpretive disciplines such as literary criticism, music, and philosophy.
Events as they happen	Observations of natural and human behaviors.	Meteorology, economics, journalism, psychology.
Experimental events (events designed to understand certain phenomena)	Observations of events that are designed to focus on specific factors while filtering or controlling for other factors. Experimental designs are often used to test hypotheses or theories.	Chemistry, physics, sometimes psychology and other medical research.

Writing about Events from the Past

The first thing you might notice about this category of writing from sources is that it addresses writing about literature, some of the sciences, and some of the social sciences. You might be thinking, huh? I typically lump the social sciences together, the natural and applied sciences together, and literature has its own special place. But there is another way to look at this, and it makes good sense in its own right.

Some of the natural or applied sciences, some of the social sciences, and most of the domain of literature deal with events from the past. Geology, for example, is a science dedicated to reconstructing events from the past that deal with the manner in which the Earth came to be in its present form and predict how it might be in the future, based on past events. Geologists examine events from the past such as strata that have similarities in different places. They look at the structure of the rocks they find and where they find them, and what resulted in their being where they are on or within the planet. These are events from the past, and the sources on which geologists rely are the geologic record that includes rocks, fossils, and evidence of significant geologic change in the past. So far, so good?

But what about history, a social science? The same is true here. Historians look for the events from the past and the historical records that document those events. Historians may not be looking at rocks and fossils, as geologists are, but they are looking at records of events through the eyes of others who were there. They may consult eyewitness accounts, government or religious records (such as birth certificates), photographic or artistic representations, and so on. They further think about those records as primary, secondary, or tertiary accounts.

What Are Primary, Secondary, and Tertiary Sources?

Primary sources tend to be written or created at the time of the event, and they have typically not been filtered through the perceptions or interpretations of others. As a result, students sometimes must be reminded that newspaper accounts, for example, might be primary sources if the reporter was on the scene, but secondary sources if the reporter collected information from witnesses and from artifacts or data after the event. Different disciplines place varying values on the journalistic account depending on the demands of the discipline as knowledge is created. Coins, pottery, first-person accounts, letters, and photographs are typically considered primary sources.

    Secondary sources are more often filtered in some way, usually because the individuals creating the account or source have some time to consider other factors. In other words, they have the benefit of hindsight. Proximity in time to the event are often considered, and which is why journalistic accounts (e.g., newspaper articles and some blog posts) are secondary sources in some cases and primary sources in others. Well-documented biographies and journal or magazine articles are often thought of as secondary sources.

    Tertiary sources tend to be compilations or syntheses such as those found in dictionaries, encyclopedias, and guide or fact books. For students in secondary schools, tertiary sources often include textbooks (although these sources can include or even be secondary or primary sources, at times). Although students increasingly have access online to primary and secondary resources, more research into how students make sense of sources is necessary. Guidance for students to use these sources is, perhaps, more important than ever.

    Ever ban your students from using Wikipedia? We say, don't. Instead, teach them to use tertiary sources as they are intended. That is, they are a gateway to inquiry. Our next section provides some guidance for using tertiary sources.

How to Use Wikipedia and Other Tertiary Resources at School

When students consult an encyclopedia or other tertiary resource (including many textbooks), they typically hold a reasonable expectation that information contained in the article will be reliable and verifiable. Educators who do not allow students to use Wikipedia as a source often cite reliability as a topic of concern. Some incidents of vandalism on the pages of Wikipedia raise the level of skepticism, and those who post and revise articles in Wikipedia may not be experts. In May 2009, Genevieve Carbery reported that a student researching journalism and globalization placed a false quote in an obituary, which was subsequently picked up and reported as factual by newspapers around the world. However, Wikipedia's reliability compares favorably to traditional encyclopedias in most regards.

When Should an Encyclopedia Be Used?

Encyclopedias, whether online or printed, are useful sources of information. Editors and contributors to encyclopedias generally set out to collect information about a wide variety of information, but may also limit the scope of articles to a specific domain (such as a medical encyclopedia). Because encyclopedias are collections of articles on a vast array of topics, they are generally excellent sources of information when students need background information.

For example, a student writing about an interest in the human genome project may decide to do a little reading on the development of the double helix. Since the main topic of the student's inquiry is the genome project, reading a Wikipedia article about the double-helix polymer would seem appropriate.

Many encyclopedia entries are well sourced; that is, they include references to other documents, media files, and experts that support the assertions found in the article. As a result, a student completing research on the genome project may find some additional sources to consult by reading the article's reference list. Savvy users of an article's reference list locate those articles, read them, and evaluate them. They also independently search for additional sources that may support, contradict, or expand on those sources. The founder of Wikipedia, Jimmy Wales, encourages students in college not to use an encyclopedia as a source in writing academic papers (Young, 2006).

Using a Collaboratively Authored Encyclopedia

The nature of the encyclopedia is that of a secondary source. Wikipedia, for example, does not claim to be a publisher of original thought, and it should not be treated as such by those consulting it as a resource. Virtually all encyclopedia articles report knowledge based on other sources; that is, original or primary sources are consulted. However, the authors, whether experts in their fields or interested parties that wish to contribute, must select from many sources and interpret those sources in writing an encyclopedia article. Thus, rather than ban the use of Wikipedia and similar collaborative projects, students and teachers can ask the following three questions when they consult any encyclopedia:

1. "Am I reading this encyclopedia article for background knowledge?"
2. "Will reading this encyclopedia article help me find sources that support, refute, or find alternatives to the main points in my own writing and presentations?"
3. "What other sources can I consult?"

Two questions specifically for online, collaborative encyclopedias:

1. "Have I checked the history tab to see who has contributed [some posts are anonymous, but the list of edits and revisions can be revealing]?"
2. "Does anything seem to be missing or not addressed in this article that is found in other sources?"

Finally, teachers may best be able to help students learn to evaluate the sources they use and when to use them rather than banning them outright.

Experts and students working with sources from the past are sometimes working to reconstruct, from sources such as artifacts and written accounts, what actually transpired. At other times, they attempt to interpret the events of the past. On occasion, they must do a bit of both.

As we will see in the next sections, choosing the most relevant evidence is very important. Just as important is noting that an examination of all the relevant evidence and the source of that evidence turns out to be critical, too. As we already know, social scientists tend to look at who is providing the evidence, but those working with the natural sciences tend to look at how the knowledge was created. In both cases, how the knowledge was reported is also of prime importance.

Writing about Events as They Occurred

As anyone who has written about events that are occurring in real time, or fairly close to it, can attest, there are mountains of information and there is always more information that can be assimilated. We should tell you that we don't mean that information is necessarily collected and analyzed at it happens, second by second (although that is sometimes possible). Rather, writing about events as they occurr tends to have the quality of timeliness, and that sources tend to be collected at the time of the event or fairly close to it.

Teachers are very familiar with this type of work, whether they are writing about it in the form of lesson plans or preparing a report for a parent conference. The quantity of data available to teachers is massive, but teachers must choose which information source requires their attention and which sources are most likely to be useful to themselves or the audience (such as a parent) in developing a lesson or a plan of action for a specific student. The data may have been collected over a brief span of time (a year or two of test score data, observations, evaluative assessments, benchmark assessments, etc.), but they all were gathered and selected in a brief period of time about events that are occurring, or have recently occurred, relative to a specific case (a classroom, a student, a lesson planning event).

The important thing to remember about sources collected about events as they occur (or close to the event) is that a clear focus is needed, and that focus is often on the procedures needed to collect and understand the data. Journalists, educators, meteorologists, and economists often grapple with this type of source because information arrives and must be analyzed and reported rather quickly for it to be of any use. Biologists and their colleagues may attempt a census of an endangered species, and then they compare that with historical data. As you can see, sometimes writing from sources means working with historical data and using current evidence to predict what could occur.

Without a clear focus, chaos tends to overwhelm the person doing the research and the writing about that research. As important, we note that most research and the writing that results from it tend to contribute to an overall conversation. Recall our discussion in Chapter 5 about arguments that are defeasible? Well-written arguments from sources tend to work from the notion that there is evidence that suggests possibilities, and it invites new inquiries based on that and other research.

Writing about Experimental Events

In many of the natural and applied sciences, researchers tend to use sources they have specifically designed to test a hypothesis. They have read the work of researchers who came before them, used their own work, and constructed a hypothesis about what would occur under very controlled circumstances. Writing about experimental research means that that the conditions must be carefully planned, and the experiment conducted just as carefully. For our purposes, it is essential that students writing about experiments learn precision and accuracy in their work (if they conducted the research) and in how they report what they did.

Wait, you say. Aren't *accuracy* and *precision* synonyms? Sometimes, they are. In experimental research, they are not the same thing, although they are closely related. Empirical research is based on evidence collected through direct or perhaps indirect observation. *Indirect observation* is actually a precise term in this context. Some kinds of phenomena cannot be observed directly by humans. For example, in particle physics, observations are indirect and based on what happens under circumstances that cannot be seen by the naked eye or even with some of the best technologies available. Rather, experiments must be set up that isolate the factors such that the indirect evidence can be detected.

Okay, what does that mean? Suppose you are a particle physicist, and you want to find evidence to support the notion of string theory, especially at the subatomic level. Directly observing subatomic strings cannot be done, at least not at the time this book went to press. Instead, physicists rely on mathematical theories and tests that are designed to determine whether strings exist by indirectly observing what happens under certain conditions. To keep it on point, we cannot see the subatomic particles, even with very sophisticated tools; however, we can see what happens when we test the conditions that would prove the existence of those particles. That is indirect observation.

Back to our argument that *precision* and *accuracy* are related terms, but not synonymous. In everyday speech, we might use the terms interchangeably, but in math and sciences, these terms can't be used as synonyms. Accuracy always has to do with how close a result (say of an experiment) to known results that the community of scientists agree is generally so. If I shoot a rifle at a target, and I hit the bullseye or close to it, my shooting is accurate.

On the other hand, if I shoot that rifle and hit the lower left corner over and over, I am precise in my shooting, but not accurate. That can actually tell me something useful. Maybe my sights are not calibrated correctly, or maybe there is a question of accuracy (is the target correctly placed?). Just the same, accuracy and precision mean different things in the sciences and mathematical fields such as statistics then they do in everyday language.

Language is a key aspect of what we are driving at here. For example, students are often told to avoid using the passive voice. In the passive voice, the person who acts is obscured. In some types of writing and in some disciplines, avoiding the passive voice is appropriate. However, in science writing, passive voice plays an important role. Wilson (2006) conducted statistical analyses that showed that essays receiving passing scores used a much higher percentage of passive voice constructions than essays that did not make extensive use of the passive voice. Passive voice constructions are widely criticized in K–12 settings, yet much university writing demands it. It can be argued that the passive voice hides the agent in order to focus attention on the object of the action, as in this sentence. If we consider what we know about literacy in the sciences, this makes sense. The focus is and should be on the processes or proofs involved and not as much on who conducted the analysis.

Passive voice can be fun to teach—really, it can! Johnson (2012) proposed that her students, who liked zombie films and related material, learned to detect the passive voice by adding the phrase "by zombies" after the main verb. It works often, but not always. For example, Johnson suggested that the sentence "The house was haunted" is a passive construction because the actor (the person doing the haunting) is not present in the sentence. The test is to add "by zombies" and see if that identifies the actor in some fun way without being the subject of the sentence. So . . . "The house was haunted, by zombies." Yep, it works. By contrast, one cannot logically state, "Zombies haunted the house, by zombies." The sentence, "Zombies haunted the house" is already in the active voice. If zombies don't interest your students, substitute something or someone else. Try "by Darth Vader," perhaps. The house was haunted by Darth Vader. Yep—passive voice. But what was Darth Vader doing haunting that house?

Precise and accurate language use is very important in the sciences and in mathematics. Sometimes the most obvious term from everyday language is not the best term to use in speech or writing that describes the results of an experiment. Two examples may help. A student author may write that the number of divorces in the state of Maine declined at the same time the consumption of margarine decreased. The statement is precise, but it is not accurate. According to Vigen (n.d.), the divorce rate in Maine did decrease, and so did the amount of margarine consumed; thus there is a correlation. However, the accuracy of the report is in question because there is no reason to believe that either factor caused the other condition. Want to have some fun with correlations? Take a look at the spurious correlation between U.S. science spending and suicides in Figure 8.1, as well as the other examples on this website: *www.tylervigen.com/spurious-correlations*. Students must learn to be precise in their writing as well as accurate.

Power writing supports students in developing writing precision and prowess. Watch a sixth-grade science teacher as she engages her students in power writing at *www.learner.org/courses/readwrite/video-detail/power-writing-science.html*.

THREE TRAPS TO AVOID WHEN YOU WORK WITH YOUR STUDENTS

Some things we say don't come across in the way we mean. Here are three of them.

Spelling Doesn't Count

Spelling does count, but not the way students sometimes think it does. When a teacher says, "Spelling doesn't count," students hear, "Spelling doesn't count, ever." Instead, try telling students this: "I won't take points off your score at this point in your writing [perhaps it's a draft], but spelling does matter." DeVere remembers submitting an essay about rock climbing his early college years, but he misspelled the word *rappelling* as *repelling*. The instructor courteously but firmly reminded him that you can't be respected as an authority on any topic related to climbing if you don't know the words used to describe the sport. He was right, and DeVere never forgot that. Spelling does count, but it may not count against your score until you have had time to revise and consider the complexities of writing about any complex topic.

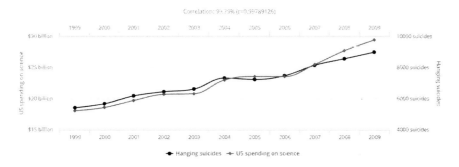

FIGURE 8.1. Correlation of U.S. science spending and suicides. Data from U.S. Office of Management and Budget and Centers for Disease Control and Prevention. Reprinted with permission from *www.tylervigen.com*. Creative Commons License: *https://creativecommons.org/licenses/by/4.0*.

If You Can Say It, You Can Write It

Thinking about a topic and being able to do so accurately is incredibly important. However, the modes of expression are not exactly interchangeable. The capacity to speak and the capacity to write about a given topic share some cognitive skills, but just because an intelligent student can speak about a topic does not mean he or she has the ability to write about it. Instead, help the student writer to use his or her speaking ability to develop the new or developing skill of writing about and within a discipline.

It's Just 500 Words . . .

In our work, we often find that length requirements are part of the job when it comes to writing; thus it is not a surprise that students sometimes ask, "How long does it have to be?" Almost all written material for publication must fit within specified boundaries that include page lengths or word counts because of economic limitations (e.g., an entire journal might have room for only 150 pages per issue) or space limitations (a letter to the editor of a newspaper that may have many letters to publish). However, the number of words in the final piece is rarely an indication of how much time was spent writing it. As you know, from reading this book, 500 words may not be many, but for well-written content, those 500 words probably represent a great deal of research to get the facts right, many revisions to make sure the words and syntax convey just the right meaning, and many hours of editing to make sure that ideas are not misconstrued. Five hundred words (or any word length or page count) is always a very rough guide, but the work that thoughtful students put in to those 500 words is often much more than one might think.

CHAPTER 8 ACTIVITY

In this chapter, we described writing about events or artifacts from the past, events that are happening in the present, and experimental events. Think of one piece you have written that fits in each category. With what discipline was each most closely aligned?

Next, think of three writing tasks you assign to your students or that you might assign to your students. Are they about events or artifacts from the past, events currently under way, or experimental? How do they align with the traditions of the discipline?

PART III

ROUTINES THAT SUPPORT LEARNING IN THE DISCIPLINES

Chapter 9

Organizing It Well

Using Graphic Organizers in the Disciplines

Story
I step into the story.
I leave my words behind.
I let the walls of the story
Be the walls of my mind.
  —GREENFIELD (2004)

As these lines from Eloise Greenfield's wonderful poem identify, one must see the images and visualize the message the author is conveying in order for deep comprehension and analysis to be possible. Knowing how to visualize information is essential to understanding any discipline. Biologists look for similarities among animals that result may result in a taxonomy with grouping by cell structure, organs and organ systems, and so on. The result is an organizational pattern that begins with a domain, followed by kingdom, phylum, and so forth. Geologists also organize knowledge by common features; for example, rocks are classified according to the way they are formed. In literature, experts think of four main types of written work with subcategories: poetry, fiction, nonfiction, and drama. In any discipline, organization is important to understanding.

That's where teachers of specific content come in. As a teacher of mathematics, art, or history, you know how content is organized. When you are not sure, you know where to look. Gladwell (2005) recounts the story of sculptures that may have been faked. The experts knew the sculptures were faked but they couldn't say why. Expertise is like that at times. Sometimes what we know is so ingrained we have to look closely at it, break it down, and almost learn it again. However, as experts, we know just how to do that in our fields.

Combining visual information with text is a time-honored way of making the complex comprehensible. Graphic organizers are one way—an important way, actually. We wrote with colleague Karen Wood, "How can a tool, made up of simple shapes and a mere sprinkling of words, possibly serve to take students where they need to go?" (Lapp, Wolsey, & Wood, 2015, p. 1).

But the not so surprising truth is that graphic organizers can take students to extraordinary new places and depths of understanding in the disciplines. They are relatively easy to use, simple to create when you understand the content, and rigorous fun. Rigorous fun? Yes, we have learned that students who learn how to make sense of complex information actually enjoy doing so. In this chapter, we share ideas about graphic organizers as a structure to help your students understand the content of the discipline and gain a deeper appreciation of it.

Above, we pointed out some macro-scale structures that are common in the sciences and in literature. However, texts in these and other disciplines are often far more nuanced than what these structures suggest. Graphic organizers don't just simplify; they build on the principle that brains need graphical information as well as textual (including spoken language) in many cases.

Scientists, for example, approach science reading tasks somewhat differently than other readers do. They tend to read a bit, then look at the graphs and charts accompanying the text. Back and forth, back and forth. They read to verify and compare the information contained in both sources of information. Remember what Dr. Devin Burr told Maria Grant in the interview in Chapter 2 about how he reads? There was a lot in that chapter, but take a minute to review it (and stick a bookmark on this page!).

As Burr implied, scientists often tend to look for things that don't quite add up. They like disequilibrium because it leads them to ask questions (see Bresser & Fargason, 2013). Questions lead to experiments, to reading, to discussions with other scientists. What happens if we put this knowledge to work through the power of graphic organizers?

There is not space in this book to cover all the graphic organizers that might be adapted for specific disciplines. Besides, we encourage you to think of new ways to represent knowledge graphically. If you have an idea, please let us know! We'd love to help you share it. For now, we would like to offer a couple of graphic organizers with some suggestions regarding how they may be adapted to help students focus on key features from several disciplines. We know you will come up with many more. We also encourage you to offer this opportunity to your students. Invite them to create graphic organizers that help them to chunk information into manageable pieces that support their comprehension. Once they have created their organizational graphics they can return to them to add more detail as they read related pieces, to use as a study guide, and to support their sharing of information. Model a few graphic organizers for them and then invite them to create ones that work for them; encourage them to view graphic organizers as note-taking guides.

COMPARISON AND CONTRAST

Let's say that we want to ask our students to look at the words of a text and verify them by looking at a visual, such as a picture, graph, or table. Or perhaps it is more accurate to say that effective readers of science texts look at the pictures, graphs, and tables, then read to verify. Either way, the idea is to help students become better readers of the science materials (in this case) they encounter.

Take a moment to look over the article "Planning Tiger Recovery: Understanding Intraspecific Variation for Effective Conservation," available at *http://advances.sciencemag.org/content/advances/1/5/e1400175.full.pdf*. This is a challenging article about tigers, the number of subspecies of tigers, and what that means for conservation efforts. We chose this piece because it is challenging to read unless you happen to be a specialist in biology. The article includes four figures (often with multiple figures embedded into one larger representation; see Figure 9.1) and two tables along with text that explains the study, discussion of the results, and conclusions.

One very common graphic organizer used for comparison and contrast is the Venn diagram (see Figure 9.2). It is very popular, but we don't like it. We know, we know. But Venn diagrams are widely used and time tested. Why don't we like it, you ask? When comparison and contrast are called for, students who struggle with complex texts and ideas tend to go for the superficial. A simple Venn diagram does nothing to call attention to the features of the items to be compared that students might not notice right away.

How do we solve that? A graphic organizer, of course. The organizer in Figure 9.3 is simple, but it reminds students to look for important attributes of the items or ideas to be compared and contrasted. If students struggle, teachers might put in some of the key attributes themselves. Students then can use a text or even multiple texts to figure out just what the important attributes are that the discipline feels are important.

This graphic organizer is just a standard one that could be used in almost any discipline. How might we modify it to call attention to the way that scientists or literary critics read and respond to text? That's the hard part, right? But maybe it's not so hard.

While we might compare two ideas using the graphic organizer above, we might also ask students to compare information within a single document. Remember we mentioned that scientists tend to read the graphics and charts back and forth with the text? In general, graphics and text should agree, but each conveys information that the other does not or cannot.

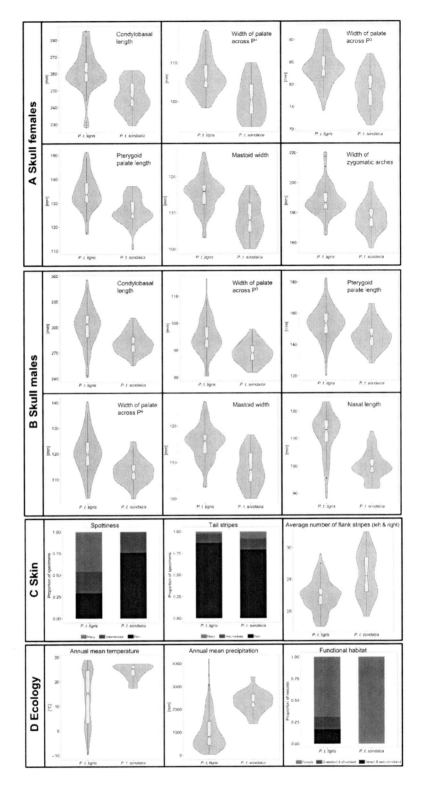

FIGURE 9.1. Example of a complex figure from a science article (Wilting et al., 2015). Copyright © The Authors. This work is licensed under CC BY-NC (*http://creativecommons.org/licenses/by-nc/4.0*).

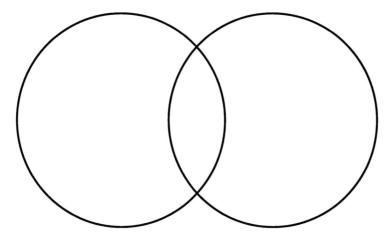

FIGURE 9.2. Venn diagram.

What might students learn by examining the graphics and what might they learn by close reading of the text itself? Although compare and contrast graphic organizers are often used to compare two ideas, they can also be used to compare the features found in a document. Why not ask students to compare what they learn from the graphics and what they learn from the written text? The only thing that needs to be changed is the label on the contrast sections of the organizer. On one side, label the differences "graphics," and on the other side, the label will read "text."

Sometimes, it does not take a lot of effort to highlight the unique features of any discipline. In the example above, it is just a matter of changing a couple of labels. And, of course, it is important to know that scientists tend to look at the graphics and the text flexibly. Historians tend to look at perspectives and who the actors (the persons doing something, not persons on a stage necessarily) are. Here, again, it is easy to adapt (Gillis, 2014) the graphic organizer to highlight what social scientists think is important (Nokes, 2010). Historians look at multiple documents and they consider the source in terms of primary or secondary and sometimes tertiary sources. For a quick refresher on what this means, please see page 174 in Chapter 8.

An easy adaptation to the compare and contrast organizer is in order. Just change the attributes section to "main ideas" and reorder the boxes for comparisons and contrasts (see Figure 9.4). A larger worksheet can accommodate more than two documents or points of view. Now students are positioned to think about what they learn from each source of information. More important, they avoid the trap of binary thinking.

Binaries tend to force thinkers into one choice or the other. Because of their either/or approach, they exclude other possibilities (Hayakawa & Hayakawa, 1990). For example, it might be possible to position students to choose the account of a

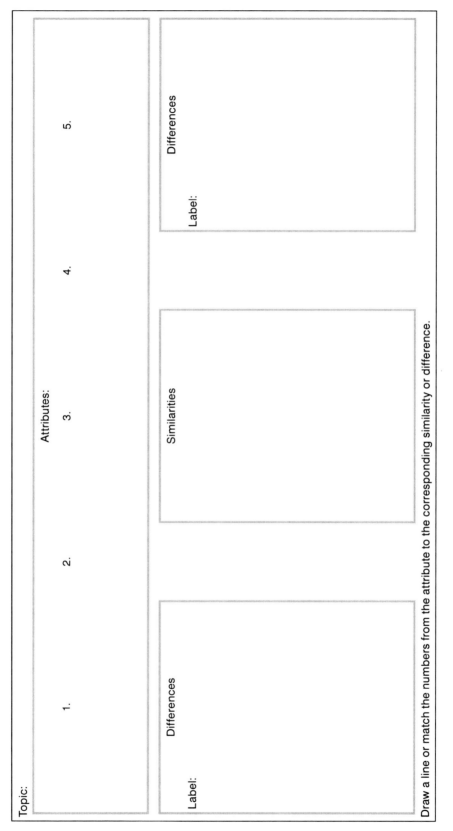

FIGURE 9.3. Basic compare–contrast graphic organizer.

From *Literacy in the Disciplines: A Teacher's Guide for Grades 5–12* by Thomas DeVere Wolsey and Diane Lapp. Copyright © 2017 The Guilford Press. Permission to photocopy this material is granted to purchasers of this book for personal use or use with individual students (see copyright page for details). Purchasers can download enlarged versions of this material (see the box at the end of the table of contents).

Topic:

Main Points:

1.   2.   3.   4.   5.

Comparisons or similarities

Contrasts
Primary Secondary Tertiary
Document 1

Contrasts
Primary Secondary Tertiary
Document 2

Draw a line or match the numbers from the attribute to the corresponding comparison or contrast.

FIGURE 9.4. Compare–contrast graphic organizer for history.

British regular over that of a Boston patriot (or the other way around) in recounting the events that led to what is now known as the Boston Massacre. However, doing so presents several problems. Historians tend to avoid choosing one account over another and instead weigh the evidence from multiple perspectives. A graphic organizer might be constructed to evoke a choice of one over another, but historians and teachers of history know that working with multiple sources toward a richer understanding is the better approach.

Through follow-up discussion and effective feedback, student can avoid the pitfalls of the binary argument. Keep reading for more about how arguments are constructed in the disciplines.

 Also view the video *Organizing Ideas from Multiple Sources* on how students in a seventh-grade science class crate a graphic organizer to support their investigation of multiple sources. Go to *www.learner.org/ courses/readwrite/video-detail/organizing-ideas-multiple-sources.html.*

ADAPTING KWL FOR THE DISCIPLINES

One of the most elegant graphic organizers we know promotes solid thinking about any topic. It has been adapted in many ways to fit different circumstances, and it builds on what students know, what they might learn as they engage with resources, and what they actually learned through a reflective process. We bet you have already figured out that we are talking about KWL, or "Know, Want to know, Learned" (Ogle, 1986). This graphic organizer is very adaptable, even as most of the more than one dozen versions we found preserve the essence of the original structure.

The idea is that students always know something that informs their approach to content. Moreover, they know something about text and can make some predictions about it even before they read it. They draw on a great deal of knowledge, then plan what they might learn as they approach new text. We refer to text here, but that text could be a lecture, a video, an article, or even an accumulation of information students can document or source. After they have engaged with the text, they take the time to reflect on what they have learned and how their knowledge has grown and expanded. Pretty neat, huh?

The basic KWL organizer is shown in Figure 9.5. Notice that there is a section for students to categorize their initial thoughts as they think about what they know. This step is often overlooked. However, it is worthwhile to have students stop and categorize their thoughts prior to reading. When they do so, they establish a framework, temporary perhaps, that they might use as they explore new content in their explorations of the content.

Okay, you say. That's great, and I use KWL all the time. Sometimes students say they do not "want" to learn anything, so I ask them what they "need" to know.

What I know	What I want or need to know	What I learned
Categories:		

The original KWL organizer.

But how can this organizer be used to emphasize what is important about learning and literacy in my discipline? We're glad you asked.

KWL in Mathematics

Mathematics is a good place to start. Hyde (2006) adapted KWL to become KWC. In KWC, in the first column, students identify "What do you know for sure?" In the second column, they grapple with "What are you trying to find out?" In the third column, they determine "Are there special conditions [the C] or precise definitions of words to watch for?" A space underneath asks students to show how they solve the problem using pictures, numbers, and words (see Figure 9.6).

What do you know for sure?	What are you trying to find out?	Are there special conditions or precise words to address?
Solution:		

FIGURE 9.6. KWC organizer.

See what Hyde did here? He took Ogle's premise and made it a tool for looking at mathematics in a way that promoted disciplinary thinking. The KWC pattern is built on the original KWL, but he turned it to meet his purposes in promoting mathematical thinking. What would happen if we tried this with another discipline? Let's see.

KWL in History

Historians value the ability to handle dissonance or noise (VanSledright, 2012) between and among accounts of the events that make up the historical record. Remember earlier in the chapter when we discussed the notion of actors? Those people who did something, not usually on a traditional stage with curtains and an intermission? The actors in a historical account and how their involvement was recorded is very important to historians. We modified to increase understanding of history as a discipline (see Figure 9.7).

Once again, you can see what we did here. We turned the basic KWL format to serve the particular features that historians value. What might you do to attend to the persons who are "actors" in the narrative, whether they are the authors of the narrative or not? For example, a newspaper account, usually a secondary source, would be written by a journalist but perhaps with quotes from one or more of the actors in the event. How might that be reflected in the KWL for multiple historical accounts chart? What would you change or add?

KWL in Science

Reading in science is a bit different in that there are many graphs, charts, and images. Scientists read back and forth, matching what they read with the graphics. The heart of science is inquiry. Draper and Adair (2010) remind us that when it comes to science, an informed public that can understand scientific principles is of utmost importance. Just what is scientific inquiry? Bresser and Fargason (2013) summarize the process with elementary-grade students in mind. Inquiry starts with wonder (Carson, 1956). Inquiry, in Bresser and Fargason's view, includes all of the following while integrating the Next Generation Science Standards (NGSS Lead States, 2013):

- Asking questions.
- Developing and using models.
- Planning and carrying out investigations.
- Analyzing and interpreting data.
- Using mathematics and computational thinking.
- Constructing explanations and designing solutions.
- Engaging in argument from evidence.
- Obtaining, evaluating, and communicating information. (p. 12)

	What I know about the document before reading	What I need to learn as I read	What I learned about this document and its author
Document A			
Document B			
Document C			
Synthesis and Conclusions:			

FIGURE 9.7. KWL adapted for analysis of multiple historical accounts.

A significant part of inquiry is mastering scientific knowledge as it currently exists and then wondering "what if." The KWL model can be adapted easily for the sciences. Although there are many aspects of science that might be reflected in KWL, in this version we examine how reading texts in science include attending to visual information such as a graphic. Consider the KWL adapted for science in Figure 9.8 (see Lapp, Wolsey, & Wood, 2015).

Now consider this. What if they needed to gather, interpret, and analyze a data set? Wouldn't that be a good fit for the KWL format? Let's adapt it and see what the result might be (Figure 9.9).

We have included two organizers that promote inquiry as well. The I-chart (Figure 9.10; Hoffman, 1992) and the I-guide (Figure 9.11; Wood, Lapp, Flood, & Taylor, 2008) also build on the original KWL model. The I-chart promotes inquiry by breaking down a question into subquestions as students examine various sources. The I-guide is similar, but it favors the overarching themes surrounding a given topic.

Graphic organizers are very useful and powerful tools in the hands of teachers who know how to use them. We think that using the same graphic organizers over and over and year to year do little to help students work with complex texts and ideas. Organizers can help students with generic structures such as problem–solution or cause–effect. However, if students are to be prepared to contend with challenging texts, they must know how to do so in context of the disciplines that are exploring the frontiers of those ideas. Teachers can adapt what they know about the discipline they teach to the structures represented in graphic organizers and help students think more like experts in the field. Be sure to invite students to create graphic organizers that support their note-taking and presentation of information.

CHAPTER 9 ACTIVITY

View this webcast: *http://go.turnitin.com/webcast/ssw15/writing-visual*. Using a literacy task for your content area, design an online graphic organizer that is flexible and that students can adapt to fit the needs of what they plan to write or how they plan to make sense of a complex text.

Text and page or chapter numbers:

What I know about this topic	What I need to know about it	What I learned from the written text	What I learned from the graphics or data
Categories:		**Synthesis of text and graphics/data:**	

FIGURE 9.8. KWL for science texts with graphics.

My hypothesis or research question	What are the data?	Evidence that supports my hypothesis
	Categorize the data	Evidence that does not support my hypothesis
Conclusion:		
Limitations:		

FIGURE 9.9. Hypothesis and data KWL.

Topic	Question	Question	Question	Question	Other interesting facts and figures	New questions
What we know						
Sources						
Synthesis:						

FIGURE 9.10. I-chart.

Topic or question	Major subtopics or themes			Summary of each text	Importance or relevance of the information
What we know					
Sources					
Synthesis:					

FIGURE 9.11. I-guide.

Chapter 10

Presenting It Well

Using Multimodal Tools in the Disciplines

In Chapter 9 we began an exploration of how graphic organizers can be used within disciplines to highlight the features of each specialized content. In this chapter, we continue that exploration by illustrating how multimodal tools permit students to make the content of their work obvious through multiple formats. Our use of the verb *make* was no accident. As the makers or creators of today's information, students are working to change tomorrow's world. Their presentations of information now have the potential to be conveyed in innovative ways rather than just shared through well-known templates

In this chapter, we focus on the interactions of visual elements, text, and the ways information can be presented. Lapp and colleagues (2009) discussed the value of public speaking and even in our digital age, the value of speech holds its spell on an audience, perhaps now more than ever. In the age of YouTube, Vimeo, and Periscope, everyone has a digital podium if they want to make use of it. Here is the essence of what Lapp and colleagues said, with slight adaptations for the 2016 audience.

Do you enjoy speaking to large groups of people? If you said "no," you are similar to many other adults who cited fear of public speaking more often than any other fear, including death (Bruskin Associates, 1973). More recently, 55% of randomly selected survey participants in a Canadian study listed public speaking as their most feared social situation (Stein, Walker, & Forde, 1994). Contrast this information with the importance of speaking, of conversing, of conversational interaction that is illustrated by the data cited above. Does this contrast suggest that on a grand level we understand the importance of communication, of conversing, but not to a large group until we are ready? In 1923, an article by Winans in *The English Journal* proposed that exercises in speaking, and particularly public speaking, had been pushed aside in favor of curricula that can be more easily measured by paper-and-pencil tests. Winans wrote, "I confess that I know no better way to improve speaking of all kinds than to encourage and help pupils to acquire something to say worth saying, to think straight, and practice saying it to their fellows" (p. 228). Still, 94 years later, we value the talents of those who can compose their thoughts orally and have something worth saying but remain concerned that attention given to public speaking is not a focus in many classrooms (Lapp et al., 2009). Unfortunately, this is still true, but we are hopeful that as the language and speaking and listening standards of the CCSS (2010) are implemented, more focus will be placed on the preparation of students to share their ideas orally and as noted in anchor standard four of the CCSS, students will become proficient at presenting their ideas orally.

Even though speaking in public, even the removed public of digital environments such as those found on video channels or voice tools such as Voki, can be daunting, we have learned in our work with students that they have important things to say, and using multimodal presentation tools helps them to find their voice. Those tools can be shared online or presented in front of classmates. The more opportunities students have to prepare and give presentations of their ideas, the more comfortable they will become with the technologies they select and the practice of presenting.

MULTIMODAL TOOLS DEFINED

Multimodal tools are those that involve more than one receptive or expressive channel. Receptive channels include listening, reading, and viewing, while expressive channels include speaking, writing, and creating visual information. Kinesthetic information (obtained through touch and muscle activity) are not to be overlooked, either. More often, the modes are layered, and in our digital era they are often built right into the tools we use. Discussion, for example, may include speaking and listening in an overlapping or turn-taking manner, and it may also make use of written text or visual diagrams. On an elementary level, then, discussion and conversation are the most recognizable of multimodal tools.

As images are increasingly available in digital form, the possibility of including them in presentations and online formats increases. While students must learn to attribute sources in their presentations and other digital works (see Wolsey, 2013, at *http://literacybeat.com/2013/08/14/copyright-fair-use*), images can transform presentations in significant ways. In Figure 10.1, compare the slide at the top with the slide at the bottom. Which do you think most complements the speaker without distracting the viewer? Both of these are presentations DeVere gave and both represent the same topic.

Buchko, Buchko, and Meyer (2012) found that PowerPoint slides did not significantly improve recall in presentations in the form of religious sermons. They

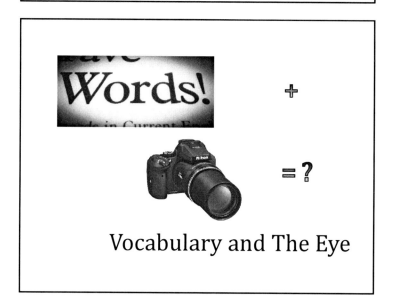

0 Provide a description, explanation, or example of the new term.

0 Ask students to restate the description, explanation, or example in their own words.

0 Ask students to construct a picture, pictograph, or symbolic representation of the term.

0 Engage students periodically in activities that help them add to their knowledge of the terms in their vocabulary notebooks.

0 Periodically ask students to discuss the terms with one another.

0 Involve students periodically in games that enable them to play with terms. (Marzano, 2009)

Literature Review

Vocabulary and The Eye

FIGURE 10.1. Images can transform presentations.

further pointed out that poor PowerPoint use actually detracted from what the audience (or congregation, in this case) was intended to recall. They suggested that:

1. Images should not compete with language, spoken or written. The audience should not have to try to attend to the speaker and written text at the same time.

2. Images can enhance what the speaker is saying (or the written text is conveying).

3. Images add emphasis to a presenter's main point.

4. Images can also stand on their own as powerful sources of information in many circumstances.

Presentations that are considered *zen* increasingly use images in the slide deck (think PowerPoint or Prezi). Keep in mind there are many types of presentation tools besides PowerPoint and Prezi. Be sure to visit our disciplinary literacy multimedia page at (*www.literacybeat.com/literacy-in-the-disciplines*) to view a multimedia presentation by high school students working in the field of physics. In Figure 10.2, notice how a student in Ms. Thayres's English class portrayed the topic of gender stereotyping based on appearance through the use of images.

Here are some guidelines:

- Include fewer words on the slides.
- Provide students with lots of examples that will encourage them to let their spoken words do the work while the images enhance what we say. (Sometimes it works the other way around, too.)
- On-screen captions or a transcript can help those who are hearing impaired, however.

FIGURE 10.2. Gender stereotyping.

One approach that can easily help you to inform students is suggested by Garr Reynolds (see *www.garrreynolds.com/preso-tips*). One of his most important points is that the audience is there to see you, the presenter. They did not come to see your slide deck. In school, sometimes the audience is captive; that is, the student in first period is going to present to the other students in first period who have to be there. But the truth of Reynolds's point remains. If we are going to expect students to learn the literacy and the content of the discipline, then the audience wants to hear a well-executed presentation by one of their peers. Nifty slides can't make up for what the presenter does not know well.

We like to use the term *conversant* when we talk about literacy in the disciplines. Content-area teachers want their students to be conversant in science, physical education, history, technology, and all the other aspects of our world that are part of school. That is, they can discuss ideas fluently using the conventions of the discipline and demonstrate knowledge of the content that is appropriate for their age and grade.

Students who are conversant in science or with literature can engage with others academically. They can have a conversation with a professional or the teacher that reflects the way that discipline approaches its work. Students who are conversant build an understanding of content by questioning it more effectively because they understand the concepts behind the words. When students give presentations, how conversant they are with the topics they address, the ideas they plan to generate, and their ability to work with ideas fluidly are represented through their graphics.

Notice in the video *Peer Teaching,* which can be found at *www.learner. org/courses/readwrite/video-detail/peer-teaching.html,* how the ninth-grade student uses his PowerPoint presentation to share information with his peers. What is so positive about his presentation is that he is using his slides to support the information he is sharing. He is not reading his slides but is instead referencing them. The next steps for him are of course to add a few graphics to make his slides less wordy and more zen.

WHAT ROLE DOES TECHNOLOGY PLAY?

One of the most ubiquitous of presentation tools in our digital age is the slide deck, often a PowerPoint. Visuals have supplemented presentations at least since Hamlet's monologue for the audience when he held up Yorick's skull to emphasize his thoughts on mortality. Thirty-five millimeter slides, flip charts, posters, and props augment the message of the presentation. In our digital age, presentation tools can either improve the presentation or send the audience skidding toward boredom. Graphics in a presentation, according to Miller (2015), can provide information in a way that text, whether spoken or written, cannot. At the same time, purely decorative graphics seem to interfere more they help. To empower students as researchers and communicators we must teach them some communication principles that are general, yet adaptable to specific disciplines.

Business: The 10/20/30 Rule

The 10/20/30 rule is easy to remember, and it can come in handy when you are helping your students create a presentation. Guy Kawasaki (2005) is a businessman with a wealth of experience in listening to and giving presentations to others. The 10/20/30 rule keeps presentations focused, according to Kawasaki, by attending to three things.

1. The presentation should have only 10 slides that focus on what the audience needs to hear. Being concise is highly valued in this model. Second, the presentation should be no more than 20 minutes in length.
2. Length matters. Classroom presentations are 5–10 minutes, with 5 minutes for discussion, questions, and answers. Students should be held to the agreed-upon time limit. Precision with language will be illustrated through their presentations.
3. Fonts must be 30 points or larger. This should be obvious, but so many presentations consist of slide after slide of tiny fonts that no one can read. Visuals should replace words. Presentations with a great deal of text are usually a crutch for a speaker who is not prepared rather than a useful way to convey information.

While your students may not have 20 minutes for a presentation, we think Kawasaki's methodology provides a useful guide if we adopt the underlying principles of 10/20/30. They include being concise, providing engagement with the audience, and making the content of every slide count for the audience. You can adapt this formula as Harden (2008), who gives presentations in the medical field, suggests to tell a story, use animations that are useful to the audience, avoid bullet points, and make effective use of visuals such as an image or video.

Remember our earlier point about being conversant? A great deal of the value of student-led presentations comes as students compose the presentation, discuss (if with a team) what elements to include, and come to a real understanding of the topic long before they ever take up the laser pointer. Equally important: Students who are conversant on the topic are well prepared and can engage the audience during the presentation and during the discussion period to follow. Everyone learns this way.

Science

LaPorte and his colleagues (2002) wrote about the value of presentations in science. The authors suggested that scientists share findings. Put another way, they use language and other modalities to do that. They argue that the traditional manner of sharing findings has been through publication in scientific journals. Two things stood out to us about their work comparing the time-honored journal to the newer medium of digital presentations that are worthwhile for teachers to consider. One is that journals require a high degree of reading proficiency in the sciences that is typically achieved at the graduate school level. Most articles are a bit beyond the reach of middle or high school students. The other is that presentation software makes it possible to report findings very quickly. Whereas a study published in a traditional journal might take years to make it into print, a presentation can be created to communicate and disseminate results quickly. The scientist further owns not just production of the research, but also the review process and distribution of the work.

Presentations in science classes may require students to present work from investigations they have conducted. Typically, these follow the traditions of the scientific method, which are built around a question based on background research, a hypothesis, and experiment to test the hypothesis, and analysis of the results. The last step of the scientific method is communicating results. That sounds like an interesting presentation!

You can see that for students in science classes, there are clear implications. If students are "doing" meaningful science work in class as they learn the ways of the scientist, presentations permit them to share their ideas in a quick and comprehensible manner, compared to a written report.

Social Studies

Presentations in social studies need not be a review of famous presidents or battles fought long ago. Here are some possibilities to make presentations engaging:

1. Instead of a biography of some famous person, ask students to construct a dialogue between two individuals who share something in common, but are separated in some way. DeVere calls this "meeting of the minds." For example, what kind of conversation would John Jay and Sonia Sotomayor have? To create this presentation, students would have to know what the Supreme Court does and what role these two justices played in United States history. In other words, they would have to conversant on the topics without boring their peers with nonessential biographical details such as where they were born or when they were appointed to the court. Consider what Admiral Zheng He of China would say to Christopher Columbus.

2. Make it a game. PowerPoint and other presentation software is actually a very powerful tool that makes use of hypertext. One of the most popular is based on

the television game show *Jeopardy!* PowerPoint easily replicates the *Jeopardy!* Game board because it need not move in the linear fashion so common in other presentations. When students create the games, they potentially have the opportunity to demonstrate that they are conversant in the topic by crafting the moves within the game. Hint: Use Bloom's taxonomy (Anderson & Krathwohl, 2001) to promote the use of thoughtful questions or activities. There are many sites on the Internet where PowerPoint templates for games can be downloaded. Here is one from the University of North Carolina at Wilmington maintained by Dr. Jeff Ertzberger: *http://people.uncw.edu/ertzbergerj/ppt_games.html.*

Math

1. Ask students to be creative. Really. Math is fun, and an inventive presentation will engage the humorous side of mathematics while delving into a topic in a meaningful way. Want to see an example? Check this video on YouTube: *https://youtu.be/EdyociU35u8.* Logarithms will never seem the same to you again.

2. Consider the needs of the math audience. The Massachusetts Institute of Technology (2013) offers these suggestions specific to the math audience when comparing chalk talks (most of the material remains visible on the board) and slide presentations:

- When slides contain large amounts of text (or equations), the audience cannot read and listen at the same time, so strategies are needed either to reduce the content on the slides or to guide the audience through the content.
- The audience needs time to absorb math concepts, but it is very easy to click through slides too quickly, especially when the presenter is nervous, so strategies are needed to give the audience time to think.
- The audience cannot refer to past slides to remind themselves of the meaning of new notation or of the purpose of details being presented, so strategies are needed to help the audience remember important points. (¶ 2)

For students in mathematics, presentations can be enhanced, as the folks at MIT suggest, by allowing the presenter to consider these elements and choose the best presentation tools and format.

CONSIDER THE FORMAT

A classic presentation is a speaker at the front of the room and an audience. In school, that audience is often, but not always, a group of peers. However, we have learned that students often benefit from presenting their ideas in other ways, too. With tablets or laptops, students might present their ideas to a small group in a roundtable format. Of course, online presentations are possible and offer additional interactive opportunities, as well.

Whole-Class and Large-Audience Presentations

When students speak to a large group, say a full class of peers, they must consider elements of public speaking. Here are several tips that you can share with your students.

- Project your voice so that others who are at the back of the audience can hear you. Practice is the key here.
- Don't be thrown by interruptions. Go with them.
- Be your conversational best. Most presentations are more successful when the speaker connects to the audience in a conversational way. Very formal language, even when addressing a topic of great importance, can put an audience off.
- Speak slowly and distinctly. Earlier, we suggested that students be conversant (which is different than being conversational); however, presenters who have a great many ideas often rush to present everything speaking so fast that the audience cannot keep up.
- Rehearse. Yes, practice in front of a mirror, your parents, your dog. Don't worry about getting every word right. Instead, focus on the tips above and the presentation planning guide elements: be conversant, be aware of what the audience expects, be concise. Some of the most well-known speakers today can be found on TED Talks. Tips from TED speakers can guide us all: *http://blog.ted.com/a-ted-speaker-coach-shares-11-tips-for-right-before-you-go-on-stage*.

Small Groups

One of our favorite presentation techniques is to use small groups or roundtables. The presentation is in a friendly, less intimidating setting. Students are encouraged to interact with the presenter (the conversant expert on the topic), and a great many more presentations fit in a small time period. Ask students to prepare small-group presentations often. A simple checklist or rubric helps keep students on the right track and accountable, and the teacher is free to move among groups. Moreover, the small-group audience is authentic. Remember the meeting of the minds scenario we suggested a few pages ago? Perfect for small group presentations. Students in group 1 present their material, and students move from presentation to presentation every 15 minutes or so. The time is not overwhelming for presentation, and students don't face the fear of speaking to an entire class with the spotlight directly on them. It's a good place to start students as presenters and conversant novices in the discipline of the class.

Online

Online presentations can take many forms. Grisham, Lapp, Wolsey, and Vaca (2014) (whom you met in Chapter 2) described several ways of creating e-posters to share information. Using online discussion tools, students explored the topics first presented on the e-posters students created using Prezi and Glogster. Infographics are also a good way to create useful online presentations of information that might foster further discussion (Wolsey, 2013). Read these two articles online:

1. The Info on Infographics: *http://literacybeat.com/2013/05/01/ infographics*.

2. Combining Print and Visual Information Via ePosters: Generating and Displaying Learning: *http://goo.gl/RSrrNU* (opens as a PDF).

LEARN MORE

One of our favorite sources of information for presentation delivery is State-of-the-Art Presentations (or SoAP). They offer a number of free resources that address topics such as body language during a presentation, using templates, building audience connections, and many more. Not all the topics will be useful to students and their teacher since they are focused on business presentations, but many of them definitely are very useful. Visit SoAP at *http://soappresentations.com/free-downloads*.

 We also invite you to view eighth-grade mathematics teacher Leon Young, who so successfully utilizes technology to support his teaching and his students learning, at *www.learner.org/courses/readwrite/video-detail/learning-blended-classroom.html*.

CHAPTER 10 ACTIVITY

During your career in education, you have probably given your fair share of presentations. Find one you have saved and evaluate it using Figure 10.3 as your framework. Update it using the principles from this chapter. Alternatively, if you have a presentation that you plan to give to your students or colleagues, plan it according to the ideas in this chapter. Note what differences it makes to the audience, and perhaps even ask them for feedback.

	Key Questions	My Response
I am **conversant** on the topic.	• Am I able to respond to questions and give the presentation without looking at the slides? • Does the presentation fit the demands of the discipline?	
I will **engage** the audience.	• Am I confident enough to respond to questions? • Have I included participation points where I ask the audience questions?	
My slides are **concise** in every way.	• How many slides do I need? • What should be on each slide? • Do I have a balance between words and graphics?	
Every element on my slides is **legible** for the audience.	• Will everyone in the room be able to read my slides (font size and color is appropriate)? • Does every item on the slides (text, animations, visuals) contribute to the presentation? • Am I not overwhelming my audience with too many words? • Are my slides zen?	

FIGURE 10.3. Presentation planning tool.

Chapter 11

Conclusion

Looking Forward

ASSESSMENT

Assessment and feedback go hand in hand in secondary classrooms. When teachers know how language figures into a content-area task, they can help students think more accurately and more precisely about the discipline. For this to work to students' advantage, there must be a clear flow from teaching objectives and standards to instruction that includes assessment and feedback. Notice that here we include assessment and feedback as part of instruction. There are many good books and articles about the role of evaluation, so we will leave discussion of that topic to those sources.

When students put their fingers on the keyboard or their pens to paper, we have to consider what is important. When we think about our disciplines in terms of how they use language, as all do to some extent, it is helpful to students to know just how their use of language informs their understanding of the content of the discipline and how those disciplines construct knowledge.

At Health Sciences High and Middle College in San Diego, California, teachers consider their content goals as well as their language goals relative to the content goals. They call these "purpose statements." For example, a social studies teacher might expect students to do the following (adapted from Health Sciences High and Middle College, 2015):

During the Industrial Revolution, examine how scientific and technological changes and new forms of energy brought about massive social, economic, and cultural change. And the language goal, relative to the goal and the use of language, could be "Extend ideas presented in primary or secondary sources through original analysis, evaluation, and elaboration.

As students work with language to increase their understanding of the discipline, they need to know what they are to learn, have reasonable models of what the learning might look like, know how to interact with others, and be able to obtain feedback about how they are doing in regard to their learning. From a disciplinary literacy standpoint, that means knowing just how language can help students learn about biology, algebra, and literature, for example.

Feedback is important in many ways. Let's consider what teachers and peers say to each other as they construct knowledge through text. We argue that students need guidance with unfamiliar content and the language structures used to construct an understanding of that content. What the teacher or perhaps peers say is ultimately very helpful if students are receiving the feedback they need while the writing is in progress.

What we mean here is that students do not seem to have a lot of use for feedback they receive, typically as a score with some annotated notes from the teacher, once a writing task is complete. Too late, then. Instead, students tend to find that guidance as they write is most helpful, and that means that at least some of the writing needs to be done in class or with appropriate technology that permits useful feedback from teacher and peers. Consider this situation: Carlos is writing a constructed response about the effect of boosterism on the California economy. His teacher walks by the computer praising, prompting, and moving on (Jones, 2007) as students work. He notices that Carlos has used the word *art* to describe a historical artifact, the label on a California orange crate. These are beautiful works of art, to

> The Society of American Archivists defines *ephemera* as "materials, usually printed documents, created for a specific, limited purpose, and generally designed to be discarded after use." For example, the labels on orange crates are regarded as *ephemera* in Figure 11.1.

be sure, but the teacher reminds Carlos of a word he just learned, *ephemera*.

Through this simple exchange, Carlos's teacher helped him remember a word he knew but could not yet use conversantly, and incorporate it into his writing. In this way, Carlos becomes more proficient with the terms that historians and archivists use when they are describing printed documents in some instances.

RUBRICS

We use rubrics all the time in our work with students at all levels, but we also recognize the limitations of rubrics, especially when it comes to expression through language and other modalities. We think of them as scaffolds or starting points. At times, rubrics provide the necessary constraints to help students learn; at other times, they provide the restraints the prevent exploration and engagement with peers and with the teacher (Broad, 2003; Wilson, 2006). Only expert guidance and thoughtful teacher decisions can fill the gaps.

Rubrics, in our experience, tend to work well when they highlight overall goals (for example, standard spelling and grammar or citation of sources) with goals that are specific to the content to be learned in the discipline and the language goals that might be evident in that particular task.

We shared a rubric for argumentation (Chapter 5) that can serve as a starting point for you (see Figure 11.2). Please take these ideas and adapt them to the content goals and the language goals for the task. Generic rubrics, we frequently say, lead to generic results.

There are many additional ways to gauge student learning in an informal manner. Twelfth-grade English teacher Kaila Tricaso, at Health Sciences High, uses exit slips to assess students' grasp of a daily topic as well as the next directions her instruction should take. Students write their understanding of a topic the teacher assigns, or that they choose to address, then deposit them in the appropriate bin. This quick assessment helps her to know what students have learned and what are the next instructional scaffolds they need. She can then plan her next day's instruction using these student-based data. Figure 11.3 says it all, because students tell the teacher just how well they are understanding the discipline and the concepts. Isn't this a neat way to make inquiry the norm in the classroom?

FIGURE 11.1. Orange crate labels are examples of ephemera. Public-domain image available at *www.apu.edu/library/specialcollections/folder/citr.*

	"4" Essay	"3" Essay	"2" Essay	"1" Essay
Argument/ Claim/Stance	States and supports a meaningful argument—claim that clearly presents the writer's position and addresses the topic.	States the argument—claim that clearly presents the writer's position and addresses the topic but does not provide strong evidence.	Provides an argument that does not match the topic.	There is no claim or argument stated.
Supporting Evidence (Details and Examples)	Thoroughly supports the thesis with specific examples and ideas from the text(s).	Supports the thesis with some details and examples from the text(s).	Supports the thesis with limited details and/or examples using only one of the texts.	Fails to support the thesis with details and/or examples from either text.
Warrant	Provides a logical assumption that supports the connection between the claim and evidence.	Provides a logical assumption but does not make a connection between the evidence and claim.	Attempts a logical assumption that merely repeats the evidence.	No logical assumption follows the evidence provided.
Counterclaim/ Counter-argument	Provides a meaningful counterargument that clearly readdresses the initial claim and supports the topic.	Provides an unclear counterargument but addresses the prompt.	Provides a weak counterargument.	No counterargument is stated.
Counter to Counterclaim	Provides a strong counter to counterclaim that is not only related to the counterclaim but "knocks" it down.	Provides a counter to counterclaim that is related to the counterclaim but does not "knock" it down.	The counter to counterclaim is not connected to the counterclaim.	There is no counter to counterclaim and this evidence ends with the opposing side.
Transitional Words and Phrases	Uses appropriate sentence frames and a variety of transitions that make all components of the argument clear and easily understood.	Uses appropriate language, but the argument and counterargument are only somewhat clear.	The language used minimally supports an easy understanding of the claim or counterclaim.	The language used does not support an easy understanding of the components of the argument.
Conventions	No errors in the conventions of punctuation, capitalization, grammar, spelling.	One to two errors in conventions.	Three to four errors in conventions.	Five or more errors in conventions.

FIGURE 11.2. Argumentation rubric, designed by Diane Lapp and Amy Miles in response to a schoolwide essential question.

FIGURE 11.3. Exit-slip bins.

TEACHER DISPOSITIONS

For years, teachers have heard that every teacher is a teacher of reading. The idea was a good one, but some teachers found that hard to enact when they heard the message that reading as a separate subject was suddenly their job, too. Of course, every teacher has a responsibility to help students succeed, but we now have several challenges before us as educators.

1. Content-area teachers are experts in the disciplines for which they are responsible to teach, and that includes the idea that they are experts in the literacies common to those disciplines. There are no better teachers to apprentice students into the discipline as knowledgeable citizens, consumers, and life long learners than the discipline expert we call "teacher." *Challenge*: Literacy in the disciplines is not just a new buzzword for "content-area literacy." Rather, it is an invitation to involve your students as participants in a society that values your discipline and the literacies that inform it.

2. The best teachers Diane and DeVere know are always immersed in learning about and through the disciplines in their content areas. Science teachers we know give lectures on astronomy at the Grand Canyon and provide their own sophisticated telescopes to the public to experience the wonder of the cosmos. They use language, in part, to convey the excitement and the processes of the discipline. Other teachers of history spend vacations in the special collections sections of university libraries because they are so intrigued with the past that they want to share it with the future historians sitting in their classrooms. We could go on and on, and perhaps that is a separate book. Teachers are experts, they love their work, and they think it's so important that they use the language of the discipline as well as the other tools available to convey enthusiasm to the students they meet every school day. *Challenge*: The literacies of specific disciplines are often transparent to teachers and other experts. What are the literacies of your discipline? How do you make those literacies plain to your students?

3. We know a great deal within our disciplines, but we know less about what the literacies of the disciplines should look like as we apprentice our students into the fields we teach. *Challenge:* How do we make expertise accessible to students who are not experts?

WHAT'S NEXT FOR LITERACY IN THE DISCIPLINES?

There are still many things we do not know about disciplinary literacy. We do not know what it looks like vertically from one grade level to another in any useful way. There is more to study about the texts students encounter and the degree to which those reflect the types of texts experts and professionals use. For that matter, we do not know much about the degree to which students compose written work or multimedia deliverables that are effective guides as they move into the world of college, work, citizenship, and lifelong learning.

We agree with Draper and her colleagues (2010) that a good start is to begin thinking of teachers as collaborative partners when it comes to literacy. That is to say, literacy coaches and mentors are not experts in the ways of every discipline, and they cannot be. Through partnerships where literacy coaches collaborate to explore the disciplines with the teachers who are experts, much can be learned and much can be translated into action in the classroom. We hope you will join us on this journey, and that you will share your thoughts and insights with us as we move forward. Are you in?

References

Adler, M. J., & Van Doren, C. (1940/1972). *How to read a book.* New York: Simon & Schuster.

Allen, S. (1985). How to enjoy the classics. In B. S. Fuess (Ed.), *How to use the power of the printed word* (pp. 50–60). Garden City, NY: Anchor.

Alvermann, D. E., Dillon, D. R., O'Brien, D. G., & Smith, L. C. (1985). The role of the textbook in discussion. *Journal of Reading, 29*(1), 50–57.

American Psychological Association. (2009). *Publication manual of the American Psychological Association* (6th ed.). Washington, DC: Author.

Anderson, L. W., & Krathwohl, D. R. (Eds.). (2001). *A taxonomy for learning, teaching, and assessing: A revision of Bloom's taxonomy of educational objectives.* New York: Longman.

Anderson, R. C., Nguyen-Jahiel, K., McNurlen, B., Archodidou, A., Kim, S., Reznitskaya, A., et al. (2001). The snowball phenomenon: Spread of ways of talking and ways of thinking across groups of children. *Cognition and Instruction, 19*(1), 1–46.

Baumann, J. F., Jones, L. A., & Seifert-Kessell, N. (1993). Using think alouds to enhance children's comprehension monitoring abilities. *The Reading Teacher, 47*(3), 184–193.

Bazerman, C. (1995). *The informed writer: Using sources in the disciplines* (5th ed.). Boston: Houghton Mifflin.

Bazerman, C. (2010). *The informed writer: Using sources in the disciplines* (5th ed., adapted). Fort Collins, CO: WAC Clearinghouse. Available at *http://wac.colostate.edu/books/informedwriter.*

Beck, I. L., McKeown, M. G., & Kucan, L. (2002). *Bringing words to life: Robust vocabulary instruction.* New York: Guilford Press.

Bennion, J., & Olsen, B. (2002). Wilderness writing: Using personal narrative to enhance outdoor experience. *Journal of Experiential Education. 25*(1), 239–246.

Blachowicz, C., & Fisher, P. (2000). Vocabulary instruction. In M. L. Kamil, P. B. Mosenthal, P. D. Pearson, & R. Barr (Eds.), *Handbook of reading research* (pp. 503–523). Mahwah, NJ: Erlbaum.

Bork, P., Bowler, C., de Vargas, D., Gorsky, G., Karsenti, E., & Wincker, P. (2015). *Tara* Oceans studies plankton at planetary scale. *Science, 348,* 873.

Bresser, R., & Fargason, S. (2013). *Becoming scientists: Inquiry-based teaching in diverse classrooms, grades 3–5.* Portland, ME: Stenhouse.

Broad, B. (2003). *What we really value: Beyond rubrics in teaching and assessing writing.* Logan: Utah State University Press.

Brown, S., & Kappes, L. (2012). *Implementing the Common Core State Standards: A primer on "close reading of text."* Washington, DC: Aspen Institute.

Brozo, W. G., Moorman, G., Meyer, C., & Stewart, T. (2013). Content area reading and disciplinary literacy: A case for the radical center. *Journal of Adolescent and Adult Literacy, 56*(5), 353–357.

Bruner, J. (1960). *The process of education.* Cambridge, MA: Harvard University Press.

Brush, T. A., & Saye, J. W. (2002). A summary of research exploring hard and soft scaffolding for teachers and students using a multimedia supported learning environment. *Journal of Interactive Online Learning, 1*(2), 1–12.

Bruskin Associates. (1973). *What are Americans afraid of?* (The Bruskin Report, 53). Edison, NJ: Author.

Buchko, A. A., Buchko, K. J., & Meyer, J. M. (2012). Is there power in PowerPoint?: A field test of the efficacy of PowerPoint on memory and recall of religious sermons. *Computers in Human Behavior, 28*(2), 688–695.

Burns, M. (2004). Writing in mathematics. *Educational Leadership, 62*(2), 30–33.

Candler, L. (n.d.) Literature circle models [blog post]. Retrieved from *www.lauracandler.com/strategies/litcirclemodels.php#LitCircleswithRoles.*

Carbery, G. (2009, May 6). Student's Wikipedia hoax quote used worldwide in newspaper obituaries. Retrieved from *www.irishtimes.com/news/student-s-wikipedia-hoax-quote-used-worldwide-in-newspaper-obituaries-1.759391.*

Carson, R. (1956). *The sense of wonder.* New York: HarperCollins.

Cazden, C. B. (2001). *Classroom discourse: The language of teaching and learning* (2nd ed.). Portsmouth, NH: Heinemann.

Cohen, E. G. (1994). *Designing groupwork: Strategies for the heterogeneous classroom* (2nd ed.). New York: Teachers College Press.

Coxhead, A. (2000). A new academic word list. *TESOL Quarterly, 34*(2), 213–238.

Daniels, H. (2002). *Literature circles: Voice and choice in book clubs and reading groups* (2nd ed.). York, ME: Stenhouse.

Dash, J. (2000). "A most terrible sea" in *The longitude prize* (pp. 3–24). New York: Farrar, Straus & Giroux.

Davey, B. (1983). Think aloud: Modeling the cognitive processes for reading comprehension. *Journal of Reading, 27*(1), 44–47.

Draper, R. J., & Adair, M. (2010). (Re)imagining literacies for science classrooms. In R. J. Draper (Ed.), *(Re)imaginng content-area literacy instruction* (pp. 127–143). New York: Teachers College Press.

Draper, R. J., Broomhead, P., Jensen, A. P., & Siebert, D. (2010). Aims and criteria for collaboration to content-area classrooms. In R. J. Draper (Ed.), *(Re)imaginng content-area literacy instruction* (pp. 1–19). New York: Teachers College Press.

Erickson, B. (1996). Read-alouds reluctant readers relish. *Journal of Adolescent and Adult Literacy, 40,* 212–214.

Farley, M. J., & Elmore, P. B. (1992). The relationship of reading comprehension to critical thinking skills, cognitive ability, and vocabulary for a sample of underachieving college freshmen. *Educational and Psychological Measurement, 52,* 921–931.

Fisher, D., Flood, J., Lapp, D., & Frey, N. (2004). Interactive read alouds: Is there a common set of implementation practices? *The Reading Teacher, 58*, 8–17.

Fisher, D., Frey, N., & Lapp, D. (2008). Shared readings: Modeling comprehension, vocabulary, text structures, and text features for older readers. *The Reading Teacher, 61*(7), 548–556.

Fisher, D., Frey, N. & Lapp, D. (2012). *Text complexity: Raising rigor in reading.* Newark, DE: International Reading Association.

Fisher, D., Frey, N., & Rothenberg, C. (2008). *Content-area conversations.* Alexandria, VA: ASCD.

Flanigan, K., & Greenwood, S. C. (2007). Effective content vocabulary instruction in the middle: Matching students, purposes, words, and strategies. *Journal of Adolescent and Adult Literacy, 51*(3), 226–238.

Gillis, V. (2014). Disciplinary literacy: Adapt not adopt. *Journal of Adolescent and Adult Literacy, 57,* 614–623.

Gladwell, M. (2005). *Blink.* New York: Little Brown.

Gladwell, M. (2008). *Outliers: The story of success.* New York: Little Brown

Graff, G., & Birkenstein, C. (2007). *They say, I say: The moves that matter in persuasive writing.* New York: Norton.

Graves, M. F. (2000). A vocabulary program to complement and bolster a middle-grade comprehension program. In B. M. Taylor, M. F. Graves, & P. van den Broek (Eds.), *Reading for meaning: Fostering comprehension in the middle grades* (pp. 116–135). Newark, DE: International Reading Association.

Graves, M. F., August, D., & Mancilla-Martinez, J. (2013). *Teaching vocabulary to English language learners.* New York: Teachers College Press.

Greenfield, E. (2004). Story. In *In the land of words: New and selected poems* (p. 30). New York: HarperCollins.

Grisham, D. L., Lapp, D., Wolsey, T. D., & Vaca, J. (2014). Combining print and visual information via ePosters: Generating and displaying learning. *Journal of School Connections, 5*(1), 59–75.

Habermas, J. (1991). *The structural transformation of the public sphere: An inquiry into a category of Bourgeois society* (T. Burger, Trans.). Cambridge, MA: MIT Press.

Haggard, M. R. (1985). An interactive strategies approach to content reading. *Journal of Reading, 29*(3), 204–210.

Harden, R. M. (2008). Death by PowerPoint: The need for a "fidget index." *Medical Teacher, 30*(9/10), 833–835.

Harvey, S., & Goudvis, A. (2000). *Strategies that work: Teaching comprehension to enhance understanding.* Portland, ME: Stenhouse.

Hawking, S. (1996). *The illustrated brief history of time.* New York: Bantam.

Hayakawa, S. I., & Hayakawa, A. R. (1990). *Language in thought and action* (5th ed.). San Diego, CA: Harcourt.

Health Sciences High and Middle College. (2015). Curriculum information. Retrieved from *http://hshmc.org/about/curriculum.*

Heller, R. (2010). In praise of amateurism: A friendly critique of Moje's "Call for Change" in secondary literacy. *Journal of Adolescent and Adult Literacy, 54*(4), 267–273.

Hemingway, E. (1952). *The old man and the sea.* London: Jonathan Cape.

Hillocks, G. (2011). *Teaching argument writing, grades 6–12.* Portsmouth, NH: Heinemann.

Hmelo-Silver, C. E., & Barrows, H. S. (2006). Goals and strategies of a problem-based learning facilitator. *Interdisciplinary Journal of Problem-Based Learning, 1*(1).

Hoffman, J. V. (1992). Critical reading/thinking across the curriculum: Using I-charts to support learning. *Language Arts, 69,* 121–127.

Holt, J. (1982). *How children fail* (rev. ed.). New York: Dell.

Hyde, A. (2006). *Comprehending math: Adapting reading strategies to teach mathematics, K–6.* Portsmouth, NH: Heinemann.

Irvin, J. L., Lunstrum, J. P., Lynch-Brown, C., & Shepard, M. F. (1995). *Enhancing social studies through literacy strategies* (Bulletin 91). Washington, DC: National Council for the Social Studies.

Ivey, G., & Broaddus, K. (2001). "Just plain reading": A survey of what makes students want to read in middle school classrooms. *Reading Research Quarterly, 36,* 350–377.

Joki, K. (n.d.). A scary–easy way to help you find passive voice! [blog post]. Retrieved from *www.grammarly.com/blog/2014/a-scary-easy-way-to-help-you-find-passive-voice.*

Jones, F. (2007). *Tools for teaching* (2nd ed.). Santa Cruz, CA: Fredric H. Jones & Associates.

Kawasaki, G. (2005). The 20/30/30 rule of PowerPoint [blog post]. Retrieved from *http://guykawasaki.com/the_102030_rule.*

Klein, M. L. (1988). *Teaching reading comprehension and vocabulary: A guide for teachers.* Upper Saddle River, NJ: Prentice Hall.

Lankshear, C., & Knobel, M. (2006). *New literacies: Everyday practices and classroom learning* (2nd ed.). New York: Open University Press and McGraw-Hill.

LaPorte, R. E., Linkov, F., Villasenor, T., Sauer, F., Gamboa, C., Lovlekar, M., et al. (2002). Papyrus to PowerPoint (P 2 P): Metamorphosis of scientific communication. *British Medical Journal, 325,* 1478.

Lapp, D., Fisher, D., & Wolsey, T. D. (2009). *Literacy growth for every child: Differentiated small-group instruction K–6.* New York: Guilford Press.

Lapp, D., Moss, B., Grant, M., & Johnson, K. (2015). *A close look at close reading: Teaching students to analyze complex texts (K–5).* Alexandria, VA: ASCD.

Lapp, D., Wolsey, T. D., & Wood, K. (2015). *Mining complex texts: Using and creating graphic organizers to grasp content and share new understandings, 6–12.* Thousand Oaks, CA: Corwin.

Lieberman, G. A. (2013). *Education and the environment: Creating standards-based programs in schools and districts.* Boston: Harvard Education Press.

Louv, R. (2008). *Last child in the woods: Saving our children from nature deficit disorder.* Chapel Hill, NC: Algonquin Books.

Manzo, A. V. (1969). The ReQuest procedure. *Journal of Reading, 13*(2), 123–126.

Marzano, R. J. (2009). Six steps to better vocabulary instruction. *Educational Leaddership, 67*(1), 83–84.

Massachusetts Institute of Technology. (2013). Presentations. Retrieved from *http://ocw.mit.edu/courses/mathematics/18-821-project-laboratory-in-mathematics-spring-2013/.*

Massey University. (2004). Academic word list. Retrieved May 22, 2008, from *http://ksngo.org/images/download/LDOCE_AWL.pdf.*

Math Open Reference. (2009). Angle. Retrieved from *www.mathopenref.com/angle.html.*

Mehan, H. (1979). *Learning lessons: Social organization in the classroom.* Cambridge MA: Harvard University Press.

MetaMetrics. (2014a). Typical reader measures by grade. Retrieved from *www.lexile.com/about-lexile/grade-equivalent/grade-equivalent-chart.*

MetaMetrics. (2014b). Typical text measures by grade. Retrieved from *www.lexile.com/about-lexile/grade-equivalent/grade-equivalent-chart.*

Metzger, M. (1998). Teaching reading beyond the plot. *Phi Delta Kappan. 80*(3), 240–256.

Michaels, S., O'Connor, M. C., & Hall, M. W. (2010). *Accountable talk® sourcebook for classroom conversation that works.* Pittsburgh: University of Pittsburgh.

Miller, M. D. (2015, September 24). Learning from PowerPoint: Is it time for teachers to move on?

[blog post]. Retrieved from *https://theconversation.com/learning-from-powerpoint-is-it-time-for-teachers-to-move-on-45146*.

Moje, E. B. (2007). Developing socially just subject-matter instruction: A review of the literature on disciplinary literacy teaching. *Review of Research in Education, 31,* 1–44.

Moje, E. B. (2008). Foregrounding the disciplines in secondary literacy teaching and learning: A call for change. *Journal of Adolescent and Adult Literacy, 52*(2), 96–104.

Moje, E. B. (2013). Disciplinary literacy: Navigating literacy contexts in secondary schools [Webinar]. TextProject. Retrieved from *www.textproject.org/archive/webinars/common-core-state-standards-webinar-series-2/disciplinary-literacy-why-it-matters-and-what-we-should-do-about-it*.

Moss, B., Lapp, D., Grant, M., & Johnson, K. (2016). *A close look at close reading: Teaching students to analyze complex texts (grades 6–12).* Alexandria, VA: ASCD.

Nagel, R. (2007). Geology. In R. Nagel (Ed.), *U*X*L encyclopedia of science* (Vol. 10, 2nd ed.). Farmington Hills, MI: Gale Cengage Learning.

Nagy, W. E., & Anderson, R. C. (1984). How many words are there in printed school English? *Reading Research Quarterly, 19,* 304–330.

National Governors Association Center for Best Practices & Council of Chief State School Officers. (2010). Common Core State Standards for English language arts and literacy in history/social studies, science, and technical subjects. Retrieved from *www.corestandards.org/assets/CCSSI_ELA%20Standards.pdf*.

NGSS Lead States. (2013). *Next Generation Science Standards: For states, by states.* Washington, DC: National Academies Press.

Nokes, J. (2010). (Re)imaginging literacies for history classrooms. In R. J. Draper (Ed.), *(Re)imaginng content-area literacy instruction* (pp. 54–68). New York: Teachers College Press.

Ogle, D. (1986). K-W-L: A teaching model that develops active reading of expository text. *The Reading Teacher, 39,* 564–570.

Orion. (Ed.). (2013). *Leave no child inside: A selection of essays from Orion Magazine.* Great Barrington, MA: Author.

Palinscar, A. S., & Brown, A. I. (1986). Interactive teaching to promote independent learning from text. *The Reading Teacher, 39,* 771–777.

Palinscar, A. S., & Herrenkohl, L. R. (2002). Designing collaborative learning contexts. *Theory into Practice, 41*(1), 26–32.

Pearson, D., & Gallagher, M. C. (1983). The instruction of reading comprehension. *Contemporary Educational Psychology, 8,* 317–344.

Pearson, P. D., & Johnson, D. D. (1978). *Teaching reading comprehension.* New York: Holt.

Pearson, S. J. (2011). *The rights of the defenseless: Protecting animals and children in Gilded Age America.* Chicago: University of Chicago Press.

Peterson, R. K. D. (2005). Why scientists can never prove that biotech crops are safe: How does science work? [blog post]. Retrieved from *http://agbiosafety.unl.edu/science.shtml*.

Popper, K. R. (1963). *Conjectures and refutations.* London: Routledge & Kegan Paul.

Porter, J. E., Sullivan, P., & Johnson-Eilola, J. (2009). *Professional writing online.* Upper Saddle River, NJ: Pearson.

Powell, J. W. (1895). *The exploration of the Colorado River and its canyons.* New York: Dover.

Raphael, T. E. (1984). Teaching learners about sources of information for answering questions. *Journal of Reading, 27,* 303–311.

Raphael, T. E. (1982). Teaching children question-asking strategies. *The Reading Teacher, 36,* 186–191.

Raphael, T. E. (1986). Teaching question–answer relationships, revisited. *The Reading Teacher, 39,* 516–520.

Rapparlie, L. (2011). *Writing and experiential education: Practical activities and lesson plans to enrich learning.* Bethany, OK: Woodnbarnes.

Richardson, J. S. (2000). *Read it aloud!: Using literature in the secondary content classroom.* Newark, DE: International Reading Association.

Richardson, J. S., & Gross, E. (1997). A read-aloud for mathematics. *Journal of Adolescent and Adult Literacy, 40,* 492–494.

Rosenblatt, L. (1995). *Literature as exploration* (5th ed.). New York: Modern Language Association of America.

Rosenshine, B., & Meister, C. (1994). Reciprocal teaching: A review of the research. *Review of Educational Research, 64,* 479–530.

Rous, E. W. (2000). *Literature and the land: Reading and writing for environmental literacy.* Portsmouth, NH: Boynton/Cook.

Ruddell, M. R., & Shearer, B. A. (2002). "Extraordinary," "tremendous," "exhilarating," "magnificent": Middle school at-risk students become avid word learners with the vocabulary self-collection strategy (VSS). *Journal of Adolescent and Adult Literacy, 45,* 352–363.

Samenow, S. E. (2007). The myth of the street gang as a "family substitute." *Psychology Today.* Retrieved from *www.psychologytoday.com/blog/inside-the-criminal-mind/201203/the-myth-the-street-gang-family-substitute.*

Seidule, T. (2015, August 10). Was the Civil War about slavery? [Video file]. Retrieved from *https://youtu.be/pcy7qV-BGF4.*

Shanahan, C. (2012). How disciplinary experts read. In T. L. Jetton & C. Shanahan (Eds.), *Adolescent literacy in the academic disciplines: General principles and practical strategies* (pp. 69–90). New York: Guilford Press.

Shanahan, C., Shanahan, T., & Misischia, C. (2011). Analysis of expert readers in three disciplines: History, mathematics, and chemistry. *Journal of Literacy Research, 43*(4), 393–429.

Shanahan, T. (2006). Relations among oral language, reading, and writing development. In C. A. MacArthur, S. Graham, & J. Fitzgerald (Eds.), *Handbook of writing research* (pp. 171–183). New York: Guilford Press.

Shanahan, T. (2012). Discipline literacy is not the new name for content area reading. Retrieved from *www.shanahanonliteracy.com/2012/01/disciplinary-literacy-is-not-new-name.html.*

Shanahan, T. (2015, July 8). Disciplinary vocabulary [blog post]. Retrieved from *www.shanahanonliteracy.com/2015/07/disciplinary-vocabulary.html.*

Shanahan, T., & Shanahan, C. (2008). Teaching disciplinary literacy to adolescents: Rethinking content-area literacy. *Harvard Educational Review, 78*(1), 40–59.

Short, K. G., & Harste, J. C., with Burke, C. (1996). *Creating classrooms for authors and inquirers* (2nd ed.). Portsmouth, NH: Heinemann.

Siebert, D., & Draper, R. J. (2012). Reconceptualizing literacy instruction for mathematics classrooms. In T. L. Jetton & C. Shanahan (Eds.), *Adolescent literacy in the academic disciplines: General principles and practical strategies* (pp. 172–198). New York: Guilford Press.

Society of American Archivists. (2015). Ephemera. Retrieved from *www2.archivists.org/glossary/terms/e/ephemera.*

Stein, M. B., Walker, J. R., & Forde, D. R. (1994). Setting diagnostic thresholds for social phobia: Considerations from a community survey of social anxiety. *American Journal of Psychiatry, 151,* 408–412.

Stromberg, J. (2013, January 1). What is the Anthropocene and are we in it? Retrieved from *www.smithsonianmag.com/science-nature/what-is-the-anthropocene-and-are-we-in-it-164801414.*

Strunk, W., & White, E. B. (2000). *The elements of style* (4th ed.). New York: Longman.

Swift, K. R. (2004). The writer's corner: Making policy arguments. *Bench and Bar, Official Publication of the Minnesota State Bar Association, 61*(9), n.p. Retrieved from *www2.mnbar.org/benchandbar/2004/Oct04/law_at_lrg.htm.*

Toulmin, S. E. (2003). *The uses of argument* (updated ed.). New York: Cambridge University Press.

Trelease, J. (2006). *The read-aloud handbook* (6th ed.). New York: Penguin.

VanSledright, B. (2012). Learning with texts in history: Protocols for reading and practical strategies. In T. Jetton & C. Shanahan (Eds.), *Adolescent literacy in the academic disciplines: General principles and practical strategies* (pp. 199–227). New York: Guilford Press.

Vigen, T. (n.d.). Spurious correlations. Retrieved from *http://tylervigen.com/spurious-correlations.*

Visual Thesaurus. (2013, January 9). Science words with multiple meanings. Retrieved from *www.visualthesaurus.com/cm/lessons/science-words-with-multiple-meanings.*

Vygotsky, L. S. (1978). *Mind in society: The development of higher psychological processes.* Cambridge, MA: Harvard University Press.

Wade, S. E., & Moje, E. B. (2000). The role of the text in classroom learning. In M. L. Kamil, P. B. Mosentahl, P. D. Pearson, & R. Barr (Eds.), *Handbook of reading research* (Vol. 3, pp. 609–628). Mahwah, NJ: Erlbaum.

Walton, D., Reed, C., & Macagno, F. (2008). *Argumentation schemes.* Cambridge, UK: Cambridge University Press.

Whitehead, M. (2001). The concept of physical literacy. *European Journal of Physical Education, 6,* 127–138.

Wiggins, G., & McTighe, J. (2005). *Understanding by design* (expanded 2nd ed.). Alexandria, VA: ASCD.

Wilson, M. (2006). *Rethinking rubrics in writing assessment.* Portsmouth, NH: Heinemann.

Wilting, A., Courtiol, A., Christiansen, P., Niedballa, J., Scharf, A. K., Orlando, L., et al. (2015, June 26). Planning tiger recovery: Understanding intraspecific variation for effective conservation. *Science Advances, 1,* 1–13.

Winans, J. A. (1923). Aims and standards in public speaking work. *The English Journal, 12,* 223–234.

Wolsey, T. D. (2004). Literature discussion in cyberspace: Young adolescents using threaded discussion groups to talk about books. *Reading Online, 7*(4). Retrieved from *www.readingonline.org.*

Wolsey, T. D. (2009, October 15). How to use Wikipedia at school [blog post]. Retrieved from *https://suite.io/tom-wolsey/2e16247.*

Wolsey, T. D. (2010). Complexity in student writing: The relationship between the task and vocabulary uptake. *Literacy Research and Instruction, 49*(2), 194–208.

Wolsey, T. D. (2013a). Copyright and fair use in the classroom [blog post]. Retrieved from *https://literacybeat.com/2013/08/14/copyright-fair-use.*

Wolsey, T. D. (2013b). The info on infographics: Synthesizing multiple sources with text and visuals [blog post]. Retrieved from *https://literacybeat.com/2013/05/01/infographics.*

Wolsey, T. D. (2014). Accuracy in digital writing environments: Read up, ask around, double-check. *Voices from the Middle, 21*(3), 49–53.

Wolsey, T. D., & Lapp, D. (2009). Discussion-based approaches for the secondary classroom. In K. Wood & B. Blanton (Eds.), *Literacy instruction for adolescent learners: Research-based instruction* (pp. 368–391). New York: Guilford Press.

Wolsey, T. D., & Lapp, D. (in press). Teaching/developing vocabulary using think-aloud and read-aloud. In K. M. Reynolds (Ed.), *TESOL encyclopedia of English language teaching.* Somerset, NJ: Wiley Blackwell and TESOL International Association.

Wolsey, T. D., Lapp, D., & Fisher, D. (2012). Students' and teachers' perceptions: An inquiry into academic writing. *Journal of Adolescent and Adult Literacy, 55*(8), 714–724.

Wolsey, T. D., Lapp, D., & Wood, K. (2015). *Mining complex texts: Using and creating graphic organizers to grasp content and share new understandings, 2–5.* Thousand Oaks, CA: Corwin Press.

Wolsey, T. D., Smetana, L., & Grisham, D. L. (2015). Vocabulary plus technology: An after-reading approach to develop deep word learning. *The Reading Teacher, 68*(6), 449–458.

Wood, D., Bruner, J. S., & Ross, G. (1976). The role of tutoring in problem solving. *Journal of Child Psychology, 17,* 89–100.

Wood, K. D., Lapp, D., Flood, J., & Taylor, B. T. (2008). *Guiding readers through text: Strategy guides in "new times."* Newark, DE: International Reading Association.

Worthy, J. (2002). What makes intermediate-grade students want to read? *The Reading Teacher, 55,* 568–569.

Young, J. R. (2006, June 12). Wikipedia founder discourages academic use of his creation. *The Wired Campus.* Retrieved from *http://chronicle.com/blogs/wiredcampus/wikipedia-founder-discourages-academic-use-of-his-creation/2305.*

Index

Page numbers followed by *f* indicate figure, *t* indicate table

CPSIA information can be obtained at www.ICGtesting.com
Printed in the USA
BVOW01*2041191016

464789BV00016B/8/P